BUSINESS & ADMINISTRATION

Nigel Parton

Bernadette Watkins

www.pearsonschoolsandfe.co.uk

✓ Free online support
✓ Useful weblinks
✓ 24 hour online ordering

0845 630 44 44

Heinemann is an imprint of Pearson Education Limited, Edinburgh Gate, Harlow, Essex, CM20 2JE.
www.heinemann.co.uk

Heinemann is a registered trademark of Pearson Education Limited

Text © Pearson Education Ltd 2011
Edited by Lucy Tritton
Designed by Lorraine Inglis
Typeset by Tek-Art, Crawley Down, West Sussex
Illustrated by Tek-Art, Crawley Down, West Sussex
Original illustrations © Pearson Education Ltd 2011
Front cover photograph © Alamy Images, Westend61 GmbH
Picture research by Melissa Allison

The rights of Nigel Parton and Bernadette Watkins to be identified as authors of this work have
been asserted by them in accordance with the Copyright, Designs and Patents Act 1988.
First published 2011

14 13 12 11
10 9 8 7 6 5 4 3 2 1

British Library Cataloguing in Publication Data
A catalogue record for this book is available from the British Library

ISBN 978 0 435 04688 0

Websites
There are links to relevant websites in this book. In order to ensure that the links are up-to-
date, that the links work and that the sites are not inadvertently linked to sites that could be
considered offensive, we have made the links available on our website at www.pearsonhotlinks.
co.uk. Search for this title NVQ/SVQ Business & Administration or ISBN 9780435046880.

Contents

www.contentextra.com/businessadmin

The accompanying website includes the following additional units for this qualification:

Q113 Use occupational and safety guidelines when using keyboards

Q208 Use a diary system

Q211 Provide reception services

Q219 Store and retrieve information

Q220 Archive information

Q221 Use office equipment

Q227 Respond to change in a business environment

Q256 Meet and welcome visitors

Plus additional coverage of the Technical Certificate units

Credits and Acknowledgements

The publisher would like to thank the following for their kind permission to reproduce their photographs:
(Key: b-bottom; c-centre; l-left; r-right; t-top)

Alamy Images: Andrew Holt 198tr, Image Source 172, INSADCO Photography 52, Mike Booth 198bl, moodboard 99, Rob Walls 58; **Corbis:** Pete Leonard 1; **Getty Images:** Hill Creek Pictures 90, Iconica 170, OJO Images 187; **Robert Harding World Imagery:** John Miller 49; **iStockphoto:** Dominik Pabis 227, Gary Woodward 183, Jacob Wackerhausen 5, Juanmonino 174, Lazarev 3, Slawomir Fajer 14, spxChrome 182; **Masterfile UK Ltd:** R. Ian Lloyd 161; **Pearson Education Ltd:** David Sanderson 11, Lord & Leverett 216; **Plainpicture Ltd:** Canvass 77, Jeff Spielman 107; **Shutterstock.com:** 32, Adam Gregor 36, Ajay Bhaskar 240, Alexey Malashkevich 147, angelo gilardelli 201, AVAVA 30, Baloncici 25, Best Studio 194, Daisy Daisy 33, De-V 236, Denis Babenko 215, Felix Mizioznikov 22, fotograaf limburg 177, Francesco Ridolfi 100, gifted 58, Glovatskiy 68, Guilu 44, Jaimie Duplass 47, Kaspri 146, Kzenon 251, lenetstan 19, Liv friis-larsen 52, Losevsky Pavel 95, Lucian Coman 211, Monkey Business Images 110, 134, Neil Rouse 50, paulaphoto 157, Radoslaw Korga 121, Rihardzz 8, Sergej Khakimullin 165, Villiers Steyn 260, Vladitto 243, wavebreakmedia ltd 148, Wolfgang Schaller 127, Yuri Arcurs 110, 202, 223, 260, Yuri Arcus 131; **Superstock:** 132

All other images © Pearson Education

The following public sector information has been licensed under the Open Government Licence v1.0:

p.59 HSE leaflet INDG163(rev2), Figure 303.2 Five step process for putting together a risk assessment p.59 http://www.hse.gov.uk, Figure 303.3 Sample risk assessment document

The following materials have been reproduced with kind permission from the following organisations:

- p.38 Sainsbury's logo reproduced by kind permission of Sainsbury's Supermarkets Ltd.
- p.38 Sainsbury's Mission statement reproduced by kind permission of Sainsbury's Supermarkets Ltd.
- p.39 Figure 302.1 flow diagram showing how the mission statement of an organisation can be achieved reproduced by kind permission of Sainsbury's Supermarkets Ltd.
- p.63 Figure 303.4 The Envirowise hierarchy of waste management, text reproduced by kind permission of WRAP (Waste & Resources Action Programme).
- p.81 Figure 305.3 Tesco job description reproduced by kind permission of Tesco Stores Ltd.
- p.113 Figure 308.3 Team model as defined by Dr Meredith Belbin, reproduced by kind permission of www.belbin.com.
- pp.225, 253 'Positive about Disabled People' logo reproduced by kind permission of Jobcentreplus.
- pp. 225, 254 'CustomerFirst' logo reproduced by kind permission of Customer First UK.
- p.249 Vale of White Horse District Council Customer Service Charter and image reproduced by kind permission of Vale of White Horse District Council.

Every effort has been made to trace the copyright holders and we apologise in advance for any unintentional omissions. We would be pleased to insert the appropriate acknowledgement in any subsequent edition of this publication

How to use this book

This book has been written to help you achieve your NVQ (or SVQ, if you are based in Scotland) Level 3 qualification. It covers the mandatory units and a range of optional units from the 2010 standards, giving you a broad choice of content to match your needs.

Throughout you will find the following learning features:

✓ Checklist

These features help you to identify important information or steps in a task that need to be completed.

Key terms

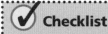

Essential terminology and phrases are explained in clear and accessible language. Where these appear in the book, the first instance of the word appears in **bold** so you know there is a definition nearby.

Activity

Use these tasks to apply your knowledge, understanding and skills. These activities cover a wide variety of subjects and will help you to expand and develop your understanding of the underpinning theory and key techniques you will need in your day-to-day working life.

Portfolio task

These are tasks that cover grading criteria from the NVQ standards. You can use these tasks to generate evidence for your portfolio. Some portfolio tasks will be supported by downloadable editable forms, which are available from www.contentextra.com/businessadmin.

Functional skills

You may be taking Functional skills alongside your NVQ – if so, these are opportunities for you to apply your English, mathematics or ICT skills in a business environment.

Office life

See how the unit applies to the real world of work, and receive best-practice hints and tips for making the most of your time in the workplace.

Doing an apprenticeship

If you are taking your NVQ as part of an apprenticeship, you will need to complete a Technical Certificate qualification. This will link to the knowledge and understanding of the NVQ, and these features will tell you about additional information provided on www.contentextra.com/businessadmin to help you complete your Technical Certificate. (See page vii for more information on the website.)

Check your knowledge

At the end of each unit, use this feature to check how well you know the topic and identify any areas you need to recap. The answers for these questions can be found at www.contentextra.com/businessadmin.

About the website

www.contentextra.com/businessadmin

Username: BALevel3

Password: Admin

The website accompanying this book will support you in a number of ways as you complete your NVQ.

Welcome to Business & Administration

This website provides additional support to complement the Heinemann NVQ/SVQ Level 2 Business & Administration and NVQ/SVQ Level 3 Business & Administration Candidate Handbooks. For information on how the unit numbers link to the different awarding organisation specifications, click here for Level 2 or here for Level 3. Here you will find the following.

Additional content for book units

Including web links, answers to questions and sample forms to use when completing Portfolio Tasks.

Additional optional units

Full coverage of additional popular units from the NVQ/SVQ, including units at different levels so you can develop a spiky profile.

Technical Certificate units

Doing an Apprenticeship? Use the dedicated Technical Certificate units to revise for your on-screen assessment or develop your knowledge and understanding to help you produce a portfolio.

Getting started

Log into the website using the user name and log-in details given in the Introduction of the book, and select the content you want to see from the left-hand menu.

About | Privacy Policy | Terms and Conditions | Contact Us | © Copyright 2011 Pearson Education Ltd

Extra free support

For the units covered in this book, you will find the
following additional support materials:

- downloadable forms and templates for portfolio tasks
  and activities
- answers to 'Check your knowledge' questions.

Manage own performance in a business environment

Activity 1

Key tasks which you carry out each week	Estimated time required
1	
2	
3	

Typical issues which interrupt your work schedule	What you
1	
2	
3	

Communicate in a business environment

Portfolio task 309.24

Task	Evidence collected
1 Find and select information that supports the purpose of written communications	
2 Present information using a format, layout, style and house style suited to the purpose and method of written communications	
3 Use language that meets the purpose of written communications and the needs of the audience	
4 Organise structure and present written information so that it is clear and accurate, and meets the needs of the audiences	
5 Use accurate grammar, spelling and punctuation, and plain English to make sure that meaning of written communication is clear	
6 Proofread and check written communications and make amendments as required	
7 Confirm what is 'important' and what is 'urgent'	
8 Produce written communications to meet agreed deadlines	
9 Keep a file copy of written communications sent	

Plan and organise meetings

Portfolio task 322.20

Task	Evidence collected
1 Produce a record of the meeting	
2 Seek approval for the meeting record, amend as required	
3 Respond to requests for amendments and arrange recirculation of a revised meeting record	
4 Follow up action points, if required	
5 Evaluate meeting arrangements, and external services where used	
6 Evaluate participant feedback from the meeting and share results with relevant people, where used	
7 Summarise learning points and use these to identify improvements that can be made to future meeting arrangements and support	

Additional free units

The website contains additional units, not covered in the book, providing you with a broader choice of units to better suit your needs. Each unit is available as a downloadable PDF for your personal use, and also includes answers, template forms and links to useful websites.

The additional units on the website are:

- Q113 Use occupational and safety guidelines when using keyboards
- Q208 Use a diary system
- Q211 Provide reception services
- Q219 Store and retrieve information
- Q220 Archive information
- Q221 Use office equipment
- Q227 Respond to change in a business environment
- Q256 Meet and welcome visitors

Unit Q211

Provide reception services

What you will learn
- Understand the purpose of reception services in a business environment
- Understand the procedures to be followed when providing reception services
- Understand ways of improving reception services and develop own role
- Provide a reception service

Unit Q219

Store and retrieve information

What you will learn
- Understand processes and procedures for storing and retrieving information
- Be able to store and retrieve information

Bonus support for apprentices

If you are taking the NVQ as part of an apprenticeship, you will also be taking a Technical Certificate. This qualification assesses the knowledge and understanding that underpins the NVQ.

The website includes concise unit-by-unit summaries of the key knowledge and understanding you need to complete your Technical Certificate — perfect for revising for on-screen assessment.

Unit Q301

Manage own performance in a business environment

What you will learn

- Understand how to plan and prioritise work and be accountable to others
- Understand how to behave in a way that supports effective working
- Be able to plan, prioritise and be accountable for own work
- Behave in a way that supports effective working

Introduction

As you progress through your career, you will be expected to take increasing responsibility for managing your own performance at work. In fact, your success in doing this may well help shape your future career prospects. By showing that you are capable of managing your own work schedule and responsibilities, you are learning management skills. In this unit you will explore the ways in which you can become skilled in managing and evaluating your own work performance, such as planning and scheduling your workload, to meet all your targets.

Learning how to behave in ways that support the overall effectiveness of work is central to your performance. In this unit you will investigate the issue of standards at work and look at how you can set high standards for yourself. You will also look at how pressure can arise at work and how you can manage this.

Dealing with setbacks and learning from your mistakes at work are all part of developing valuable experience. You will look at ways of dealing with setbacks and moving forward from these to go on to achieve success in your career.

Planning and prioritising work

After working through this section you will understand and be able to:

- explain the purpose and benefits of planning work, and being accountable to others for your own work
- explain the purpose and benefits of negotiating realistic targets for work and ways of doing so
- describe ways of prioritising targets and setting timescales for your own work
- describe the types of problems that may occur during work, and ways of dealing with them
- explain the purpose and benefits of keeping other people informed about progress
- explain the purpose and benefits of letting other people know in good time if work plans need to be changed

- explain the purpose and benefits of recognising and learning from mistakes
- explain the purpose of guidelines, procedures and codes of practice that are relevant to your own work.

Planning and being accountable to others for your work

In this section you will investigate the benefits from a work perspective of taking time to plan your work schedule in advance. You will also look into the issue of accountability and why you need to be accountable to others for your work.

Purpose and benefits of planning your work

Taking time at the start of your week to plan for the work that you need to get through is an essential element of good **time management**. It allows you to:

- work out time needed for each task
- see all your deadlines at a glance
- identify any **bottlenecks** so that you can prepare for these ahead of time by requesting more time or more help
- book resources needed to complete any work, such as external printers, couriers or even temps.

Without a little time spent planning your work, you will simply be responding to and completing work requests as and when they come in, without an overview. Planning means that you will be able to make better use of your time at work which, in turn, means there should be fewer last-minute snags, fewer problems with deadlines, and your week should run more smoothly and efficiently. Planning is a critical activity which reaps great rewards in terms of better time management.

Key terms

Time management – working out how to make the best use of your time.

Bottlenecks – these hold up work flow and cause delays.

What planning tools do you use?

Being accountable to others for your own work

Being accountable means that you are answerable to somebody for the work that you do. Every employee in an organisation is answerable to somebody else for their actions – usually their immediate line manager.

The reason why we are all held accountable for our work is because we are required by our contracts of employment to complete certain tasks. Failing to complete the work that is required of you means that you are not carrying out your job properly. This can result in your being **disciplined** and ultimately **dismissed** from your position if you fail to comply with the disciplinary procedure. Being accountable is a very important requirement of your job, no matter who your employer is. Even the managing directors of organisations are

Key terms

Disciplined – reprimanded for some aspect of your behaviour or performance, which is not satisfactory; in a work situation this is usually part of a disciplinary procedure.

Dismissed – told you no longer have a job.

Activity 1

1 Complete the first table by making a list of the key tasks that you are required to do each week at work, along with estimates of time required for each task.

A version of this table, ready for you to complete, is available to download from www.contentextra.com/businessadmin

Key tasks that you carry out each week	Estimated time required

2 In the second table, list some of the typical issues that interrupt your work schedule. For each issue that you identify, write down one thing that you could do in order to minimise this interruption.

A version of this table, ready for you to complete, is available to download from www.contentextra.com/businessadmin

Typical issues that interrupt your work schedule	What you could do to minimise this interruption

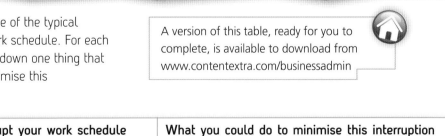

accountable for their actions to the board of directors and can be dismissed if they fail to meet the responsibilities required of them. Accountability applies equally to everyone, from the very top of the organisation down.

Portfolio task 301.1 → Links to **LO1**: assessment criterion 1.1

Write a short report which explains the purpose and benefits of:

- planning your work
- being accountable to others for your own work.

You should include examples of both planning and accountability in your report from your own work experience to illustrate your answer.

Negotiating realistic targets for work

In this section you will investigate the reasons why you need to negotiate realistic work targets. You will also look at some of the ways in which you can go about this.

Reasons why you need to negotiate realistic targets for work

Negotiation is the process of communicating with others in order to bargain for an outcome which works best for you. The overall aim of any negotiation is to reach an agreement. This means that there will need to be some flexibility on both sides.

You need to develop good negotiation skills to make sure that you do not become overburdened with a workload which is unmanageable. Colleagues who need your services at work will always want tasks completed right away. If you provide administrative services to fifteen other staff, you can see that this would be an impossible situation without some room for negotiation on deadlines.

Negotiating your work deadlines means that you can control your work rate and ensures you can devote adequate time to effectively completing each task to a high standard. You cannot work to high standards if you are rushing your way through each task in a bid to complete it in the shortest possible time.

Ways of negotiating realistic targets for work

Before you begin your negotiations you need to do the following.

- When a work request is sent to you, read it and estimate the number of hours' work that it will need.
- Make a note of the deadline given.
- Look at your existing work schedule and identify a day and time when you can begin this work.

Now you are ready to negotiate a realistic deadline. Here is a rundown of the stages which your negotiations should take:

- Reply to the person who sent you the work request, advising them of your availability and your estimate of the time needed to complete the work.
- If you cannot realistically complete the work by the deadline that you have been given, you need to alert them to this fact.
- Propose an alternative time by which you can have the work completed.
- If they accept this proposal, then you can add the work to your current schedule as planned.
- If they cannot accept this alternative deadline, then you need to repeat to them that you are unable to meet their initial deadline and outline the reasons why.
- If there is no agreement at this point, the matter needs to be escalated to a manager.
- Ask your manager to advise you on the best approach for rearranging your other work tasks, if necessary, to accommodate any urgent deadlines.

✓ **Checklist**

Negotiating realistic targets for work

Remember:

- Negotiation requires an element of flexibility on both sides.
- The overall aim of negotiating is to reach agreement.
- If no agreement is forthcoming from the other person despite your best efforts, you need to escalate the matter to a manager.

How could your manager help you with scheduling and deadlines?

Portfolio task 301.2 ➔ Links to **LO1**: assessment criterion 1.2

Write a short report which explains:

- the purpose and benefits of negotiating realistic targets for work

- ways of negotiating realistic targets for work.

You should include examples of work targets of your own in your answer to show your understanding.

Prioritising targets and setting timescales for your work

Prioritising targets

Prioritisation of your work is central to making the best use of your time. This is especially true when there is

too much to do and not enough time to get through everything. How do you decide which items should be attended to first? What, if anything, can be left until the end of the week?

> **Key term**
>
> **Prioritisation** – setting out the order in which you must do your various work tasks.

Urgent or important

The key to prioritising your work targets is to first of all distinguish between the urgent and the important work. Urgent items have immediate consequences if they are not given attention, whereas important items do not. Important items, however, still need to be completed in order to achieve work goals, but can usually be completed at a later date without causing undue problems. If they are left too long, however, important items will also become urgent.

> **Activity 2**
>
> Look over your work tasks for this week. Identify which tasks are urgent and which are important using the table below.
>
> | My urgent tasks for this week | My important tasks for this week |
> |---|---|
> | | |
>
> A version of this table, ready for you to complete, is available to download from www.contentextra.com/businessadmin

There is also some work that can be classified as urgent but not important. A good example of this is when you are interrupted by someone with a request for help because they are having a crisis with their work. This is urgent because it needs immediate attention from you, taking you away from your own work. However, it is not important to you personally because it does not necessarily contribute to your long-term goals or plans.

There are also tasks that are neither urgent nor important, such as certain phone calls, emails and some meetings.

	Urgent	Not urgent
Important	**1** Crises Deadlines Firefighting	**2** Goals and targets
Not important	**3** Interruptions from others	**4** Time-wasting activities

Table 301.1: *Urgent–Important Matrix*

These often take up a good deal of time and hold you up from getting on with the urgent and important items that need your attention.

Look at Table 301.1. This is called the Urgent–Important Matrix and you can apportion all your work tasks into one of the four boxes. Too much of your time spent in box 1, 3 or 4 is unproductive. The key aim of good time management is to work more in box 2, where you will be attending to work which is important but not urgent.

Managing your priorities at work is a fine balancing act where you need to be very clear about which are your essential work tasks and attend to these before you can deal with other matters.

Do you use an electronic diary system?

Setting timescales

Once you have identified your work priorities for the week, you will be in a position to begin setting the timescales for each job. Firstly you will need to have all the estimated time requirements for each job. From here, you can schedule them into your weekly work planner in order of priority. This will give you a very good and detailed list of your work tasks for the week.

If you use a computer-based diary system, you can enter all your work into this and then make it available as a shared document for your work colleagues, so that they can see what you are working on. This will also assist in making your negotiations simpler in the event of additional work requests coming in to you, as you can refer the requester to the online shared calendar or diary to show them your existing work commitments.

✓ Checklist

Setting timescales

Remember, when setting timescales for your work, allow additional time for:

- spellchecking
- proofreading your work.

Portfolio task 301.3 → Link to **LO1**: assessment criterion 1.3

Produce a short report which describes ways of prioritising targets and setting timescales for your own work. Remember to include examples from your own work experience in order to demonstrate your understanding.

Functional skills

English: Reading

If you carry out research involving reading texts including work-related documents as well as Internet research in order to complete your portfolio task, you may be able to count this as evidence towards Level 2 Functional English: Reading. Remember to keep records of all the documents, handbooks and guidelines which you study, along with the websites which you visit, as you will need to document any reading research you carry out.

Work problems

In this section you will investigate some of the typical problems that you may experience from time to time at work and how you can deal with these.

Types of problems that may occur during work

Some typical problems that can occur at work include:

- time constraints
- conflicting deadlines
- resource problems.

Time constraints

One of the most common problems in all organisations is lack of time – and too much to do. This is why time-management skills such as work-planning and prioritisation are so vital in order to get the most out of your time.

You should apply time-management skills to your work every day in order to compensate for any time constraints.

Conflicting deadlines

Another problem that you are very likely to experience at work is conflicting deadlines, when two (or more) colleagues need you to complete work for them at the same time.

As we have seen earlier in this unit, these types of problems are best resolved by negotiation between all the parties concerned. Sometimes, colleagues will happily agree to their work taking second place to another deadline once they see that it is more important than theirs – or has drastic consequences for the business if it is not met.

Resource problems

Resource problems arise when two or more colleagues need the use of resources (such as meeting rooms, laptops or projectors) at the same time and there are not enough of these resources for everyone to have their own. This type of problem can be quite easily remedied by using a booking system, maintained by a member of the administrative team. For example, they would keep a booking diary for each of the resources and staff would be required to book these resources ahead of time to secure their use. This type of system is a good solution to most

Using a booking system is a good method of dealing with resourcing problems

resourcing problems because it places the allocation of the resources under the responsibility of an unbiased third party, who will deal with any conflicting needs in an objective and business-focused manner.

Activity 3

List some of the problems that you have experienced at work. You can use the examples given in the section above if they are relevant to you, or else you can list examples of your own.

Problems that occur at work	Why this problem occurs

A version of this table, ready for you to complete, is available to download from www.contentextra.com/businessadmin

Portfolio task 301.4 → Link to **LO1**: assessment criterion 1.4

In order to complete this portfolio task, you need to write a short guide which could be used to help train new members of staff in your department. This guide should describe three types of problems that may occur at work, along with ways of dealing with each of them. You can include in your answer examples of problems that you have experienced at work which you mentioned in the activity above and say how you went about (or would go about) finding a solution to these.

Keeping other people informed about progress

When you are completing work requests for one or more colleagues, it is likely that you will be left alone to get on with the work. The colleagues who made the work requests will assume that all is well and the work will be completed on time as agreed unless they hear otherwise.

Sending out periodic progress updates

It is a good idea to schedule periodic reminders to yourself to send out progress updates to colleagues. This way, it becomes an automatic part of your job. This has two key advantages for you:

- It shows your colleagues that you are proactive and that you are in control of your timescales.
- It gives peace of mind to your colleagues — and prevents them from having to come to you to ask about progress.

Activity 4

Produce a draft email which could be sent out to one of your colleagues and which gives a progress update on one of their work tasks. Print it out and show it to your assessor when you have completed it. Save the draft email once you have finalised the text so that you can use it as a template for future progress updates.

Notifying colleagues of delays

It is important for you to take responsibility, as part of your role, for keeping your colleagues updated on your progress against targets and — importantly — to advise them of any unforeseen delays to the completion of their work. This is especially important for projects which are large and time-consuming, because a series of delays can impact hugely on the original deadline and push it back not just by days but by weeks or even months.

Alerting colleagues to any delays as soon as possible also means that they are better able to make a **contingency plan** and to work around the delay where possible.

Unit Q301

Key terms

Contingency plan – an alternative plan of action set up to minimise disruption to a business where an original plan did not go as scheduled.

Reflecting – looking back over a situation and considering what you might do differently next time.

Self-evaluation – looking at both the positives and negatives of some aspect of yourself.

Checklist

Informing others of progress

Remember, it is good practice to keep others informed:

- on your progress with their work requests

- if there are delays to the original deadline.

Portfolio task 301.5 → Link to **LO1**: assessment criterion 1.5

Write a short report which explains the purpose and benefits of keeping other people informed about progress. You should include examples from your own work experience which highlight why it is important to communicate your progress on work tasks.

Letting others know if plans need to be changed

As mentioned on page 8, it is crucial to alert your colleagues if, for whatever reason, work plans need to be changed. This is so that they can then make an alternative arrangement for their own work plans and to make provision for any disruption to work schedules and plans further down the line.

This is critical because these plans may involve meetings with other managers or clients of the business, which will then need to be changed. Giving others as much notice as possible allows the business to save face and avoids appearing unprofessional. It also prevents any unnecessary preparation or travelling on the part of others who would have been attending the meetings.

Checklist

Changing work plans

Remember: if work plans need to be changed, give others as much notice as possible, so that they can make contingency plans if necessary.

Portfolio task 301.6 → Link to **LO1**: assessment criterion 1.6

Write a short report which explains the purpose and benefits of letting other people know in good time if work plans need to be changed. Remember to include your own examples of work plans which might need to be changed, the reasons for this and the way in which you would let others know.

Functional skills

English: Speaking and listening

If your assessor asks you to take part in a discussion about this portfolio task as part of the assessment for this learning outcome, you may be able to count it as evidence towards Level 2 Functional English: Speaking and listening.

Recognising and learning from mistakes

One of the most valuable skills that you can learn in a work environment is, firstly, how to recognise when you have made a mistake and, secondly, how to learn from this so you do not repeat the mistake in the future. Failing to learn from mistakes will make it difficult to improve performance — or find better ways of dealing with situations in the future.

Recognising mistakes

The key way of recognising mistakes is by **reflecting** on situations and evaluating actions in the light of the results. The more you do this and the more you learn to practise **self-evaluation** skills, the quicker you will make improvements in your performance at work, which will demonstrate that you are an experienced member of staff.

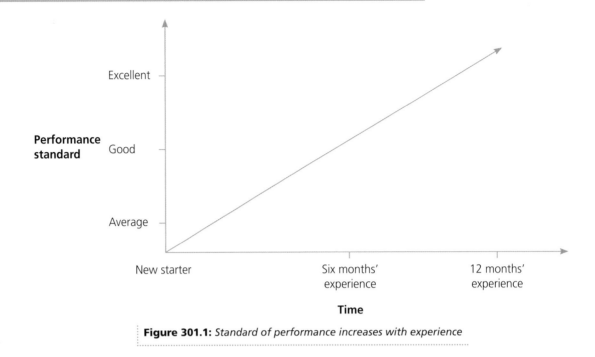

Figure 301.1: *Standard of performance increases with experience*

Learning from mistakes

Learning from experience is precisely what makes you better at your job over time. It is this experience which also allows you to progress to more senior positions within the organisation and attract an increased salary in the future. To underline just how much organisations value experienced employees, take a look at the jobs pages in your local newspaper and look at the proportion of vacancies advertised which require experienced staff.

> **Portfolio task 301.7** → Link to **LO1**: assessment criterion 1.7
>
> Produce a short written guide which clearly explains the purpose and benefits of recognising and learning from mistakes. Your guide needs to be short but informative, so remember to give explanations for each point that you make. You can also include examples of your own to show how you have both recognised and learned from mistakes.

Explain the purpose of guidelines, procedures and codes of practice that are relevant to own work

In this section you will look at the reasons why guidelines, procedures and codes of practice are so important at work.

Why do we need guidelines, procedures and codes of practice at work?

Guidelines, procedures and codes of practice are very important for us all in our working environment as they guide and, in some cases, direct our behaviour. They protect us from harm, they make sure tasks are carried out in the correct manner and they create a consistent approach, so that all staff perform the same tasks in the same way. If guidelines, procedures and codes of practice are followed, difficult situations and injury are minimised.

Some typical examples of guidelines, procedures and codes of practice include:

● health and safety guidelines for the safe handling of office equipment such as print cartridges

● procedures for reporting employee absence

● organisational codes of practice for dealing with customer complaints.

In the next activity, you are going to identify some of the relevant guidelines, procedures and codes of practice which apply to you in your job.

Activity 5

Carry out some research of your own at work to identify all the guidelines, procedures and codes of practice that are relevant to your work. Once you have located the necessary documents, complete the table. Keep a copy of your findings as they will be very useful to you in completing the next portfolio task.

Guidelines, procedures and codes of practice that are relevant to my work	How this affects the work that I do

A version of this table, ready for you to complete, is available to download from www.contentextra.com/businessadmin

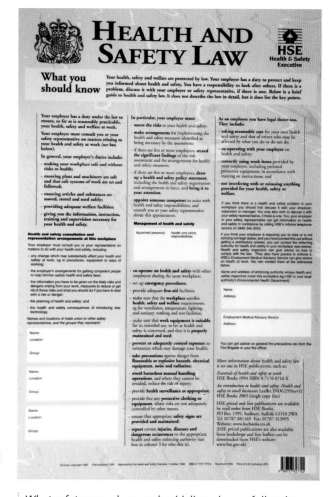

What safety procedures and guidelines do you follow in your work?

Portfolio task 301.8

→ Link to **LO1**: assessment criterion 1.8

Produce a short guidance document which could be used to train new members of staff in your department and which explains the purpose of any three guidelines, procedures and codes of practice that are relevant to your own work. You can use the guidelines, procedures and codes of practice which you identified in the activity earlier in this section on which to base your answer.

Functional skills

English: Reading

If you carry out research involving reading texts including work-related documents as well as Internet research in order to complete your portfolio task, you may be able to count this as evidence towards Level 2 Functional English: Reading. Remember to keep records of all the documents, handbooks and guidelines which you study, along with the websites which you visit, as you will need to document any reading research you carry out.

Understand how to behave in a way that supports effective working

After working through this section you will understand and be able to:

- explain the purpose and benefits of setting high standards for your own work

- describe ways of setting high standards for your own work

- describe ways of dealing with pressure arising from work tasks

- explain the purpose and benefits of accepting setbacks and dealing with them

- explain the purpose and benefits of being assertive and its meaning in work tasks

- give examples of work situations where it is necessary to be assertive

- explain the purpose and benefits of being ready to take on new challenges and adapt to change

- explain the purpose and benefits of treating others with honesty, respect and consideration

- describe types of behaviour at work that show honesty, respect and consideration and those that do not

- explain the purpose of helping and supporting others at work, and the benefits of doing so.

Explain the purpose and benefits of setting high standards for your own work

In this section you will examine the reasons why it is important to set high standards for your own work.

What are high standards?

High standards are standards which result in the best levels of performance and productivity. They can be defined in terms of:

- work rate
- service levels
- error rate.

Reasons why setting high standards is important

High standards are important at work because they set out the targets that you should aim to meet in many areas of your work and which require:

- practice
- learning
- focus
- motivation.

High standards are to be expected in any professional organisation and employees are equally expected to work towards these as a part of their job. Setting high standards ensures that the work of the organisation is carried out as efficiently and productively as possible. It also ensures that customers are satisfied, products are error-free and processes run smoothly and to schedule.

Activity 6

Identify three examples of high standards that are relevant to your job. For each one, say what the benefit is of having that standard.

A version of this table, ready for you to complete, is available to download from www.contentextra.com/businessadmin

High standards relevant to my job	Benefit of this standard to my job

Portfolio task 301.9 → Link to **LO2**: assessment criterion 2.1

Produce a written report which explains the purpose and benefits of setting high standards for your own work. Remember to include three examples from your own experience where you have – or could – set yourself high standards and give an outline of the benefits of this.

Functional skills

English: Writing

If you take care to produce a professional and well-presented report for your answer to this portfolio task, you may be able to count it as evidence towards Level 2 Functional English: Writing. Remember to use headings and subheadings, check you have used correct spelling and grammar and then print out the final corrected version of your report, once you have made all your corrections.

Which arrow represents your work?

- replying to all customer queries within 24 hours
- being helpful and polite to all contacts, both internal and external.

Describe ways of setting high standards for your own work

There are a number of ways in which you can set high standards for your own work. A useful starting point is to begin by:

- listing the main duties that you undertake each day
- working out how many items you usually process per minute or per hour
- identifying specific work tasks that take you the longest time to complete
- listing the main contacts – both internal and external – you speak to each day.

Once you have produced a list with all of this information, you can go through each point and identify where you can usefully set yourself high targets to work towards, such as:

- increasing your work rate by 10%
- achieving zero spelling errors in typed documents
- responding to all work requests within two hours
- meeting all work deadlines

Portfolio task 301.10 → Link **LO2**: assessment criterion 2.2

Produce a written report which describes ways of setting high standards for your own work. You can base your answer on the three examples which you used in the previous portfolio task and, for each one, outline the ways in which you either have set – or could go about setting – high standards for your work.

Dealing with pressure from work

When work is arriving on your desk faster than you can process it, inevitably you will feel under a certain amount of pressure. Pressure is something that you need to learn to identify and to deal with in work situations, as failure to do this could result in:

- reduced performance due to stress
- lower morale, as you cannot cope with the workload
- errors in work, due to being overloaded with tasks
- a breakdown in relationships with colleagues, as you cannot meet their needs.

Unit Q301 Manage own performance in a business environment

Identifying pressure

It is important that you are able to identify the key triggers of pressure in your job. Perhaps there are certain times of the year, month or even the week when workloads become regularly heavy with too much to do. Whatever the pattern of peaks and troughs in demands made on you at work, the better you can prepare ahead to cater for these situations, the better you will perform and be able to cope during these times.

How well do you deal with pressure at work?

Pressure can also arise at work from having to carry out certain tasks that are unpleasant. An example could include having to take regular calls from a customer who is particularly demanding or difficult. It could also be due to difficult colleagues. In these types of situations, it is important to find ways of coping — or avoiding — certain situations if at all possible. If this is not possible, then coping strategies are a good idea.

Activity 7

Make a list of three sources of pressure in your current job. For each one, list one way in which you could better prepare yourself to cope with this pressure.

Ways of dealing with pressure

Once you have identified the key sources of pressure in your job, you can begin to find the best ways in which to deal with them. Here is a practical guide which offers some useful advice:

- Set aside some quiet time each day when you turn off your email and mobile phone and set your desk phone to voicemail. Use this quiet time to think about your work priorities in a calm manner.

- Write your work list down. Don't attempt to keep everything in your head — you are risking forgetting something important if you do this.

- Prioritise by setting out what needs to be done first, second, third, and so on.

- Always request more time and even some help if you feel that this is necessary.

- If your manager gives you two urgent things to do, ask them which one you should prioritise.

- Take a short break from your desk in between tasks to gather your thoughts and prepare for the next task.

- Never be afraid to speak up and say when someone has given you an impossible deadline to meet — it is quite likely that they do not in fact know how many hours' work the task entails.

Apart from the practical and very work-focused guide given above, you can also deal with pressure by:

- taking regular exercise
- eating healthily
- getting rest.

These are general lifestyle guidelines, but it is well documented that a good diet and exercise contribute greatly to relieving stress.

Activity 8

Think about the ways in which you deal with pressure in your work and other areas of your life. List three things that you do (or would like to do) which would help you to deal with pressure.

✓ Checklist

Remember:

- A certain amount of pressure can be a good thing as it motivates us to work hard to achieve goals.

- Pressure can, however, escalate into unmanageable stress if it is not adequately dealt with.

- You need to devise a set of ways that will help you deal with your own particular work-based pressures.

> **Portfolio task 301.11** → Link to **LO2**: assessment criterion 2.3
>
> Produce a short written report which can be distributed to members of staff in your organisation and which describes ways of dealing with pressure arising from work tasks. Remember to include examples from your own experience outlining ways in which you have dealt with such pressure. It may strengthen your answer if you carry out your own additional research into pressure at work and include some of your findings from this in your report.

Accepting setbacks and dealing with them

Setbacks at work are unfortunate events which happen to us all from time to time, causing us problems in terms of completing a task or performing to the required standards. They are a fact of life at work. What is important is the way in which you choose to respond to them.

When you become frustrated and upset by a setback at work, a potentially large amount of time can be lost due to the disruption which this causes. This amount of lost time will depend essentially on the way in which you choose to react to it.

Discussing your misfortune with colleagues at length, for example, is not a very constructive way to deal with such a situation. A better approach would be not to take the matter personally and instead:

● accept that it has happened and identify what you can now do, in view of the setback, to move forward in the most effective way

● ensure that you do not waste your valuable time worrying about things over which you have no control

● learn from any mistakes that you have made – this will enable you to do better next time.

Benefits of accepting setbacks and moving forward

It is better to adopt an accepting attitude and move forward with your job in the aftermath of a setback as this minimises time lost at work and it avoids your becoming overly focused on errors of the past. Focusing

on past errors can hamper your work performance and relationships with colleagues, especially if you blame others for the setback. It is better to acknowledge the setback, identify any suitable damage limitation actions and, if necessary, discuss the situation with your manager.

> **Portfolio task 302.12** → Link to **LO2**: assessment criterion 2.4
>
> Write a short guide for staff in your organisation which explains the purpose and benefits of accepting setbacks and dealing with them. Include examples from your own experience and say why you think it is a better approach to accept setbacks which occur at work and to find ways of dealing with them.

Being assertive at work

In this section you will look at what it means to be assertive at work. You will also investigate the reasons why being assertive is important and the benefits that this has for you and your work.

What does 'assertive' mean?

Being assertive means expressing your ideas, comments and opinions freely without being either aggressive or submissive. Assertiveness is considered to be a very important communication skill in business, so much so that an entire industry has evolved over the last forty years, which deals with techniques for the development of assertiveness skills.

> **Activity 9**
>
> Carry out some Internet research to find some assertiveness training websites. Read about the various techniques that you can adopt in order to act assertively. Find and list three things you can try to do at work in order to be more assertive.

Being assertive means that you are aware of your own rights and needs, but you also respect the rights and needs of your colleagues. It means that you will not allow others to violate your rights and needs and are able to express your thoughts and opinions objectively with the goal of completing a work-related task.

Table 301.2: *Response to work pressures: aggressive, assertive, submissive*

State	Typical response to work pressures
Aggressive	Domineering, controlling, bullying. Insists on getting own way with no consideration of the other's position.
Assertive	Rational, well considered. Explains own view in a way which is confident and proactive.
Submissive	Typically says yes to all work requests and does not attempt to negotiate with others or put forward own opinions and ideas.

Purpose and benefits of being assertive in work tasks

Being assertive is the ideal communication strategy to adopt in work situations. It means that you will be able to stand up for yourself adequately, while not being domineering or aggressive towards others. Being aggressive is something that you should avoid at all costs, as this type of behaviour can result in allegations of workplace bullying, which is covered by employment legislation, such as the Equality Act 2010. Similarly, being submissive and taking on all work tasks without considering the pressure which this will put you under is also something that you should avoid.

Activity 10

Think about two of your usual work tasks. In what ways could you try to be more assertive in managing these tasks?

Portfolio task 301.13 → Link to **LO2**: assessment criterion 2.5

Write a brief report which explains the purpose and benefits of being assertive. Remember to begin by stating what you understand by the term assertive in relation to work tasks. Then outline the reasons why you need to be assertive at work and the benefits that this has for both you and your work colleagues.

Work situations where you need to be assertive

There are certain times at work where being assertive is necessary. For example:

- when dealing with particularly difficult or aggressive colleagues or customers
- when being asked for your opinion in meetings
- in performance appraisals
- when requesting a pay rise
- when applying for a promotion
- when asking for better working conditions from your manager, such as new office equipment or furniture.

The list above is just a selection of situations when you will need to be prepared to speak up and assert yourself in order to be heard and listened to. If you do not find it possible to behave in an assertive manner in these situations, you are likely to come off worse and it is almost certain that you will not achieve what you want.

How to behave assertively

Some people find it difficult to behave in an assertive manner because they are either too passive or too aggressive by nature. Our behaviour is the result of many factors and is so deeply ingrained in our personalities that to suddenly have to change the way in which we respond to others or conduct ourselves can be difficult.

However, that is not to say that it is impossible. With a little practice and preparation, most people can alter the way in which they communicate their opinions and conduct themselves with others in work situations.

Unit Q301

Manage own performance in a business environment

Activity 11

Practice some assertiveness skills of your own by doing the following exercises:

1   Imagine that your manager wants you to take on a large new project but you already work late most nights and you cannot possibly take on any additional work at the moment. Rehearse your response to your manager (which is a polite refusal) in the mirror or role-play it with a friend or colleague.

2   Imagine that you are in a meeting and you disagree with the point that is being made by a very opinionated and aggressive manager. How would you act and what would you say in order to get your opinion across to the members of the meeting?

✓ Checklist

Being assertive

Remember:

* Assertiveness is about speaking up for yourself in a way that is neither aggressive nor overbearing.

* Assertive people have respect for the opinions of others and are able to listen to them.

Portfolio task 301.14

→ Link to **LO2**: assessment criterion 2.6

Write a short guide which gives three examples of work situations where it is necessary to be assertive. Include examples from your own work experience to highlight instances where you found it necessary to act assertively and, for each one, say what the benefit was of being assertive in that particular situation.

Taking on new challenges

In this section you will look at the purpose and benefits of being ready to take on new challenges and adapt to change.

Being ready to take on new challenges

Being ready and willing to take on new challenges at work is simply a state of mind. Those who have this readiness and willingness will benefit from opportunities to develop new and enhanced skills, learn new technologies and work with new people and processes. All of these opportunities are extremely valuable from a career-development point of view. They will provide you with a better skill set, a well-rounded CV and a greater chance of being selected for promotion in the future.

Apart from the advantages which this will bring to your career and skills, being ready and willing to take on new challenges will make your working experience more varied, interesting and rewarding. Staying in the same role can become dull and repetitive once you have become fully skilled in a certain area and have done it for a long time. By simply being willing to accept new challenges at work, you are adding to the variety and interest of your work. You are greatly improving your future prospects at the same time.

Being able to adapt to change

A central part of being willing to take on new challenges is the ability to adapt to change. If you become fixed in a certain way of working, you will not find it easy to become adaptable to changes that occur at work. Adaptability — just like willingness to take on new challenges — is just a state of mind. You can even train yourself in positive thinking techniques to help you to be more adaptable to change. To succeed, however, you need to be prepared to leave behind the current routines and processes which you have become used to at work. You will also need to be open to learning any required new skills.

✓ Checklist

Techniques to help you adapt to change

Some of these techniques may be helpful in allowing you to be more adaptable to change:

- Look for the positive, rather than the negative effects of the change.

- Look at the long-term, not the immediate short-term view. This will help to allay immediate worries concerning changes to your work routine. It may be unsettling now, but you will soon get used to new ways of working.

- Focus on the fact that you are fully capable of coping with this change.

Activity 12

Think of three ways in which you could become more adaptable to change at work. Give one benefit for each method that you identify.

Portfolio task 301.15 → Link **LO2**: assessment criterion 2.7

Write a short report which explains the purpose and benefits of being ready to take on new challenges and adapt to change. Use examples from your own experience to show the benefits of this.

Treating others with honesty, respect and consideration

It is essential at work to behave in ways which demonstrate your honesty, respect and consideration for others. This does not just mean behaving in this way towards your manager and colleagues, but it also extends to all the people with whom you may come into contact during the course of your work.

Being honest

Honesty, as the saying goes, is always the best policy. If you can be honest in your interactions and discussions with others, this will go a long way towards gaining a good reputation among your colleagues. Honesty also requires an element of tact. Tact involves taking care when putting across your opinions and thoughts so as to avoid offending or hurting the feelings of others.

Being respectful and considerate

Being respectful and considerate of others requires the ability to acknowledge that colleagues may have a completely opposing view to yours, but at the same time to demonstrate that you respect their opinion and welcome the opportunity to discuss your views in a polite and considered manner.

Portfolio task 301.16 → Link to **LO2**: assessment criterion 2.8

Write a short guide which can be distributed to staff in your organisation and which explains the purpose and benefits of treating others with honesty, respect and consideration. Use examples from your own experience which highlight the reasons why this is important.

Types of behaviour at work that show honesty, respect and consideration

There are a number of types of behaviour which people can display at work which show honesty, respect and consideration. These can be grouped under the umbrella heading of 'good manners'. Here is just a selection of these:

- Owning up to errors is a very good example of honesty at work. It is surprisingly difficult to do, especially if you work in an organisation where people do not generally own up to any errors unless they are found out.

- Listening to others without interrupting or speaking over them is a very good skill to learn as it shows respect and consideration for others' opinions.

- Taking on board the opinion of a colleague with whom you disagree is a mark of respect and demonstrates that even though you have opposing views you acknowledge that each of you has the right to your own opinion and to voice that opinion in an open and frank discussion.

Are you a good listener?

Failure to show honesty, respect and consideration

You may have noticed that certain colleagues at work have unfortunate tendencies to:

- speak over others in meetings – constantly interrupting and not allowing others to speak
- intimidate or even bully staff into taking on tasks that make their workloads unmanageable
- ridicule colleagues behind their back.

All of these behaviours are unprofessional and are not what is expected of professionals working in organisations.

The way in which people behave in meetings is a good indicator of their general respectfulness. Next time you are in a team meeting at work, take a few minutes to observe the way in which people speak and interact with one another. You will notice that some people speak over others, while some raise their voices to make themselves the centre of attention. Others may even stand up or bang the desk to demonstrate their strong feelings about an issue. These are all examples of disrespectful behaviour.

Activity 13

Make a list of three types of behaviour in a work environment which you consider to lack honesty, respect and consideration. For each example, give reasons to explain your opinions.

Portfolio task 301.17 → Link to **LO2**: assessment criterion 2.9

Write a short guide which describes types of behaviour at work that show honesty, respect and consideration and those that do not. Include two types of behaviour for each in order to demonstrate your understanding of the correct way to behave towards colleagues at work.

Helping and supporting others at work

In this section you will look at the reasons why you should be prepared to help and support others at work and at the benefits of this.

Why provide help to others?

Sometimes workloads in a team or department become uneven with the result that certain members of staff become overloaded while others may not be very busy at all. The solution from a business point of view is for those with free time to take a share of the work from those who are extremely busy. In this way the required work will be completed quickly and efficiently. The whole team or department also benefits from this as, by helping individuals to complete work tasks, the whole team's or department's targets will be met.

Another example of a situation where you should be prepared to help and support others is when new or inexperienced colleagues may need your help. As you gain more experience and learn more about the way in which your department operates, you are also gaining valuable skills within the organisation from which younger and less experienced colleagues can benefit. You are very well placed therefore to provide **on-the-job training** so that they can become more proficient at their job in a shorter time.

Key term

On-the-job training – training which is provided to staff while they are at work doing their job.

Activity 14

Think of three ways in which you could provide help and support to new or inexperienced colleagues at work.

Benefits of being helpful and supportive

There are a number of benefits — both to you and to your team or department — of being helpful and supportive to colleagues at work. For example, being supportive brings about:

- a much more positive and pleasant working environment for everyone
- better **productivity** in the department because people are helped to develop new skills and become better at their job

- improved morale as people realise they can ask for and receive help when they need it
- a climate of trust and cooperation.

Key term

Productivity – the rate at which work is completed.

Portfolio task 301.18 → Link to **LO2**: assessment criterion 2.10

Write a brief report which explains the purpose of helping and supporting others at work, and the benefits of doing so. Give examples from your own experience to strengthen your answer.

Evidence collection

In order for you to complete the remaining assessment criteria to successfully pass this unit, you will need to carry out various tasks at work and then produce evidence to show that you have demonstrated the required skills and competence.

Evidence can be collected in a number of different ways. For example, it can be in the form of a signed witness testimony from a colleague or line manager, a copy of any related emails or letters you have produced, or a verbal discussion with your assessor.

Speak to your assessor to identify the best methods to use in order to complete each portfolio task and remember to keep copies of all the evidence that you produce.

Be able to plan, prioritise and be accountable for own work

Portfolio task 301.19

→ Links to **LO3**: assessment criteria 3.1, 3.2, 3.3, 3.4, 3.5, 3.6, 3.7, 3.8 and 3.9

Gather evidence of your work to show your assessor that you have successfully carried out the tasks outlined in the table below. Check with your assessor on the best ways of gathering evidence for each of the tasks before you begin.

Task	Evidence
1 Negotiate and agree realistic targets and achievable timescales for own work. 2 Prioritise targets for own work.	

A version of this form, ready for you to complete, is available to download from www.contentextra.com/businessadmin

Behave in a way that supports effective working

Portfolio task 301.20

→ Links to **LO4**: assessment criteria 4.1, 4.2, 4.3, 4.4, 4.5, 4.6 and 4.7

Gather evidence of your work to show your assessor that you have successfully carried out the tasks outlined in the table below. Check with your assessor on the best ways of gathering evidence for each of the tasks before you begin.

Task	Evidence
1 Set high standards for own work and demonstrate drive and commitment in achieving these standards. 2 Adapt work and working methods to deal with setbacks and difficulties.	

A version of this form, ready for you to complete, is available to download from www.contentextra.com/businessadmin

Office life

Julie's story

My name is Julie Holmes and I'm 19 years old. I've been working as an administrative assistant for a national chain of insurers for five months now. My job involves providing administrative and secretarial support to a team of ten agents. My working day is quite varied and I enjoy dealing with different colleagues.

However, one issue I am noticing at the moment is that I am increasingly being put under pressure by being given work with urgent deadlines from several people at once. I also receive no advance warning of this work. I have been working long hours over the last couple of weeks to try to stay on top of the workload, but it never seems to be enough. A friend of mine says I should start telling people that I cannot do the work for them when they want it because I am already working at full capacity. However, I do not wish to be seen as uncooperative or rude. I cannot continue under this level of pressure, but I do not know what to do.

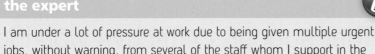

Ask the expert

Q I am under a lot of pressure at work due to being given multiple urgent jobs, without warning, from several of the staff whom I support in the office. This is making my working day overly hectic and stressful. What can I do about this?

A You need to change the way in which you deal with these work requests. Otherwise the situation will not change. You need to become more assertive and negotiate with these people with the aim of pushing back some of the deadlines. If the staff whom you support cannot agree some flexibility, you need to escalate this matter to your line manager.

Top tips

Providing support to multiple staff will always carry the risk of being presented with the challenge of conflicting deadlines. This is why Julie needs to become assertive and negotiate with her colleagues to reach agreement on securing more time to complete the work.

The key to being assertive lies in the ability to stand up for oneself whilst also respecting the needs of others and, importantly, without coming across as overbearing or rude. Assertiveness is a communication skill which can be learned and developed over time and which will be of huge benefit to people during their career.

Unit Q301 Manage own performance in a business environment

Check your knowledge

1 What is a benefit of planning your work?

a) You can extend your work deadlines.

b) You can see clearly which work tasks you have to complete and by when.

c) You can keep your work area tidy.

d) You can leave some of your tasks until next week.

2 What does the term 'prioritising' mean?

a) It means filing your paperwork.

b) It means rearranging deadlines however you wish.

c) It means doing your favourite tasks first.

d) It means organising work into the order in which it needs to be done.

3 Why is it good practice to keep others informed about your progress?

a) So that they can tell your manager if you are late completing work.

b) So that they can give you additional tasks to complete.

c) So that you can keep practising your work.

d) So that they have advance warning in case there is a problem with schedules.

4 What is the main advantage of learning from past mistakes?

a) You will not make the same mistake again.

b) You will never improve your performance.

c) There are no advantages to learning from past mistakes.

d) Mistakes stay on your personnel file forever.

5 How could you set a high standard for your own work?

a) By working out your average typing speed and working at this rate.

b) By making sure you meet minimum work requirements.

c) By looking at your weekly work rate and aiming to increase this by ten per cent.

d) By asking your colleagues to time you making phone calls to customers.

6 What is the main advantage of accepting setbacks at work and dealing with them?

a) You can move forward with your other work commitments with minimum disruption.

b) You can just forget that the setback occurred.

c) You can deny any involvement in the setback.

d) You can take the blame for the setback.

7 What do you understand by the term 'assertive'?

a) Being bossy.

b) Standing up for yourself without being aggressive.

c) Never listening to others.

d) Doing everything that is asked of you.

8 Which of these is a benefit of taking on new challenges at work?

a) You will take on too much work and suffer from stress.

b) You will experience new areas of work and develop new skills.

c) You will not learn anything new.

d) You will be entitled to a pay rise.

9 Why is it important to show honesty, respect and consideration to others at work?

a) Because this is the type of behaviour expected from you as an employee.

b) Because you are told to do so.

c) Because inconsiderate behaviour might backfire on you.

d) Because otherwise you might lose your job.

10 Why do you think you should be prepared to help and support others at work?

a) There is no need to help others at work.

b) Because this contributes both to team spirit and to the wider work goals of the team.

c) Because you will get noticed by your manager.

d) Because then you can take the credit for the work.

Answers to the Check your knowledge questions can be found at www.contentextra.com/businessadmin

What your assessor is looking for

In order to prepare for and succeed in completing this unit, your assessor will require you to be able to demonstrate competence in all of the performance criteria listed in the table below.

Your assessor will guide you through the assessment process, but it is likely that for this unit you will need to:

- complete short written narratives or personal statements explaining your answers
- take part in professional discussions with your assessor to explain your answers verbally
- complete observations with your assessor ensuring that they can observe you carrying out your work tasks

- produce any relevant work products to help demonstrate how you have completed the assessment criteria
- ask your manager, a colleague, or a customer for witness testimonies explaining how you have completed the assessment criteria.

Please note that the evidence which you generate for the assessment criteria in this unit may also count towards your evidence collection for some of the other units in this qualification. Your assessor will provide support and guidance on this.

The table below outlines the portfolio tasks which you need to complete for this unit, mapped to their associated assessment criteria.

Task and page reference	Mapping assessment criteria
Portfolio task 301.1 (page 4)	Assessment criterion: 1.1
Portfolio task 301.2 (page 5)	Assessment criterion: 1.2
Portfolio task 301.3 (page 7)	Assessment criterion: 1.3
Portfolio task 301.4 (page 8)	Assessment criterion: 1.4
Portfolio task 301.5 (page 9)	Assessment criterion: 1.5
Portfolio task 301.6 (page 9)	Assessment criterion: 1.6
Portfolio task 301.7 (page 10)	Assessment criterion: 1.7
Portfolio task 301.8 (page 11)	Assessment criterion: 1.8
Portfolio task 301.9 (page 13)	Assessment criterion: 2.1
Portfolio task 301.10 (page 13)	Assessment criterion: 2.2
Portfolio task 301.11 (page 15)	Assessment criterion: 2.3
Portfolio task 301.12 (page 15)	Assessment criterion: 2.4
Portfolio task 301.13 (page 16)	Assessment criterion: 2.5
Portfolio task 301.14 (page 17)	Assessment criterion: 2.6
Portfolio task 301.15 (page 18)	Assessment criterion: 2.7
Portfolio task 301.16 (page 18)	Assessment criterion: 2.8
Portfolio task 301.17 (page 19)	Assessment criterion: 2.9
Portfolio task 301.18 (page 20)	Assessment criterion: 2.10
Portfolio task 301.19 (page 21)	Assessment criteria: 3.1, 3.2, 3.3, 3.4, 3.5, 3.6, 3.7, 3.8 and 3.9
Portfolio task 301.20 (page 21)	Assessment criteria: 4.1, 4.2, 4.3, 4.4, 4.5, 4.6 and 4.7

Unit Q302

Evaluate and improve own performance in a business environment

What you will learn

- Understand how to evaluate and improve own performance
- Be able to evaluate and improve own performance using feedback from others
- Be able to use evaluation of own performance to agree, develop and use a learning plan

Introduction

This unit explains the principles and benefits of continuously improving your own performance to help develop the overall efficiency of the organisation. It also explains the sources and value of feedback on your own performance.

Planning your objectives and day-to-day work tasks can assist in helping you become more efficient. By setting SMART objectives you will also be able to be more specific about what you want to achieve.

By evaluating your current performance, you will be able to identify if you have any further training or development needs and then formulate a learning plan to action any specific areas. This will ultimately ensure that you extend your skills and knowledge and improve your performance.

The unit will also look at the different learning and development opportunities that may be available to you and also provide you with some information on possible career progression.

Doing an apprenticeship?

If you are taking your NVQ as part of an apprenticeship, you will find that the knowledge and understanding for this unit links to your Technical Certificate. Go to www.contentextra.com/businessadmin to find summaries of the Technical Certificate units.

How to evaluate and improve own performance

After working through this section you will understand and be able to:

- explain the purpose and benefits of continuously improving own performance in a business environment
- explain the purpose and value of encouraging and accepting feedback from others
- describe ways of evaluating own work

- explain the purpose and benefits of trying out possible improvements to own work, benefit organisations and further own career
- compare possible career progression routes
- describe possible development opportunities
- justify the value of developing a learning plan.

The purpose and benefits of continuously improving own performance in a business environment

It is important to know that you are improving in your work role as this will ensure that you are **motivated** and enjoy your job. As you become more experienced in the workplace you will get better at what you are doing and you will become more **efficient**.

Being efficient means undertaking a task quickly and to a high standard. It is important to understand that you may well be good at what you do already, but it is likely that you will get better with time as you extend your skills and knowledge.

If all the staff in an organisation try to improve their performance, then this should improve the performance of the organisation as a whole.

Key terms

Motivated – has the desire to do something, such as to work hard.

Efficient – able to complete a task quickly and to a high standard.

Checklist

Improving performance

Remember, improving performance is not all about increasing sales or meeting targets. Improving performance can be measured in many different ways. For example, spending longer on the telephone with a customer to ensure that all their needs are met is a way to demonstrate improved customer care. This may lead to better customer retention and improved customer care performance.

Portfolio task 302.1 → Links to **L01**: assessment criterion 1.1

List three reasons why it is important to continuously improve own performance.

Most organisations will have some form of staffing structure in place. The benefits of a structure are that:

● all staff have specific roles and responsibilities and by completing their tasks, they should help the organisation to achieve its objectives

● all staff should know what is expected of them

● staff are likely to have an awareness of how what they do fits with the other parts of the organisation

● all staff should know what authority they have and what decisions they can make.

As you can see from the points detailed above, a structured organisation should ensure that staff know their role and are clear about what is expected of them. It also allows staff to see how their role fits within the organisation as a whole and how it links into all the other parts of the organisation. By working within this type of framework, it is possible to create **empowerment** by developing the capability of extending the employees' skills and knowledge to constantly develop the organisation.

Empowering employees can assist in preparing the organisation towards long-term success by developing key individuals and groups of people who may generate a **competitive advantage** for the organisation. This can be achieved by the organisation having more effective employees because they are more highly trained and have better skills than their competitors' employees. This may also enable the organisation to link into new processes and innovative ways of working.

Key terms

Empowerment – the process of enabling or authorising an individual to think, behave, take action, control their work and take part in decision-making processes.

Competitive advantage – when an organisation is able to secure profits above the average gained by its competitors.

Planning your work more effectively

As discussed later in the unit, new systems, processes and equipment may make the organisation more efficient, but another important factor to consider is how you plan your work and how you can improve your own performance.

As part of your job, you will be able to plan some of your own work. For regular and routine jobs, you might prepare a 'to do' list of things that you need to do that day or that week or you may use a 'task manager' system on your computer. By prioritising your tasks you will be able to plan your work more effectively.

✓ Checklist

Planning your work

The following checklist will help you plan your work:

● Write down all your tasks and when you need to achieve them by.

● Highlight any specific deadline dates and try to achieve them one day ahead of the deadline.

● For larger jobs, break down the tasks into more manageable elements if required.

● Classify your tasks by deciding how important they are and when they need to be completed by. Then use a rating system, for example, 1, 2, 3 or A, B, C, to help prioritise them.

● Think about what you *must* do, *should* do and *could* do.

● Identify at the outset any targets that may be difficult to achieve and try to negotiate extra time or resources if required.

● Check your list each day and work through your tasks in the order that you have rated them.

● Don't panic if a new urgent task comes up. Just slot it into your list in the appropriate place and carry on with your current task.

● Always review your plan at the end of each day and reschedule any new targets into the plan.

Managing tasks

> ### ✓ Checklist
>
> **Best use of time**
>
> Remember to ensure that you make the best use of your time:
>
> - Don't make unnecessary trips away from your desk.
> - Don't over-use your email and be checking it all the time.
> - Don't waste time chatting to colleagues for long periods.
> - Don't put off jobs that you don't like doing.
> - Don't take on too much and try to deal with lots of tasks all at once.
> - Don't dither and be unable to decide what to do first.

We have already discussed how to prepare a list of all your tasks and how you can classify them in terms of importance and target dates. Also consider:

- Delegation – it is likely that you are not the only person in the office who can carry out a particular task. Can you delegate a particular task to a colleague?
- Must, should, could – try to prioritise your work into these three areas: work that I must complete this week; work that I should complete this week; and work that I could complete if I had some spare time.

One-off jobs and longer-term targets

For one-off jobs or longer-term targets/objectives, you may find an approach called setting SMART objectives useful.

SMART means:

- **S**pecific – it says exactly what you intend to do.
- **M**easurable – you can measure progress and show that you have completed it.
- **A**chievable – the targets are not beyond your reach.
- **R**ealistic – the target is not too optimistic.
- **T**ime-bound – you have a specific deadline for completion.

If you set any SMART objectives, make sure that they make sense, that they are understood by you and your colleagues and that you have agreed them with your manager.

- An example of a non-SMART objective:

  'I'm an administrator, but I want to become an IT expert as soon as possible.'

This is not SMART, as it is not specific, measurable or realistic. Also, there is no specific completion date and it is questionable whether it is achievable.

- An example of a SMART objective:

  'I want to learn how to use spreadsheets by completing a course at my local college which will finish in June next year.'

  Looking at this example in more detail, it is possible to check each element to see if it is SMART:

  Specific – the objective is fairly detailed and it does state what the intention is.

  Measurable – the objective says that the intention is to 'complete' the course. By this it will be possible to measure the success or not, as the course will either be completed or not.

  Achievable – the objective is achievable as it doesn't say that you want to become an expert; it just says that you want to learn one specific element (spreadsheets).

  It is **R**ealistic as you have not overestimated your capabilities and you have set enough time to complete the course.

  It is **T**ime-bound as there is a clear end date.

The advantage of setting SMART objectives is that because they are specific they define each element. As a result you are more likely to achieve them.

> ### Portfolio task 302.2 Links to **LO2**: assessment criterion 2.3
>
> Write a SMART objective for your job that you can achieve sometime in the near future. Explain how you will complete the objective and how you will measure it. This will be useful evidence for your portfolio.
>
> #### Functional skills
>
> **English: Reading**
>
> If you carry out research involving reading texts including work-related documents as well as Internet research in order to complete your portfolio task, you may be able to count this as evidence towards Level 2 Functional English: Reading. Remember to keep records of all the documents, handbooks or guidelines which you study, along with the websites which you visit, as you will need to document any reading research you carry out.

The types of changes that could be made to improve your own performance

Most organisations have an agreed **working culture**. In simple terms, a work culture means 'this is how we do things round here'. At work, you will notice how people communicate and interact with each other and how people plan their work.

Key terms

Working culture – the way that an organisation works, based on its history, traditions, values and vision.

Self-motivated – be able to work independently and with enthusiasm without pressure from others.

Job satisfaction – being happy in your job.

It is also likely that there will be some performance standards in place which you will need to work to. These may include some specific targets that you need to achieve on an ongoing basis and also may include some general standards. For example, if you work as an administrator, based in the main reception, then you will interact with your customers and colleagues on a daily basis, and some of the general performance standards that you will need to meet may be things like:

- dealing with people quickly and efficiently
- dealing with people in a courteous manner
- treating everyone equally and fairly.

It is worth remembering that not all standards will be written down or communicated to you. There may often be an assumption that you will just behave to this standard anyway. From the organisation's perspective, it would be an acceptable assumption, for example, for your behaviour to be professional, courteous and non-discriminatory at all times.

One of the key elements for improving performance is making sure you are **self-motivated** and enjoy your job. Being self-motivated means that you are able to come into work each day in a positive frame of mind and you are able to complete the tasks by taking ownership of your job. This will improve your **job satisfaction** and should get you thinking about how you might be able to improve your job.

By being accountable for your job, you are taking responsibility for your actions. By adopting this frame of

mind, this enables you to plan your work and to start to set yourself some meaningful objectives to achieve.

Once you have been in your job for a while, you will have a fairly detailed understanding of how it works. You will then be in a position to see if you can make any changes that could improve your own performance. Think about what you do, how you do it and what effect your role has on other parts of the organisation.

The following questions should provide you with a starting point for some ideas:

- Do I enjoy my job? Am I self-motivated? Can I make any improvements in my own performance?
- Do I take responsibility for my job and complete the tasks to the best of my ability and within the agreed time frames?
- Can any of the existing procedures or processes be eliminated or combined?
- Are there any new systems or technology that can be used to do this task more efficiently?
- What do my colleagues think – do they have any ideas for areas that could be improved?

Make sure that you discuss your ideas with your manager, test out any proposals with a trial to see if they work and seek feedback to refine your ideas further if necessary. Ultimately, any changes should result in some or all of the following outcomes being achieved:

- The task or process is more efficient than before.
- The improvement provides a better service to the customer.
- The organisation is saving money by adopting the new way of working.
- You and your colleagues are happy and motivated.

The purpose and value of encouraging and accepting feedback from others

Generally speaking, feedback of any type is useful, particularly if it is constructive. To be constructive the feedback must be meaningful, have value and be accepted by you. You may receive some positive feedback and there may not be any action required from you as a result of such feedback, but the important thing is to ensure that you understand what all feedback means and how to put this into context in relation to your whole job. If you receive some feedback from a customer or a colleague and you are not sure what it means, then ask them to clarify in more detail.

It is important not to become upset or down if someone gives you some negative feedback about your performance. Take the comments on board and make sure you get it right next time.

Remember to consider any feedback in the context of your whole job. For example, if your manager said that you did not meet one of your performance targets for the month, then you might well be disappointed, but if you had ten targets in total and you met the other nine, then most people would accept that as very competent performance. However, if you had not met this target for several months in a row or you began to fall short of some of your other targets as well, then you would need to take the appropriate action to resolve the issues. A good idea is to make a list of the issues and then pull together an action plan in order that you can then begin to manage the situation. This could then be transferred onto your learning plan as an area for development.

By accepting feedback from your colleagues and customers, it should help you to improve your own performance. By improving your performance, you should become more efficient in your role. If all your colleagues are also doing the same, then the whole organisation should improve and become more efficient. Regular constructive feedback within an organisation could create a learning organisation.

Also remember that some people never give verbal feedback, but you will usually instinctively know if they are happy with your performance or not. Finally, don't forget that you can always ask someone for some feedback on your performance — 'How did I do?'

✅ Checklist

Feedback

How to accept and value feedback:

- Listen to what people have to say about you.
- Avoid overreacting and let people have their say; don't let your emotions get in the way.
- Pay attention to what is being said; clarify what the issue is or what you need to do to improve in the future.
- Be prepared to respond and explain what action you might take.
- Take the feedback on board and, if it is valid and constructive, follow it up with some positive action.
- Feed back to the person at a future date to let them know what you have done.

Portfolio task 302.3 → Links to **L01**: assessment criterion 1.2

Make a list of any feedback that you have recently received from any source. If you have any written feedback, for example, an email or an appraisal/review document, print it out for use as evidence in your portfolio. Consider the feedback that you received and whether it was of value. Consider any responses that you will make to this feedback.

Functional skills

English: Reading

If you carry out research involving reading texts including work-related documents as well as Internet research in order to complete your portfolio task, you may be able to count this as evidence towards Level 2 Functional English: Reading. Remember to keep records of all the documents, handbooks or guidelines which you study, along with the websites which you visit, as you will need to document any reading research you carry out.

What kind of feedback might this customer be giving?

The various types and sources of feedback

Feedback can be formal or informal. An example of informal feedback might be a colleague saying to you, 'Well done, you dealt with that difficult customer really well.' This is obviously positive information, and if you are doing something well, just carry on doing the same. It is likely that your colleague might try to adopt the same approach when they next deal with a difficult customer. By doing this, you will be sharing **best practice** and you will start to develop positive vibes in your team.

Sometimes, you will get more formal feedback. This will normally come from your line manager or a colleague that you work closely with. Another common source of feedback is from customers or from other organisations that you work closely with. If you have received some positive feedback from a customer, for example, an email thanking you for assisting them, print this out as it will be a valuable piece of evidence for your portfolio.

The table below shows some examples of feedback and how you might respond appropriately:

Appraisal and 360-degree feedback

The most common formal feedback that you are likely to receive is from your manager through your review or appraisal meeting. Most organisations have a process in place to allow for meetings between individual employees or teams and their managers to review performance and capability. At these meetings, you are likely to discuss and agree the following elements:

- your achievements for the previous year
- setting some specific goals or objectives for the forthcoming year
- a review of your training and development needs.

This appraisal meeting would normally take place once a year, with perhaps a quarterly- or six-monthly review meeting to track progress. Some organisations have a

Table 302.1: *Types of feedback and action to take*

Type of feedback	Action/follow-up
Customer email 'Thank you for resolving my problem.'	Keep up the good work and continue to deal with all customers politely and efficiently.
Colleague 'Thank you for sending those urgent documents through to me.'	Keep up the good work and ask your colleagues if there is a quicker or more effective way to send the documents through in future, maybe by email.
Supplier 'Can you make sure that you give me the correct delivery details next time?'	Learn from this and make sure that you have the correct delivery addresses for all sites, etc. Share this information with your colleagues.
Manager 'Thank you for preparing that draft report. I've made some changes and left it on your desk.'	Make the changes to the document and pass it back promptly. Make a note if there are any common errors or issues that you might need to action. Learn from the experience and make sure your report is even better next time.
Manager Comments written on your appraisal form from your appraisal meeting.	This is formal feedback that will probably link into your targets or development needs for the forthcoming year. Ensure that you are clear about the feedback and that you agree an action plan with your manager.
Director 'I have seen the good work that you are doing. I would like you to manage a project to roll out your methods of working to other parts of the business.'	Thank the director and also let your manager know that the director has approached you to do this work. Spread your positive energy and good working practices throughout the whole organisation.

Unit Q302 Evaluate and improve own performance in a business environment

The 360-degree feedback process. Why is it called the 360-degree feedback?

less structured approach in place, but it is still likely that you will discuss issues with your manager from time to time, and they will give you relevant feedback, even though this might not be written down.

Some organisations use the 360-degree feedback method to manage performance and give feedback to employees. This approach involves your manager asking a number of colleagues to comment on you and your performance. This is normally done by completing a series of answers to questions on a pre-printed form. The information is then passed to your manager who will go through it with you, and this is often linked to or forms part of your appraisal meeting. One advantage of this method is that you will get feedback from different people in different parts of the organisation and often at different tiers; for example, from senior staff and peers.

Evaluation of feedback

Always think of feedback as positive. Try to be objective in your evaluation of any feedback and try to learn from any mistakes you made. Put plans in place to make sure that you get it right next time. If you have received some negative feedback, consider the following points.

- Am I still learning the system/process?
  (If so, it may take time to be fully competent. Set yourself a target!)

- Can I ask for support or advice if the same situation occurs again?

- Perhaps I was not given enough time or the correct resources to deal with the issue.

- Do I need to write a procedure or note for myself to make sure I remember how to deal with it next time?

- Have I got a specific development need and do I need some training?

- Was the problem outside my control?

By working through these points, you will start to identify how you can improve in the future and possibly make changes to your working methods to become more effective.

Ways of evaluating own work

Improving your performance will make you more efficient in your role. Accepting feedback is very useful and your colleagues should provide you with relevant support and assistance by giving you suggestions on how to improve in your job. Remember, don't take any comments about your performance personally and remain objective.

In terms of evaluating your own work, you should do this as a matter of course. For example, when you have written a letter to a customer or prepared a spreadsheet, you should check it for accuracy. This is called **self-evaluation**, and by doing this you will quickly get to know how you are performing.

Key term

Self-evaluation – looking at both the positives and negatives of some aspect of yourself.

✓ Checklist

Checking work

Some quick checks that you can make after completion of the task:

- How long did it take me to do this job?

- What is the quality of my output?

Time and quality are both important factors and they both need to be considered. For example, it is no good producing a piece of work very quickly if there are numerous errors in it as a result. It is much better to spend a little longer and get it 'right first time'.

Sometimes, particularly if you are doing something for the first time, it is useful to review your experience to ensure that you do even better next time. You can do this by:

- making a note of everything that went well
- making a note of any problems you had and identifying solutions to deal with those issues next time
- analysing the problems and checking if they were preventable of if they were outside your control
- learning from your experiences and doing it better next time.

To evaluate your work in a more structured way, it is useful to complete a self-assessment plan (see Portfolio task 302.4). This will help to identify any areas of your role that may need further development.

How does filling in a self-assessment tick list help identify your development needs?

Portfolio task 302.4

→ Links to **L01**: assessment criterion 1.3

Table 302.2 gives some suggestions of questions that you should ask yourself. By being as honest as you can, you will get the most out of this exercise.

Think about each element individually and give yourself a score (1 is excellent and 5 is poor). After you have completed the table, you will be able to highlight those areas where you need further development. This information can then go into your learning plan which will be covered later in this section. Once you have identified your development needs, you can address them by putting in place an action plan.

Table: 302.2: *Self-assessment tick list*

Current skills, knowledge and abilities	Specific elements to consider	Score 1–5 (1 = excellent, 5 = poor)	Action Y/N
Communication skills	• Do you have good written English and oral skills? • Are you a good listener? • Are you good at face-to-face communication and using appropriate body language?		

A version of this table, ready for you to complete, is available to download from www.contentextra.com/businessadmin

The purpose and benefits of trying out possible improvements to own work

Whenever you complete a task, you will do so by undertaking various elements. This means following an agreed way of working that exists within your organisation. For example, if your manager asks you to send a standard letter to a customer, then you would probably:

- write the letter to meet the needs of the customer
- write the letter in the standard 'house style'
- write the letter in the correct format — probably formal for an external customer
- use the relevant letterheaded paper
- send the letter out within the agreed standards that your organisation works to — see note below.

Note: Some organisations have a series of set standards that they work to; for example, 'We will answer the telephone within 15 seconds' or 'We will reply to our customers' letters within five working days of receipt'. These standards are often referred to as **performance standards**.

Key term

Performance standards – the requirements that must be met for a particular level of performance.

By writing the letter to the customer, it is assumed that you have communicated to them in the correct format, with the right level of detail, and you have met their needs. You therefore might say — why do I need to do anything different or new?

Clearly, there is an argument to 'do nothing'. You may be familiar with the saying 'Don't fix it if it isn't broken', in other words, 'We have been doing it for years this way and it has worked perfectly fine so why change it?' Often, there is no need to make any changes to a procedure or a process. However, it is always worth thinking about any changes that might ultimately make your organisation more efficient and potentially provide a better service to your customers.

Looking at the letter example again, it may be possible to challenge some elements and ask the following questions:

- Is a letter to the customer actually necessary? Would it be better to phone or send an email to them: would this be cheaper and quicker?
- Is it necessary to contact them at all — could the process be eliminated?
- Could the letter be combined with something else? For example, a flyer showing a new product or service on offer.
- Is more frequent interaction with customers required?
- Is there any new technology or are there new systems that can be used to achieve this task more efficiently?

Sometimes, you might get the chance to challenge things, maybe at your appraisal meeting or at a team meeting. Quite often, new staff coming into an organisation can see where improvements could be made.

✓ Checklist

Remember, don't challenge everything, and be subtle in your approach, as sometimes people are sensitive when suggestions are made to make changes. If you have an idea for an improvement:

- you could think about it for a while
- test it out to see whether you think your suggestion would work or not
- discuss your idea with a colleague.

The business world is constantly changing and some organisations in some specific sectors, such as advertising companies, need to change continually and have to think up new and innovative ways of working. If they don't move with the times then they may go out of business. Also, technology changes frequently and it is important to update relevant processes and procedures to utilise the new technology that may be available.

If every member of a team improves their performance, then this continual improvement should ensure that the efficiency of the whole team is increased.

In summary, the benefits of introducing new ways of working are that they could make the organisation more efficient, more profitable, provide a better service to the customers and perhaps give the organisation a competitive advantage over rival companies.

Portfolio task 302.5 → Links to **LO1**: assessment criterion 1.4

Make a list of any performance standards that exist in your organisation.

Setting high standards

In your job, you should always behave in a sensible and professional manner. You should also help to support effective working. This means being positive at all times and going out of your way to provide support to your team and giving a helping hand as required. At some point, most people will feel stressed and a bit down or overloaded with work. At these times it is essential that the whole team works well together and that colleagues support each other accordingly; for example, agreeing to stay late to work an extra half an hour to assist a colleague who has an urgent job to complete.

Setting high standards for yourself doesn't mean setting unrealistic targets that you find difficult to achieve. You can set yourself some general standards to achieve; for example:

● to act in an honest and professional manner at all times

● to treat all colleagues and customers fairly and equally at all times

● to support your team and support the vision and objectives of the organisation.

You can also set yourself some specific targets to achieve; for example:

● to set or agree some specific challenges in your job role

● to agree some targets with your manager (perhaps as part of the appraisal meeting)

● to complete your learning plan.

Within each job role there will be some specific key tasks. The key tasks are the parts of your job that are most important and they are likely to be listed in your job description. There are normally approximately five to eight key tasks in a job. In order to undertake the key tasks, you will need to be competent in the different elements of your job. These **key competencies** will be things that you will normally do to meet the required standards of your job role.

Key term

Key competencies – tasks performed to meet the basic requirements of a job.

Some organisations manage employee performance based on their ability to meet the requirements of the job. To meet the required standards there will be a series of performance standards. These can then be used to ensure that you meet the required standards. If you need some additional support or training, this can link into your learning plan. (See p. 41 where learning plans and their benefits are discussed in more detail.)

Some organisations check to see if performance standards are being met on a regular basis — sometimes monthly. Other organisations review them less frequently, say once every six or 12 months. Often any review of your performance will be undertaken at your annual appraisal meeting with your manager.

The table below shows an example of the appraisal of one key task within an administrative assistant's job role. Remember, each job role will have several key tasks within it. The end column can be used to agree if the standards are being achieved or not. If the standards are not being achieved, then it is likely that some additional training may be required. For example, perhaps some one-to-one support with a colleague may help. If so, this could then be transferred into a learning plan as an action for development.

Unit Q302 Evaluate and improve own performance in a business environment

Table 302.3: *Appraisal of one key task within an administrative assistant's job role*

Key tasks	Key competencies	Performance standards to be met	Are the standards currently being met or is further training required?
• To prepare the agenda and minutes for all team meetings.	• Ability to plan the meetings effectively. • Ability to liaise effectively with all members of the team. • Ability to listen effectively and record concise and detailed minutes.	• To produce a list of all the meeting dates for the year. • To complete the draft minutes within 24 hours of the meeting. • To circulate the final agreed minutes within 48 hours of the meeting. • To produce accurate final minutes.	

As you learn more you will increase your level of competence in several aspects of your job and you will gain additional skills and knowledge that you are then able to offer to potential employers.

How learning and development can improve own work, benefit organisations and further own career

Many organisations have a structured approach to learning and development. One of the most commonly used methods is an annual appraisal meeting, which would normally take place with your manager. This meeting provides an important opportunity to discuss how you can build on your achievements and set yourself goals and objectives, and what training you might need in the coming year.

By reviewing your training and development needs, you will identify any specific issues and you will be able to link these into your learning plan. Also, the organisation that you work for will coordinate your training and development needs to ensure that you and all of the other employees attend the relevant training courses.

Benefits of training for you and the organisation

Some organisations have something called a training matrix which details all the training needs for all the employees for the forthcoming year. As part of this matrix, the company may target some specific qualifications to specific jobs. For example, if you were employed as a customer service assistant in a large organisation, you might be expected to:

● complete an internal customer care course within the first six months of your employment

● complete an NVQ level 2 in customer service by the end of your second year with the organisation

● complete a team-leading or management NVQ before you are able to progress to a job such as a customer service team leader.

Why is it important for the whole team to undergo training?

Some organisations undertake this structured training approach to ensure that the key competencies within each job role are met. Clearly, by ensuring that all staff members are trained to the same level in a relevant qualification, the organisation can then ensure that there is consistency in the way that people undertake their tasks and the way that staff interact with their customers. The theory behind this approach is that all staff (apart from new staff) will be fully trained and competent in their role. This can then potentially have the following advantages.

For the organisation:

- increased profits and growth
- a more efficient organisation
- more effective working between teams
- a happy and motivated workforce
- increased staff retention
- transforming the culture of the organisation.

For the individual:

- a better understanding of their job role
- a more comprehensive range of skills and knowledge
- improved competence in their job role
- greater job satisfaction
- a structured career plan
- more effective cross-team working.

Learning organisations

Learning organisations are those organisations that manage change well. They tend to view change positively and encourage continuous development of their employees and the organisation. It is generally accepted that these learning organisations have a more productive and happier workforce. A more productive workforce should ensure, in theory at least, that the organisation is operating in an efficient way. This could lead to competitive advantage over other similar organisations.

Key term

Learning organisations – organisations which encourage learning, thereby creating a knowledgeable workforce, or are willing to accept and adapt to new ideas and change.

Portfolio task 302.6 → Links to **L01**: assessment criterion 1.5

Look at the following attributes of a learning organisation and check to see if you think your organisation has any of these elements in place:

- continuous learning amongst the staff and a shared vision to achieve the organisation's objectives
- effective communication between all staff
- promoting new practices, viewing change positively and accepting mistakes as a 'positive learning experience'
- all employees are encouraged to share in the decision making process
- everyone is proud of the organisation and its achievements
- a strong emphasis on product quality and customer service.

Use a search engine to find 'The Sunday Times best 100 companies to work for' and have a look at some of the responses from the staff of those companies. Could you say the same about your organisation?

Functional skills

English: Reading

If you carry out research involving reading texts including work-related documents as well as Internet research in order to complete your portfolio task, you may be able to count this as evidence towards Level 2 Functional English: Reading. Remember to keep records of all the documents, handbooks or guidelines which you study, along with the websites which you visit, as you will need to document any reading research you carry out.

Changes ahead

The working environment is changing rapidly and will continue to change. There will be changes in working practices and there will be technological changes, too. Your organisation will change: it might adopt new systems or processes; there might be new products to try out; you may have new customers; your company may grow larger; or it may become smaller and more specialist. These are just some examples of the changes that could happen. From your point of view, you need to be ready to adapt to change. By continuously improving your own work, you will be regularly exploring new and more effective ways of working. As a result, you will probably take on new challenges without any particular problems. Employers value staff who are able to be positive about change.

If you are anxious about any proposed changes in your organisation, try to respond in a constructive way and 'give it a go'. The following checklist should help you.

✓ Checklist

Responding to possible changes

- If any changes are proposed, speak to your colleagues and managers about it. Find out as much as you can as this removes the fear of the unknown.

- Don't be hard on yourself — everyone needs time to adapt to change. Be patient and give yourself time to adjust over a few weeks if necessary.

- Think about things objectively. Will this change be better overall for everyone in the future?

- Try not to turn down a new challenge. If you are unsure, you could always agree a trial period.

Remember, discuss any concerns or worries that you have with your colleagues and manager and don't get things out of proportion.

Links to the mission

By continuously improving your own work, you should become more knowledgeable and possess additional and more varied skills than you had previously. As an employee, you have a responsibility to work towards achieving the organisation's **mission and objectives**. All large and most medium-sized organisations will have a mission. This is sometimes called a mission statement and is normally a few sentences detailing the organisation's overall objective or reason for being in business.

Key term

Mission and objectives – a statement outlining an organisation's overall objective and reason for being in business.

From the overall mission statement, the organisation will then plan how it is going to achieve its mission, and this will create a number of objectives. From the objectives, some more detailed action plans and targets will be generated. These action plans and targets may well form part of your job role.

J Sainsbury plc

Sainsbury's is a large company mainly focusing on operating high-street supermarkets throughout the United Kingdom. It has a mission statement, which defines its goal and vision as follows:

'Our goal — At Sainsbury's we will deliver an ever-improving quality shopping experience for our customers with great products at fair prices. We aim to exceed customer expectations for healthy, safe, fresh and tasty food, making their lives easier every day.'

As well as this overall goal, Sainsbury's will have in place a series of key objectives that it wants to achieve each year. There will then also be a series of more detailed action plans and targets for each region or individual store to achieve as shown in Figure 302.1.

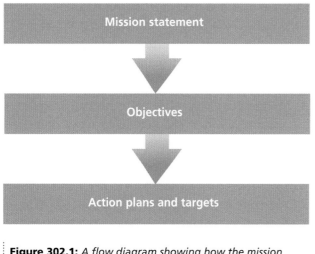

Mission statement

Objectives

Action plans and targets

Figure 302.1: *A flow diagram showing how the mission statement of an organisation can be achieved*

The action plans and targets for each individual Sainsbury's supermarket will then be broken down further and will form the action plans and targets for each individual employee.

By continuously improving your own work, you will be meeting and potentially exceeding your own targets, and as a result the overall mission and the objectives of your organisation will be achieved. Try to focus on putting your energy into what your organisation is trying to achieve. By doing this, you will help to ensure that your organisation is constantly developing and becoming more effective.

Some organisations have a system in place called total quality management (TQM). There are three main principles of a TQM system:

- getting it right first time every time
- ensuring that there are zero defects/errors
- continuous improvement.

Try to remember these principles and try to bring them into your everyday job role.

Portfolio task 302.7 → Links to **LO1**: assessment criterion 1.5

Find out if your organisation has a mission statement. Also try to obtain copies of any relevant objectives or action plans. These will provide useful evidence for your portfolio.

Career progression routes

Most administrators have transferable skills that will enable you to work in many different types of organisations and sectors. It is likely that you will:

- have good communication skills
- be self-motivated, use your own initiative and have a flexible approach to work
- have good organisational skills and be able to plan your work effectively and prioritise jobs and meet deadlines
- have the ability to extract, analyse and store information in manual and computer-based systems
- have good technical skills; for example, be competent in IT.

Administrators are often in demand and all organisations need administrative tasks to be undertaken. As you move up the career ladder, you will hopefully be able to decide what you want to do next. You may decide to specialise in a particular area, for example, accountancy or human resources, or you may want to become a team leader or a manager.

Portfolio task 302.8 → Links to **LO1**: assessment criteria 1.6 and 1.7

Find out if your organisation has any career progression opportunities. There may be some internal development courses or training programmes that you can attend. This may help you to plan your career.

Functional skills

English: Reading

If you carry out research involving reading texts including work-related documents as well as Internet research in order to complete your portfolio task, you may be able to count this as evidence towards Level 2 Functional English: Reading. Remember to keep records of all the documents, handbooks or guidelines which you study, along with the websites which you visit, as you will need to document any reading research you carry out.

Unit Q302 Evaluate and improve own performance in a business environment

What career opportunities are available to you within your organisation?

Development opportunities

A **learning plan** is used to address any development needs that have been identified. A **self-assessment questionnaire** may have identified some development needs for you, or your manager might have identified some development needs at your appraisal.

Key term

Learning plan – a plan containing specific measurable targets, drawn up for each member of staff to help plan their learning and development needs.

Self-assessment questionnaire – a questionnaire used in many organisations to identify an individual's current skills or knowledge gaps.

Once you have drawn up your learning plan, it is likely that you will need to undertake some type of training. This training should extend your skills and knowledge and there are four main ways that you can complete training:

1 On-the-job training – This would normally cover a specific skill that you could learn from a colleague. You might then be able to shadow this person for a period of time or perhaps be seconded into that team.

2 Workplace training courses – This training would be delivered by staff from within your organisation and could include training in relation to your organisation's specific policies or procedures; for example, 'A health and safety update', 'How to undertake an appraisal' or 'How to conduct interviews'.

3 College courses – Colleges offer nationally accredited qualifications including NVQs, AS and advanced levels, degrees and professional and management qualifications in areas such as marketing, human resources, accountancy and supervisory management. Some courses may be run within your organisation or may involve day release, distance learning or part-time evening sessions.

4 Specialist training courses – Private training providers offer specialist short courses normally lasting one or two days. These are often held at hotels or conference venues and can deal with a variety of issues; for example, time management, new legislation updates or team-building sessions.

Some organisations and professional bodies require their members to undertake continued professional development (CPD). This process requires employees to keep their skills and knowledge up to date by attending an agreed amount of training or update sessions in relation to their specific profession. For example, if you were a health and safety adviser, you would need to be aware of any new legislation, and it would be a requirement that you would attend some update training courses throughout the year.

The value of developing a learning plan

The principle of drawing up a learning plan is that any development needs will, once addressed, ensure that you have adequate skills and knowledge to undertake your job on a day-to-day basis — in other words, it will ensure that you are competent in your job. You may also wish to develop your skills and knowledge in readiness for another role or a possible promotion.

Not all organisations use learning plans, but when they are used, they normally link into the annual cycle, including the appraisal meetings. Once all the appraisals and learning plans have been completed, the organisation can pull together a training matrix to deliver the relevant training on either an individual or group basis.

It is best to keep the format of a learning plan as simple as possible to ensure that everyone understands it and that it can be easily monitored. The objectives in your development plan should be SMART and should state:

- what your target or objective is (sometimes called the expected outcome)
- the actions to be undertaken to ensure that the target is achieved
- any specific assistance or resources required
- a specific time frame or date for completion.

Once you have identified your development needs and a target has been set, you can consider how you will achieve the targets in a little more detail. It is likely that you will complete this process with your manager, possibly as part of your annual appraisal meeting. Don't always assume that the solution is to attend an external course. This may be relevant in some instances, but it is worth remembering that there are normally lots of 'in-house' opportunities to develop your skills and knowledge by working closely with your colleagues. Some of the development activities that can be taken to address any identified gaps are as follows:

- attending a short external training course
- completing a specific external course, for example, an NVQ
- attending an internal training course
- one-to-one training with a colleague or trainer
- shadowing or observing the way that other people perform similar roles
- understanding any internal processes in more detail; for example, any training manuals or detailed processes.

The style, format and content of a learning plan can vary, but a straightforward example is shown below:

Table 302.4: *Personal learning plan*

Target/objective	Action and resources	Target date for completion	Outcomes and reflection
1 To gain a detailed understanding of the receptionist's role by October 2011	I will shadow my colleague for 1 hour each day for 1 month • My time – 20 hours • My colleague's time – 20 hours • No other costs	30 September 2011	
2 To become first-aid qualified by January 2012	I will attend a 2-day external course • Course cost £350 • Accommodation and travel costs £150 • My time 15 hours • No other costs	31 December 2011	
3			

Remember to try to be SMART with your objectives. Record your target or objective in the first column and then state how you are going to achieve this in the second column. You need to consider how you are going to do it, what action will be required and by whom and also what the cost will be if any. The target date for completion should be agreed with your manager and it will be up to you to keep track of your actions to ensure that you achieve the objective by the agreed date.

The outcomes and reflection column should be completed after you have undertaken the objective. The outcome would be fairly specific and the reflection is more of a personal viewpoint. For example, in relation to objective 1, the outcome might be: 'I have completed 20 hours of shadowing with my colleague and I'm now competent to work on the reception.' The reflection might be: 'I enjoyed my time on the reception desk and I learned some new skills, particularly communication and interpersonal skills, which I will be able to use in my existing role — overall, I really enjoyed it.'

Note: Some organisations refer to learning plans as 'personal development plans', but they are the same thing.

Portfolio task 302.9

→ Links to **LO1**: assessment criterion 1.8

Complete your own learning plan – use the self-assessment plan to identify any development areas and try to think of some additional areas that you want to develop.

Table: 302.5: *Self-assessment tick list*

Target/objective	Action and resources	Target date for completion	Outcomes and reflection

A version of this table, ready for you to complete, is available to download from www.contentextra.com/businessadmin

---

Evidence collection

In order for you to complete the remaining assessment criteria to successfully pass this unit, you will need to carry out various tasks at work and then produce evidence to show that you have demonstrated the required skills and competence.

Evidence can be collected in a number of different ways. For example, it can be in the form of a signed witness testimony from a colleague or line manager, a copy of any related emails or letters you have produced or a verbal discussion with your assessor.

Speak to your assessor to identify the best methods to use in order to complete each portfolio task and remember to keep copies of all the evidence that you produce.

Be able to evaluate and improve own performance using feedback from others

Portfolio task 302.10

→ Links to **LO2**: assessment criteria 2.1, 2.2, 2.3, 2.4 and 2.5

Gather evidence of your work to show your assessor that you have successfully carried out the tasks outlined in the table below. Check with your assessor the best ways of gathering evidence for each of the tasks before you begin.

Task	Evidence collected
1 Encourage and accept feedback from other people.	
2 Evaluate own work and use feedback from others to identify areas for improvement.	

A version of this table, ready for you to complete, is available to download from www.contentextra.com/businessadmin

Be able to use evaluation of own performance to agree, develop and use a learning plan

Portfolio task 302.11

→ Links to **LO3**: assessment criteria 3.1, 3.2, 3.3 and 3.4

Gather evidence of your work to show your assessor that you have successfully carried out the tasks outlined in the table below. Check with your assessor the best ways of gathering evidence for each of the tasks before you begin.

Task	Evidence collected
1 Evaluate own performance and identify where further learning and development will improve own work.	
2 Agree and develop a learning plan to improve own work performance that meets own needs.	

A version of this table, ready for you to complete, is available to download from www.contentextra.com/businessadmin

Office life

Daniel's story

My name is Daniel and I'm employed as an administrative assistant in a small manufacturing company in Manchester. I work in the purchasing section and one of my main tasks is to help process the invoices that come into the office.

Recently I noticed that we were purchasing the same products from different companies in different amounts and at varying prices. I decided to arrange a meeting with my manager to discuss this inefficiency.

Before the meeting I prepared a detailed list of the prices and quantities of products. My manager was pleased with this information and surprised there was such a variation in prices. She asked me to carry out a brief review of the purchasing system to identify the main issues and how they could be resolved. She also asked me to set some SMART objectives for the review to agree before I started the work.

At the next team meeting, I decided to ask my colleagues for some help on setting SMART objectives. They were very helpful and also raised some further issues with the purchasing system, particularly the computer system we use. By the end of the meeting we had agreed some SMART objectives and some ideas to resolve the problems.

Ask the expert

Q I have to formulate a series of SMART objectives for a project that I have been asked to lead. What do I need to do?

A Gather as much information as you can and make sure that you understand exactly what is being asked of you. Consider:

- what the objectives are
- the actions to be undertaken to ensure that the objectives are met
- whether you can achieve the objectives alone or you need any specific assistance or resources from your colleagues
- a specific date for completion.

And remember what **SMART** means:

- **S**pecific — it says exactly what you intend to do.
- **M**easurable — you can measure progress and show that you have completed it.
- **A**chievable — the targets are not beyond your reach.
- **R**ealistic — the target is not too optimistic.
- **T**ime bound — you have a specific deadline for completion.

Make sure that any objectives that you set meet the SMART criteria.

Top tips

Daniel could have spoken to his colleagues first before he spoke to his manager. By doing this he would have had more information to hand.

Daniel did well to write down a list of all the issues. This demonstrated that he had thought about everything, and was structuring his approach to solving the problems.

Daniel did well to ask for his colleagues' input and comments at the meeting. The whole team could become motivated and excited about improving the efficiency of the system.

Can you think of anything else that Daniel could have done better?

Check your knowledge

1 **What is a learning organisation?**

a) An organisation that provides training for its staff.

b) An organisation with a large training budget.

c) An organisation which encourages learning by creating a knowledgeable workforce who are willing to accept and adapt to new ideas and change.

d) A college or a school.

2 **What does the term 'competitive advantage' mean?**

a) Being better at customer service.

b) Being the cheapest provider of a service/product.

c) Asking the staff to work extra hours to help out.

d) When an organisation is able to secure profits above the average gained by its competitors.

3 **What could give you job satisfaction in your role?**

a) Being paid more.

b) Being happy and motivated on a day-to-day basis.

c) Taking on new and challenging tasks.

d) All of the above.

4 **Which one of the following is an example of a SMART objective?**

a) Achieving £3,000 worth of sales by the end of the year.

b) Planning some training for the team.

c) Increasing turnover.

d) Checking out a competitor's sales methods.

5 **What does 'best practice' mean?**

a) A method seen as the most effective at achieving an outcome.

b) The 'way that we do things around here'.

c) Maximising the profits of the organisation.

d) Working in partnership with other organisations.

6 **How do you know if one of your colleagues is self-motivated in their job?**

a) They always look tired and unhappy.

b) They try to disrupt the team.

c) They try to delegate all their tasks to other people.

d) They come into work each day in a positive frame of mind, they take ownership of their job and complete tasks successfully.

7 **What does being efficient mean?**

a) Getting the job done as quickly as possible.

b) Being able to complete a task quickly and to a high standard.

c) Working through each task in a methodical way.

d) Helping the team to get their tasks completed.

8 **What information would you find in a personal learning plan?**

a) Rate of pay and holiday entitlement.

b) The main tasks in a job.

c) A target or objective that you want to achieve.

d) A training course on offer in the organisation.

9 **If you were 'shadowing' someone, what would you be doing?**

a) Following them around.

b) Helping them out with their tasks.

c) Getting assistance from them.

d) Working alongside them to gain a detailed knowledge and understanding of their job.

10 **What are the key competencies in a job role?**

a) The person specification.

b) The tasks that are performed to meet the basic requirements of a job.

c) The job description.

d) Knowing how to do your job.

Answers to the Check your knowledge questions can be found at www.contentextra.com/businessadmin

Unit Q302 Evaluate and improve own performance in a business environment

What your assessor is looking for

In order to prepare for and succeed in completing this unit, your assessor will require you to be able to demonstrate competence in:

- understanding the purpose and benefits of continuously improving your own performance
- how to encourage and evaluate feedback
- how to make changes to your working methods to become more effective
- how to formulate a learning plan and plan your career
- the benefits of learning and development to you and the organisation.

You will demonstrate your skills, knowledge and competence through the three learning outcomes in this unit. Evidence generated in this unit will also cross-reference to the other units in this qualification.

Please bear in mind that there are significant cross-referencing opportunities throughout this qualification, and you may have already generated some relevant work to meet certain criteria in this unit. Your assessor will provide you with the exact requirements to meet the standards of this unit.

As a guide, you will probably be assessed as follows:

- one observation for the whole unit

- at least one witness testimony to be produced
- a written narrative or professional discussion to be undertaken
- several work products to be produced as evidence
- a personal statement describing anything relevant; for example, any feedback that you have received.

The work products for this unit could include:

- a copy of your organisation's mission and/or goals
- a copy of any specific SMART objectives that you may have
- a copy of your review or appraisal document
- a copy of any performance standards that exist within your organisation
- a personal learning plan
- copies of any action plans or 'to do' lists
- minutes of any relevant meetings that you have attended.

Your assessor will guide you through the assessment process as detailed in the candidate logbook. The portfolio tasks will count towards some of the knowledge and understanding elements and evidence requirements for this unit. The detailed assessment criteria are shown in the candidate logbook.

Task and page reference	Mapping assessment criteria
Portfolio task 302.1 (page 27)	Assessment criterion: 1.1
Portfolio task 302.2 (page 28)	Assessment criterion: 2.3
Portfolio task 302.3 (page 30)	Assessment criterion: 1.2
Portfolio task 302.4 (page 33)	Assessment criterion: 1.3
Portfolio task 302.5 (page 35)	Assessment criterion: 1.4
Portfolio task 302.6 (page 37)	Assessment criterion: 1.5
Portfolio task 302.7 (page 39)	Assessment criterion: 1.5
Portfolio task 302.8 (page 39)	Assessment criteria: 1.6 and 1.7
Portfolio task 302.9 (page 42)	Assessment criterion: 1.8
Portfolio task 302.10 (page 43)	Assessment criteria: 2.1, 2.2, 2.3, 2.4 and 2.5
Portfolio task 302.11 (page 43)	Assessment criteria: 3.1, 3.2, 3.3 and 3.4

Unit Q303

Work in a business environment

What you will learn

- Understand the purpose and benefits of respecting and supporting other people at work
- Understand how to maintain security and confidentiality at work and deal with concerns
- Understand how to assess, manage and monitor risk in the workplace
- Understand the purpose of keeping waste to a minimum in a business environment, and the procedures to follow
- Understand procedures for disposal of hazardous materials
- Understand ways of supporting sustainability in an organisation
- Be able to respect and support other people at work in an organisation
- Be able to maintain security and confidentiality
- Be able to assess, manage and monitor risk
- Be able to support the minimisation of waste in an organisation
- Be able to follow procedures for the disposal of hazardous waste in an organisation
- Be able to support sustainability in an organisation

Introduction

In this unit you will look at some of the important issues that will affect you when working in a business environment. Showing respect and giving support to other people at work forms the basis of effective working relationships in all organisations. You will explore ways in which you can support others and help improve efficiency in working methods.

Maintaining security and confidentiality at work are critical issues that you need to understand. You also need to have a good grasp of the procedures that must be followed to maintain security and confidentiality.

Understanding how to assess risk in the workplace is important in maintaining a safe working environment, free of unnecessary hazards. You will look at likely causes of risk which you may come across in your working environment and how they can be safely dealt with and controlled.

Keeping waste to a minimum and maximising the efficiency achieved from business resources is important to the sustainability of any organisation, both in terms of cost-saving and for the protection of the environment. You will explore these issues and look at the procedures that you can follow to help maximise efficiency and minimise waste.

Respecting and supporting other people at work

After working through this section you will understand and be able to:

- explain the purpose of supporting other people at work
- explain the purpose of helping other people to work effectively and efficiently a) for individuals and b) for organisations
- explain what is meant by diversity and why it should be valued
- outline the benefits of diversity to an organisation
- explain how to treat other people in a way that is sensitive to their needs
- explain how to treat other people in a way that respects their abilities, background, values, customs and beliefs
- describe ways in which it is possible to learn from others at work.

Explain the purpose of supporting other people at work

Individuals working in organisations cannot achieve their goals and targets in isolation. Everyone is, to some extent, **interdependent** — that is, they rely on others at times to get things done. Employees need to collaborate in order to work successfully and achieve their goals.

This involves supporting others. Support can be a vital component of good interpersonal relationships at work. It creates a positive climate of cooperation and trust and helps everyone involved to achieve more — and to learn more — than they would on their own.

Benefits of supporting others

Key benefits of supporting others include:

- helping them to build their skills and competence more quickly than they would alone
- providing a way of sharing information and skills
- building good relationships and increasing trust
- setting a precedent: those whom you support are themselves more likely to be supportive to others in the future.

Key term

Interdependent – being dependent on one another.

Activity 1

List three ways in which you could lend support to others in your organisation. These can include both support that you have actually given and support that you could potentially give to others in the future.

Office life

Alicia's story

My name is Alicia Green and I am 21 years old. I have been working as an administrative assistant for a large IT services organisation for three months. I have a varied and, at times, very hectic workload.

I usually manage to cope with these peaks in workload somehow. However, I do not feel that I am being given adequate support or training by my line manager. When I ask her for help with something she is always impatient and in a hurry to get back to her own work. As a result, I often just muddle through on my own.

I feel that I am not progressing and learning as much as I should be, and I'm wondering whether it was a mistake to have taken this position. This is an important issue for me because I am hard-working and keen to develop my work skills so that I can make a successful career for myself in the future. I want to sort this issue out because overall I really like my new job, but I am unsure of how best to go about raising the issue.

Ask the expert

Q I have been working as an administrative assistant for three months and have a manager who does not, in my opinion, give me enough support at work. What should I do?

A You need to talk to someone at work about this situation. If you do not want to speak to your manager, you should go to the HR department. It might be a good idea to write down your issues and list the specific support that you would like. That way, you will have a clear picture of the situation to show to others. This could even form the basis of a training or support plan for you over the coming months.

Top tips

When new starters are recruited to an organisation, it is essential for their managers to consider the training and support needs which these new members of staff will have. Alicia's manager is responsible for Alicia's training and development and should provide support on an ongoing basis so Alicia will learn more quickly and become skilled in all the key aspects of her role. She will also be happier and more likely to remain with the organisation long term.

Portfolio task 303.1 → Links to **LO1**: assessment criterion 1.1

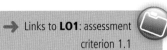

Write a short report which explains the purpose of supporting other people at work. Include examples from your own work experience where you have either provided or been provided with support, and say what the reasons for this were. Outline what you believe are the benefits of being supportive to others.

Functional skills

English: Speaking and listening

If your assessor asks you to take part in a discussion about this portfolio task as part of the assessment for this learning outcome, you may be able to count it as evidence towards Level 2 Functional English: Speaking and listening.

Have you helped out a colleague by showing them an efficient way to carry out a task?

The purpose of helping other people to work effectively and efficiently

It is always important – if not critical – to work effectively and efficiently at work because this is the way that you will make the best use of your time and effort. Working effectively and efficiently:

- takes the least amount of time
- is the most cost-effective
- causes the least amount of waste, including both time and resources.

Helping others to become more effective and efficient can involve demonstrating better working techniques to them; for example:

- quick filing techniques
- efficient document storage for ease of retrieval
- good use of computer software to keep template versions of regularly needed documents, such as sales letters and courtesy reply letters, readily available
- providing 'rules of thumb', such as when and how best to chase up individual colleagues for information

- giving opportunities to practise new skills to improve performance
- using a telephone headset instead of a handset to allow better multitasking
- using software to automate routine tasks
- explaining common errors and ways of avoiding them.

It is particularly important for you to develop skills and become competent in providing help and support to others when they need to complete work for either other individuals or other organisations.

The quality of the work that they undertake for individuals should reflect their professionalism and desire to do well and progress within the organisation. Whether they are completing work for peers or for managers, you should always support them in working to the highest standards. This may require you to carry out on-the-job training for them or to coach them in certain areas of work.

If you are providing support to others who are completing work for other organisations, you will probably need to be able to provide training for them. This could include the correct procedures to follow; any specific paperwork to complete and how to complete it; and informal advice on the best ways to deal with a particular organisation – such as who the best contact may be for them and what the generally preferred contact methods are.

Activity 2

List three ways in which you could help others with whom you work to become more effective and efficient in their work. This can include examples where they have to deal with individuals and organisations.

Portfolio task 303.2 → Links to **LO1**: assessment criterion 1.2

Write a short guide which explains the purpose of helping other people to work effectively and efficiently both for individuals and for organisations.

Explain what is meant by diversity and why it should be valued

Diversity means difference. It refers to differences in terms of:

- age
- gender
- role
- background
- skill level and type
- beliefs, customs and traditions
- sexual orientation
- ability or disability.

Legislation

Employers must ensure that they stay within the law when they employ staff. In the UK employment legislation exists to protect employees from **discrimination** on the basis of:

- gender
- sexual orientation
- ethnic background, beliefs and creed
- age
- disability.

This means that employees have the right not to be discriminated against on the basis of any of the above factors. They can also take an employer to an employment tribunal if they believe that they have been unfairly treated at work.

Key term

Discrimination – when someone is treated unfairly at work on the basis of their ethnic origin, age, sexual orientation, gender or ability.

The latest piece of legislation to come into effect which is relevant to diversity in the workplace is the Equality Act 2010, which replaces previous legislation.

Activity 3

Research the content of the Equality Act 2010 on the Internet and make notes of the key points which it covers. Make sure that you would be able to answer questions from your assessor on the contents of this new piece of legislation.

The value of diversity

The key value of a diverse workforce lies in the different experiences, opinions, perspectives and abilities which are brought together with the aim of contributing towards a common goal and adding value to the organisation.

In addition, embracing a culture of diversity reminds us all that we should have the self-assurance to look beyond our own age, ethnic and social grouping to realise that we are part of a larger group – society as a whole. This ethos allows us to build working relationships that are united by the common value of respect for others.

Diversity in teams

The value of diversity in team membership in creating high-performing and successful teams is widely recognised in many organisations, and this is especially so where teams have complex or innovative challenges to meet.

It is arguably these very differences in perspective which the various team members bring to the organisation, combined with a respectful and open-minded approach that make these teams so successful.

Activity 4

Give two reasons why you think that diversity in team membership is of such great benefit to performance. Carry out some Internet research on this subject and make notes on your key findings. Remember to properly quote any sources that you use in your answer.

✓ Checklist

Diversity

Remember, diversity can refer to:

- age
- skills and abilities
- perspectives and opinions
- ethnicity and race
- gender and sexual orientation
- beliefs and creed.

Portfolio task 303.3 → Links to **LO1**: assessment criterion 1.3

Write a short guide which could be used to train new staff in your organisation and which explains what is meant by diversity and why it should be valued. Give your own examples of diversity in your guide to demonstrate your understanding.

Outline the benefits of diversity to an organisation

Diversity brings with it a wealth of advantages to any organisation. For example, it provides:

- a wide range of skills and abilities which go towards creating an excellent talent pool
- a better understanding of customers from diverse backgrounds
- a strong and solid basis on which to deal with international and culturally diverse business partners

- an organisational culture that fosters respect for individual differences
- a dynamic and highly productive working environment in which people are proud of their individuality, and their contributions have a positive impact on the organisation.

All these factors combine to create a positive and forward-thinking business environment. Imagine if everyone in your organisation had the following identical profile, providing no diversity:

- aged 26
- attended the same school
- studied the same subject at college
- started work in the organisation at the same time.

It is hard to envisage how anyone would come up with new and better ways of working or a novel approach to product development in such a situation. There would be no buzz of different ideas being discussed over a coffee break nor a 'thinking outside the box' approach to innovation. These are the very seeds of groundbreaking new concepts that take an organisation to greatness.

Why would you not want everyone in your organisation to be of a similar age and background?

Activity 5

Carry out some Internet research to identify diversity initiatives which are currently being undertaken by organisations or the government to promote some aspect of diversity in businesses. You may wish to research the diversity policy of a well-known organisation of your choice or, alternatively, you could research a stand-alone interest group or charity. Your task is to create a computer-based presentation of your findings to show either to your assessor or to your group. Your presentation should contain at least 12 slides.

Portfolio task 303.4 ➡ Links to **LO1**: assessment criterion 1.4

Write a short report which outlines the benefits of diversity to an organisation. Include examples of your own which demonstrate these benefits.

Explain how to treat other people in a way that is sensitive to their needs

In order to be able to treat people in a way that is appropriate and sensitive to their needs, it is important to be respectful towards them. You also need to be able to show **empathy**. Whether or not you do this will be evident from your behaviour towards others, which includes both **verbal** and **non-verbal** behaviours. Verbal behaviours are how and what you say, including:

- tone of voice (sincerity as opposed to indifference)
- general temperament (genuine concern as opposed to irritation or impatience).

Non-verbal behaviours include things such as:

- eye contact (keeping good eye contact shows interest and honesty)
- facial expressions (which can often give away your true underlying feelings, especially if they differ from what you are saying)

- posture (the way you sit or stand can convey your inner feelings, so always be careful to sit up straight, facing towards your colleague and do not slouch or face away from them).

Key terms

Empathy – being understanding and sensitive.

Verbal – spoken.

Non-verbal – unspoken.

Patronising – talking down to someone.

Portfolio task 303.5 ➡ Links to **LO1**: assessment criterion 1.5

Produce a short training guide to be used in your organisation which explains how to treat other people in a way that is sensitive to their needs.

Functional skills

English: Speaking and listening

If your assessor asks you to take part in a discussion about this portfolio task as part of the assessment for this learning outcome, you may be able to count it as evidence towards Level 2 Functional English: Speaking and listening.

Explain how to treat other people in a way that respects their abilities, background, values, customs and beliefs

In order to respect others' abilities, backgrounds, values, customs and beliefs, you need to learn to treat them appropriately. This means that the following should be avoided at all times:

- **patronising** comments
- sexist language
- racist comments
- ageist remarks.

This may all sound obvious, but it is interesting to observe how some people unconsciously react to those around them from different age, ethnic or ability groups.

Unit Q303 Work in a business environment

This is due to our perceptions of **stereotypes** of certain groups of people. You need to find ways of behaving towards others which do not use stereotypes as a basis for your interactions with them. The best advice is to simply take people on their merit and take the time and effort to get to know them better. This effort will reap rewards for you in your working life as you come to learn about the special skills and abilities that others have and which you can benefit from by collaborating with them.

Key term

Stereotypes – characteristics of groups of people that are simplistic and often exaggerated.

✓ Checklist

Remember:

*   In order to be able to treat people in a way that respects their abilities, background, values, customs and beliefs, you will need to have an open mind.

*   Talking to and mixing with people from other walks of life, creeds, nationalities, age groups and abilities will not only broaden your own horizons but you will also benefit from learning about other people's experiences.

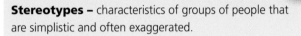

Portfolio task 303.6 → Links to **LO1**: assessment criterion 1.6

Write a short guide which explains how to treat other people in a way that respects their abilities, background, values, customs and beliefs. Include examples of your own that demonstrate ways in which people can do this.

Activity 6

Make a list of three ways in which you can act at work to avoid stereotyping people from age, ethnic and ability groups that are different to yours.

Learning from others at work

At work, we are learning all the time. We are not even aware of all of the learning that we do because some of it is unconscious — that is, we are not deliberately setting out to learn anything. Instead, learning occurs as we experience others behaving in a certain way and see the results.

'Sitting with Nellie'

'Sitting with Nellie' is a traditional method of learning used for new employees and is often considered the best way to allow them to learn their new role. The process involves a new recruit sitting alongside a more experienced employee who knows the job thoroughly. This way, they get to see the job being performed by a skilled and competent person first-hand and are shown the detailed skills and techniques which they must learn to become competent in their new job.

Informal learning

Informal learning is happening all the time when we are at work. Just by chatting to colleagues about work-related issues, seeing how processes work or observing others in conversations with customers, you are learning more about how your organisation operates. All of this is valuable in building your experience and developing your skills for your career.

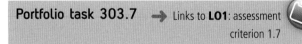

Portfolio task 303.7 → Links to **LO1**: assessment criterion 1.7

Describe ways in which it is possible to learn from others at work. Include examples of your own, showing how you or your colleagues have learned from others at work and the benefits of this type of learning.

Maintaining security and confidentiality at work

After working through this section you will understand and be able to:

● outline the purpose and benefits of maintaining security and confidentiality at work

● outline requirements for security and confidentiality in an organisation

● outline legal requirements for security and confidentiality, as required

● describe procedures for dealing with concerns about security and confidentiality in an organisation.

The purpose and benefits of maintaining security and confidentiality at work

Security and confidentiality are critical to organisations. Without these things, the existence of the organisation is at risk. You will look more closely at each of these issues next.

Security

Security relates not only to the physical security of the building and its contents, but also to the **intellectual property** of the organisation. Intellectual property consists of all the organisation's ideas, original products and services, and the brand name of the business, as well as any other copyrighted material that it owns.

> **Key term**
>
> **Intellectual property** – intangible items such as ideas, art or brands which have a value to organisations.

There must be organisational security procedures in place to protect these things. The procedures also need to be monitored and overseen by employees within the organisation, and any security alerts or breaches must be treated with urgency. Some examples of security procedures include:

● entry to and exit from the building controlled by security guards, PIN number or ID card

● password-protection of staff computers and email accounts

● physical security within the main building, such as locked or restricted access rooms to protect computer servers and data that is stored in the organisation.

The Data Protection Act 1998 affects all organisations that store sensitive personal data and requires them to have procedures in place which guarantee the safe and secure storage of both paper-based and electronic data relating to individuals.

> **Activity 7**
>
> Research the Data Protection Act 1998 in detail and make notes on the main requirements of this important piece of legislation. In what way does it impact on your organisation?

Confidentiality

Confidentiality means the protection of certain sensitive information so that it is only seen by those authorised to do so. Maintaining confidentiality is vital in order to prevent the leaking of critical business information either to employees who are not supposed to have access to it or, worse, to the general public. If such breaches occur, highly sensitive data may be given away to competitors, which can ruin the business.

Breaches of confidentiality can occur where, for example, inadequate measures have been taken to safeguard the whereabouts of information. They can also occur where the organisation has set an easily guessed password, such as 'password', allowing computer hackers the opportunity to access confidential files.

Figure 303.1: *Adequate measures must be taken by organisations to protect confidential information*

Activity 8

Find out what particular areas of information are classed as confidential in your organisation.

Portfolio task 303.8 → Links to **LO2**: assessment criterion 2.1

Produce a brief guide to be used in your organisation which outlines the purpose and benefits of maintaining security and confidentiality at work.

Requirements for security and confidentiality

Depending on the type and size of an organisation, its specific requirements for security and confidentiality will vary. For example, a business which deals with and stores a large amount of cash on its premises will have a specific need for security to protect this. The usual procedure that organisations adopt to protect the movement of cash is to employ the specialist services of a security company, which has its own uniformed guards and high security vans. Within the organisation's premises, cash is usually secured by locked doors and cupboards, along with strictly controlled staff access to it, with one employee given overall responsibility for cash control.

Other specific security measures that organisations may need to have in place include security relating to the computer network. This is especially important if employees are able to log on to the computer system remotely — either from home or while travelling on company business. Special user names and passwords need to be issued to staff and these are often changed every six weeks in order to keep security as tight as possible.

In some organisations and even industries, confidentiality is of heightened importance. This can be due to the particular nature of the work carried out in these organisations, such as new product development, and includes confidentiality over new designs, new drug formulations, new technological developments and anything else which, if it were made available to competitors, would undermine and even ruin the future of the business.

Activity 9

Think of three organisations for which you consider confidentiality to be of critical importance and, for each one, say why you think this is the case.

Portfolio task 303.9 → Links to **LO2**: assessment criterion 2.2

Write a short report which outlines requirements for security and confidentiality in an organisation. You may wish to include examples relating to your own or another organisation with which you are familiar in order to illustrate your answer.

Functional skills

English: Reading

If you carry out research involving the reading of texts including work-related documents as well as Internet research in order to complete your portfolio task, you may be able to count this as evidence towards Level 2 Functional English: Reading. Remember to keep records of all of the documents, handbooks and guidelines which you study, along with the websites which you visit, as you will need to document any reading research you carry out.

Legal requirements for security and confidentiality

Organisations are bound by certain pieces of legislation that set out requirements for security and confidentiality. For example:

- The Health and Safety at Work Act 1974 states that employers must maintain the safety of all employees, customers and any visitors who may enter the premises. This means that organisations must, by law, have safety and security procedures in place which satisfy this legal requirement.

- The Data Protection Act 1998 states that all organisations that store sensitive personal data must have adequate security measures in place to safeguard this data from misuse, which includes accidental loss or deliberate theft.

What are the benefits of an electronic key system for an office building's security?

- The Copyright, Designs and Patents Act 1998 protects the ownership and use of creative work belonging to people or organisations, preventing others from copying and reproducing them elsewhere.

Activity 10

Carry out research to identify the main legal requirements for security and confidentiality that relate to your organisation and the ways in which they are carried out.

Portfolio task 303.10 → Link to **LO2**: assessment criterion 2.3

Write a short guide which outlines legal requirements for security and confidentiality. You should also include any specific legal requirements which relate to your own organisation in your answer. You can use the research that you carried out for the activity above.

Procedures for dealing with concerns about security and confidentiality

The correct procedure for addressing any concerns that you may have relating to security and confidentiality will depend on the nature and severity of your concern. For example:

- Minor concerns, such as a colleague having left their keys or wallet lying on their desk, can be easily remedied by taking the initiative and alerting the owner yourself.

- More serious concerns, such as the suspected theft of items belonging to the organisation, or unauthorised access having been gained to the computer network, must be reported to a senior manager.

Once you have reported a serious concern about security or confidentiality to a manager, it is then their responsibility, not yours, to follow this concern up to a satisfactory conclusion using the appropriate channels.

There may be specific procedures in place that tell you to whom you should report a particular type of concern. For example:

- Computer or software concerns may be reported to the head of IT.
- Concerns about access to buildings should be reported to the building security office, if there is one, or else to the person in charge of operations.
- Concerns over suspected breaches of confidentiality should be reported to the HR manager.

Activity 11

Carry out some research on your organisation to identify any specific procedures which it has in place for the reporting of security or confidentiality concerns. Make notes on your findings as these will be useful for you in completing the next portfolio task.

✓ Checklist

Concerns about security and confidentiality

Remember:

- Any concerns about security or confidentiality require immediate action.
- If you are unsure of what to do, go directly to a manager and report it.

Portfolio task 303.11 → Links to **LO2**: assessment criterion 2.4

Produce a short written guide which describes procedures for dealing with concerns about security and confidentiality in an organisation of your choice.

Unit Q303 Work in a business environment

Assessing risk in the workplace

After working through this section you will understand and be able to:

- describe sources of risk in an organisation, including health and safety
- explain how to assess and monitor risks in an organisation
- describe ways of minimising risk in an organisation.

Sources of risk

A source of risk in an organisation is anything that can potentially cause harm to employees or to anyone else present on the premises. The types of risks that are present in organisations vary depending on the working environment. For example, the risks present in a factory that uses dangerous raw materials and heavy processing machinery would be far greater than those present in an office environment. However, offices do still contain potential hazards and you will go on to investigate these next.

Identifying sources of risk in an office environment

Sources of risk in an office environment include anything that could cause harm by tripping, slipping, falling, electric shock, contact with chemicals, scalding or injury from falling objects. As you can see, there are many different ways in which you could potentially be harmed in an office.

Possible sources of risk in a typical office might include:

- electrical equipment, such as computers and printers
- exposed cables trailing across the floor

What are the potential hazards associated with this risk?

- faulty or loose wiring
- exposure to chemicals in printer toner cartridges
- open drawers
- goods left lying on the floor
- shelves badly or over-stacked
- fire.

Activity 12

Look around your office and list as many potential sources of risk as you can. For each source of risk that you identify, give one way in which the risk of harm could be minimised.

Source of potential risk of harm	Method of minimising risk

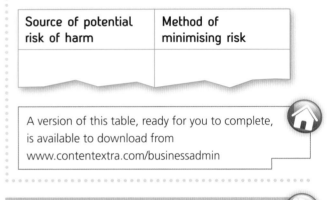

A version of this table, ready for you to complete, is available to download from www.contentextra.com/businessadmin

Portfolio task 303.12 → Links to **LO3**: assessment criterion 3.1

Write a short and informative guide to be used in your organisation which describes sources of risk, including health and safety issues.

How to assess and monitor risks in an organisation

Assessing risks in the workplace

The Health & Safety Executive (HSE) has published a very useful guide for employers and employees which details the steps that need to be taken in carrying out a risk assessment in the workplace. They outline a five-step approach which is shown in Figure 303.2.

Using the approach shown in Figure 303.2 will allow you to put together a risk assessment which can be used as a working document to record both what is already being done in the organisation to minimise risks, as well as what else needs to be done in the future, along with details

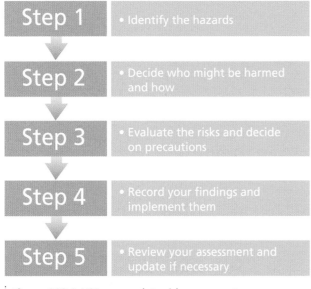

of the person responsible for implementing the action and a date by which it needs to be completed. Figure 303.3 shows an excerpt from a sample risk assessment document produced by the HSE as a guide to employers.

Figure 303.3 shows a clear and objective method for assessing workplace risks and taking action where necessary to either remove or minimise these. The responsibility for assessing and monitoring risks within an organisation ultimately rests with the employer. However, employees are also responsible for taking any necessary precautions to look after their own safety at work, such as wearing the correct protective clothing or using protective equipment, if necessary, as well as for looking out for the safety of their colleagues. Employees should always be consulted and involved in the development of workplace risk assessments as they may experience risks as part of their job which the management are not aware of, and so can provide valuable information.

Figure 303.2 *HSE approach to risk assessment*

What are the hazards?	Who might be harmed and how?	What are you already doing?	What further action is necessary?	Action by whom?	Action by when?	Done
Display screen equipment	Some staff working intensively at computers without adequate breaks risk posture problems and pain, discomfort or injuries, e.g. to hands/arms, from overuse, improper use or from poorly designed workstations or work environments. Headaches or sore eyes can also occur, e.g. if the lighting or screen image is poor.		Supervisors to monitor to ensure staff continue to get breaks away from the computer.	Supervisors	4/10/07	4/10/07
			Check that identified actions from self-assessments are followed up ASAP.	Manager	21/10/07	4/10/07
			Tell staff that they are to inform their manager of any pain they have that may be linked to computer use.	All staff	21/10/07	21/10/07
			Remind laptop users to carry out regular DSE assessment to avoid problems and identify any issues.	Manager	4/10/07	4/10/07
Work at height Changing light bulbs, cleaning TV screens	Falls from any height can cause bruising and fractures.	Appropriate stepladder in good condition provided, if needed, and staff know how to use it safely.	Remind staff to always use the stepladder when working at height and not to stand on chairs or other furniture.	Manager	20/7/07	17/7/07

Figure 303.3 *A sample HSE risk assessment document*

Unit Q303 Work in a business environment

Activity 13

Using the same approach as that outlined in the HSE sample risk assessment (Figure 303.3), identify three potential hazards which are present in your workplace. For each one, complete the table below.

What are the hazards?	Who might be harmed and how?	What are you already doing?	What further action is necessary?	Action by whom?	Action by when?	Done

A version of this form, ready for you to complete, is available to download from www.contentextra.com/businessadmin

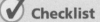

✓ Checklist

Assessing workplace risks

Remember:

- A hazard is a potential source of risk.

- A risk is a chance of people being harmed.

- A risk assessment is the way in which risks are identified and action plans are drawn up, as appropriate, to eliminate or at least minimise this risk.

Monitoring risks in the workplace

Once you have carried out a risk assessment and have planned any necessary actions, you need to constantly monitor risks in the workplace to ensure that your risk assessment remains current. Monitoring is important to take account of changes that can occur at work, including changes in:

- working methods
- staffing
- work location.

Changes in working methods, staffing or location of work may mean additional risk assessment activities must be implemented. For example, the recruitment of young or inexperienced staff will certainly incur a greater risk of accidents at work due to lack of experience. Similarly, changes in working methods may involve new hazards such as lifting, working from a height or using new equipment. Each of these will warrant special consideration.

Monitoring risk can be carried out by:

- keeping the risk assessment up to date; for example, by monthly or quarterly updates

- giving staff or staff representatives a regular forum for feeding back their own assessments to management

- involving every member of staff in workplace risk assessments.

Portfolio task 303.13 → Links to **LO3**: assessment criterion 3.2

Write a short report which explains how to assess and monitor risks in an organisation. You may wish to include examples of risk assessment methods which you are familiar with from your own organisation. You should also research the information available on the HSE website. Go to www.pearsonhotlinks.co.uk, search for this title and click on this unit before you begin writing your report.

Ways of minimising risk in an organisation

Risks can be minimised in the workplace by taking action to quickly address all the areas which are highlighted as potential hazards. This will mean:

● prioritising the actions that are to be carried out

● following up on actions taken to ensure that the plans are implemented to schedule.

Failing to implement risk-reduction actions means that employees may be exposed to unnecessary risk at work. This has two possible consequences:

● employees may suffer harm or injury

● employers may be in breach of health and safety legislation for failing to protect staff from harm at work.

In addition to swift action to reduce hazards at work that present risk to employees, organisations should provide training to employees to make sure that they know how to follow all the correct working procedures. This will protect them from potential injury and reduce the number of days lost to absence because of injury.

Activity 14

Are there any changes in your workplace which may have had implications for your organisation's risk assessment? Ask your manager or mentor for information about this if you do not know of any changes.

Portfolio task 303.14 → Links to **LO3**: assessment criterion 3.3

Write a short guide which will be used as a staff training tool and which describes ways of minimising risk in an organisation. Include three examples of actions which organisations can take to minimise risk in an office environment.

Key term

Finite – something which only has a limited supply.

Keeping waste to a minimum in a business environment

After working through this section you will understand and be able to:

● describe the purpose and benefits of keeping workplace waste to a minimum

● describe the main causes of waste that may occur in a business environment

● describe ways of minimising waste, including using technology and other procedures

● explain the purpose and benefits of recycling

● describe organisational procedures for recycling materials, and their purpose

● describe ways in which waste may be minimised by regularly maintaining equipment.

The purpose and benefits of minimising workplace waste

Costs of waste

The key purpose of keeping workplace waste to a minimum is to control costs. Waste is expensive as it means resources are being purchased, but not fully utilised, by an organisation. A large amount of waste often means that the organisation is not being effective in its management of resources and it should quickly take steps to remedy this.

Time spent planning for better and more efficient resource utilisation will reduce the amount of waste produced.

Waste and the environment

Waste has negative consequences for the environment. Most waste ends up in landfill sites. The use of landfill sites for waste needs to be kept to a minimum because:

● they emit greenhouse gases into the atmosphere

● they potentially make the land surrounding them unusable for habitation for many years

● suitable places for landfill sites are **finite**

In response to the increasing amount of waste that was being sent to landfill sites, the government introduced a landfill tax to provide businesses with a financial incentive to divert waste from landfill sites by recycling and reusing resources.

Portfolio task 303.15 → Links to **LO4**: assessment criterion 4.1

Produce a short guide which can be used to train members of staff in your organisation and which describes the purpose and benefits of keeping workplace waste to a minimum.

Functional skills

English: Writing

If you take care to produce a professional and well-presented report for your answer to this portfolio task, you may be able to count it as evidence towards Level 2 Functional English: Writing. Remember to use headings and subheadings, check you have used correct spelling and grammar and then print out the final corrected version of your report, once you have made all your corrections.

The main causes of business waste

The main causes of waste in business are:

- packaging
- energy usage – to heat and light the office buildings and to power office equipment
- water usage
- office consumables such as stationery and printer cartridges
- computers and electrical appliances
- petrol and diesel fuel for business travel.

Packaging

A casual look into the average business waste container will show clearly how much excess packaging is used in business. Once an item is unpacked, the packaging immediately becomes waste, so any initiatives to reduce and recycle as much packaging waste as possible will have an enormous impact on office waste reduction.

Energy usage

Offices need energy supplies in order to heat and light the office buildings and to power office equipment. However, much energy (gas and electricity) is often wasted in office environments due to lights, heating and appliances being left on when not needed.

Huge savings can be achieved by businesses simply by making a few alterations to their policies on energy usage.

Water usage

Water is wasted in businesses every day by taps being left running, leaks not being attended to and consumption not being adequately monitored.

Office consumables such as stationery and printer cartridges

Stationery wastage is a costly and yet easily preventable problem for businesses. Some of the reasons why there is so much wasted stationery include over-ordering, incorrectly ordered items and letterhead and compliment slips becoming out of date due to changes in business details.

Computers and electrical appliances

Computer and other electrical hardware is a cause of business waste because organisations too often replace existing equipment rather than carrying out maintenance and repairs to prolong its life.

Petrol and diesel fuel for business travel

A lot of petrol and diesel fuel is used up by business travel to meetings which in many cases could be saved by a phone call or conference call. Cutting out unnecessary travel would make a significant cost-reduction to many businesses.

Activity 15

Carry out some research within your own organisation to identify the main sources of waste.

Portfolio task 303.16 → Link to **LO4**: assessment criterion 4.2

Write a brief report which describes the main causes of waste that may occur in a business environment.

Ways of minimising waste

There are many initiatives that can be implemented to reduce the amount of waste that goes to landfill sites. The government's Envirowise programme has developed a hierarchy of waste management which shows the actions you can take to reduce costs of waste and help the environment at the same time.

Using technology to minimise waste

You should maximise the uses of the technology around you at work to minimise the amount of waste produced. For example:

- Use email as much as possible instead of sending letters in the post.
- Use the company website as a catalogue instead of producing paper brochures which need to be posted out to customers at an additional cost.
- Use electronic documents as much as possible at work; for example, to send round meeting minutes or team updates.

Activity 16

Carry out some Internet research to find out about the legislation that applies to the management of waste by UK businesses. For an overview of all the UK legislation relating to the management of waste, go to www.pearsonhotlinks.co.uk, search for this title and click on this unit.

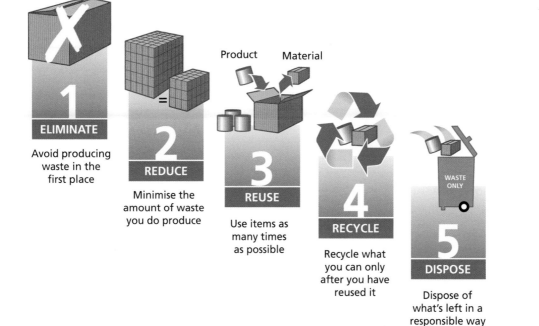

1 ELIMINATE
Avoid producing waste in the first place

2 REDUCE
Minimise the amount of waste you do produce

3 REUSE
Use items as many times as possible

4 RECYCLE
Recycle what you can only after you have reused it

5 DISPOSE
Dispose of what's left in a responsible way

Product   Material

WASTE ONLY

Figure 303.4: *The Envirowise hierarchy of waste management*

Figure 303.5: *How does recycling help the environment?*

The purpose and benefits of recycling

Recycling is the processing of used resources to turn them into new ones. They can be turned into the same thing as they were originally; however, in practice, this is often too expensive and items are often reprocessed into alternative products.

Benefits of recycling

The benefits of recycling are enormous. For example, recycling:

- reduces the quantity of waste that goes into landfill sites
- reduces the need for (and therefore the consumption of) new **virgin resources**
- reduces the cost to businesses of disposing of waste (so it makes sound financial business sense)
- increases **sustainability** by preventing the increased use of natural resources, such as trees.

Activity 17

Complete the table below to identify how each of the items can be a cause of waste, along with what actions can be taken to reduce this waste.

Cause of waste	Actions to reduce waste
Printer paper	
Packaging	

A version of this table, ready for you to complete, is available to download from www.contentextra.com/businessadmin

Key terms

Virgin resources – new resources which have not yet been processed or recycled.

Sustainability – the ability to continue with an activity without depleting the world's natural resources.

✓ Checklist

Recycling

Remember, recycling is part of the waste hierarchy:

- reduce
- reuse
- recycle.

Portfolio task 303.17 → Links to **LO4**: assessment criterion 4.3

Write a short guide which describes ways of minimising waste, including using technology and other procedures.

Portfolio task 303.18 → Links to **LO4**: assessment criterion 4.4

Produce a training information guide which explains the purpose and benefits of recycling. This guide could be used to help new members of staff learn about the reasons why it is important to recycle as much as possible at work.

Organisational procedures for recycling materials

All businesses should have procedures for recycling. A simple set of recycling procedures can be drawn up and included as part of the company manual. An outline of the steps to be taken for each type of recycling should be included. Everyone at work should be responsible for recycling as much as possible, and staff may need training to raise their awareness of this important issue.

For example, people need to know the types of materials that can be recycled and where they should be placed for processing. Recycling facilities need to be as effortless as possible to ensure that everyone uses them. Sometimes it is all too easy to simply ignore the recycling procedures and put things into the general rubbish bin, especially if you are busy and the procedures are cumbersome.

An organisation's procedure for recycling might include the following items:

- paper
- cardboard
- plastic
- print cartridges
- electrical hardware
- CDs
- glass.

For each type of item, there should be a special collection bin located in a designated position in, or nearby, the office.

✓ Checklist

Recycling procedure

A company procedure for recycling should include:

- a list of the items that can be recycled
- a designated place where they are to be placed
- information on when collections are made.

Portfolio task 303.19 → Links to **LO4**: assessment criterion 4.5

Write a short report which describes organisational procedures for recycling materials and their purpose. Use recycling examples from your own company to help you. If your company is not very active in recycling, carry out some Internet research to find out about the possibilities for office recycling and use these examples in your report.

Maintaining equipment to minimise waste

The regular cleaning, servicing and maintenance of office equipment – as with many other things – prolongs its useful life and delays the need to purchase replacement equipment.

This is beneficial to organisations in two ways:

- It reduces business costs.
- It reduces the quantity of waste produced by the business.

Costs to the business are reduced because the need to spend money on new equipment is reduced. The costs of disposing of the old equipment are also reduced.

By looking after the equipment currently in situ and keeping it in good working order, the business will effectively get more value for the money that it spent on purchasing it.

Activity 18

Find out how much of your office equipment is regularly maintained, as well as how often this equipment is replaced.

Portfolio task 303.20 → Links to **LO4**: assessment criterion 4.6

Write a short guide which describes ways in which waste may be minimised by regularly maintaining equipment. You can use examples from your own organisation to illustrate your answer.

Procedures for disposal of hazardous materials

After working through this section you will understand and be able to:

- explain the purpose of procedures for the recycling and disposal of hazardous materials
- describe procedures for the recycling and disposal of hazardous materials for an organisation.

The purpose of procedures for the recycling and disposal of hazardous materials

Hazardous materials require special procedures in the workplace in order to be recycled and disposed of. This is because they present potential dangers to employees if not handled in the correct manner, and hazardous waste is not, by law, permitted to be disposed of with the general waste.

Businesses therefore need to be able to monitor and review the company's use of such materials in order to:

- eliminate some of these hazardous materials in favour of less hazardous alternatives, where possible
- explore all options for reuse and recycling, rather than disposal.

There are several benefits for having a procedure to deal with hazardous materials:

- It ensures that the business stays within the law.
- It ensures that staff and visitors to the premises are kept safe from the harmful effects of these materials.
- It ensures that the community and environment outside the business are kept safe from the harmful effects of these materials.
- It reduces the company's costs associated with disposing of hazardous waste.
- It controls the flow of hazardous materials through the organisation.
- It will help to identify all the options for reuse and recycling.

If a business did not have a procedure for dealing with hazardous materials, there would always be the risk that the materials could be disposed of in an unmonitored or uncontrolled way and the business could be prosecuted as a result of this.

There are a number of professional agencies that can provide businesses with support, advice and guidance on matters relating to hazardous materials in the workplace.

While businesses must meet legal requirements, they can do more by producing less hazardous waste in the first place. This will benefit the company as the costs of dealing with and disposing of such items will be lower. It will also benefit the environment.

Activity 19

Find out what hazardous materials are used by your organisation and the procedures that are in place for their recycling and disposal.

Portfolio task 303.21 → Links to **LO5**: assessment criterion 5.1

Write a short report which explains the purpose of procedures for the recycling and disposal of hazardous materials. Include examples from your own organisation or another organisation of your choice to illustrate your answer.

Procedures for the recycling and disposal of hazardous materials

A typical procedure for the recycling and disposal of hazardous materials within an office-based business might include the following:

- Nominate a person responsible for the management of hazardous materials within the business.
- Identify and list all the hazardous materials that must be monitored.
- Establish the steps to be taken to deal with each hazardous material (reusing, recycling or disposal).

- Specify the dates and times when external waste contractors and recycling companies will collect certain types of hazardous materials.

- Make sure all staff are aware of the procedure, the specific items concerned and the legal requirements relating to the management of hazardous materials.

How much hazardous office waste can be reused or recycled?

In a typical office environment, hazardous materials might consist of:

- printer toner cartridges
- fluorescent light tubes
- old computers
- lead-acid batteries
- other types of old electrical equipment.

Firstly, printer cartridges can be reused by being refilled. Secondly, all the remaining items in the list can be recycled, so none of the hazardous materials will end up in landfill. By simply following a good procedure for the recycling and disposal of hazardous materials, and by liaising with waste and recycling partners, a business can drastically reduce its waste costs.

Portfolio task 303.22 → Links to **LO5**: assessment criterion 5.2

Produce a short guide which describes procedures for the recycling and disposal of hazardous materials for your organisation. Remember to write your guide clearly so that it can be easily understood and followed by members of staff in your organisation.

Supporting sustainability

After working through this section you will understand and be able to:

- explain the benefits to an organisation of improving efficiency and minimising waste over time

- describe ways of continuously improving own working methods and use of technology to achieve maximum efficiency and minimum waste

- outline ways of selecting sources of materials and equipment that give best value for money.

The benefits of improving efficiency and minimising waste

Waste represents an inefficient use of resources and also bears a significant cost to the business. Therefore, any reductions in waste represent a huge benefit to organisations.

Efficiency in business means getting the best use out of your existing resources. This can be achieved by finding ways to improve processes, increase speed and productivity, and reduce error rates and delays.

Purpose of improving efficiency

A business must strive to improve efficiency as this is a key method of:

- improving business performance
- reducing costs relative to output
- improving productivity
- improving the financial and environmental health of the organisation.

Purpose of minimising waste

For a business, the purpose of minimising waste includes:

● focusing on using only those resources that are necessary for the business

● carefully monitoring purchases made by the organisation so that they can be evaluated and justified — increasing accountability for spending is a very good way to avoid over-purchasing and the waste that this produces

● reducing the amount that needs to be taken away by waste contractors, and therefore reducing this business cost

● reducing the impact of waste on the community and the environment.

Benefits over time

Small improvements in efficiency throughout the organisation coupled with a reduced waste burden will bring about noticeable benefits over time. This type of incremental change in business is one of the best ways to bring about improvements as it is gradual, relatively easy to implement and causes minimum disruption to business processes. However, it does require perseverance and tenacity to maintain new processes when there is no immediate benefit to be gained. This type of initiative is change by evolution rather than revolution.

Activity 20

Carry out some research to identify three ways in which your organisation could improve efficiency and reduce waste.

Portfolio task 303.23 ➜ Links to **LO6**: assessment criterion 6.1

Write a short report which explains the benefits to an organisation of improving efficiency and minimising waste over time. Include examples which are relevant to your own organisation in your answer.

Continuously improving working methods to maximise efficiency

There are many ways in which you can make small changes to the way you do things at work in order to improve efficiency and reduce waste.

Ways of improving efficiency and reducing waste

In an office environment, you could:

● email documents rather than printing them and sending them

● use the company website to do as much as possible for the business, such as manage customers and suppliers online, as well as having an online sales brochure

● restrict the use of printing to a minimum — with the aim of becoming a paperless office (or as close to this as possible)

● set the default settings on printers and copiers to double-sided to use less paper.

Longer-term plans for waste reduction

The changes listed above can largely be put in place quickly and with minimal expense. In the medium term, however, further changes can be made to the way the office is run. These will require approval from senior management as they will involve capital expenditure to set up. For example:

● Install motion sensors on lights in the office building. This will reduce unnecessary use of electricity for lighting, as lights will go out when no one is around.

● Make sure all unnecessary lights and heaters are turned off outside office working hours. This can be set up centrally.

● Use energy-efficient technology around the office – invest in low-energy consumption, eco-friendly computers and monitors.

● Install a video-conferencing facility to reduce the number of miles staff travel for meetings.

Portfolio task 303.24 ➡ Links to **LO6**: assessment criterion 6.2

Write a short report which describes ways of continuously improving your own working methods and use of technology to achieve maximum efficiency and minimum waste. Give two examples from your own work experience to show how you have done (or could do) this.

Ways of selecting materials to get best value for money

Purchases of materials and equipment by businesses often represent a large expense. These costs can reduce the overall profitability of an organisation if they are not ruthlessly controlled. It is for this reason that businesses must constantly evaluate the amount of expenditure on such materials and work out how they can get more for their money.

Shopping around

The main thing that you need to do is to compare the prices and products available from several different suppliers. Simply sticking with one supplier for the sake of convenience cannot be justified from a cost or value perspective.

Value for money consists of two elements: cost and quality. If costs are lower but quality is poor, then a decision needs to be taken on the level of quality which is required versus the cost savings desired.

Ways of getting the best-value sources of materials and equipment involves the following:

● speaking to as many potential suppliers as possible

● trying to negotiate a deal with suppliers on price, based on your intended regular custom with them

● developing long-term relationships with suppliers to get better terms.

Considering the environment

A key consideration in selecting from alternative sources of materials and equipment will be their impact on the environment. Selecting the more environmentally friendly products will have a positive effect on the business from a cost perspective and will also lower energy usage.

There are many ways in which you can purchase more environmentally friendly materials for the office, from light bulbs and computer monitors to staplers and recycled rather than virgin paper.

Activity 21

Carry out some Internet research to identify an environmentally friendly office equipment supplier and list some of the materials and equipment which they can supply.

✔ **Checklist**

Being environmentally friendly

Remember, selecting environmentally friendly materials and equipment:

- saves the business money — by lower energy bills and lower waste-disposal costs
- helps the environment.

Portfolio task 303.25   → Links to **LO6**: assessment criterion 6.3

Produce a short report which outlines ways of selecting sources of materials and equipment that give best value for money. Give three examples of materials or equipment in your answer and, for each one, show how you could select these to get the best value for money.

Evidence collection

In order for you to complete the remaining assessment criteria to successfully pass this unit, you will need to carry out various tasks at work and then produce evidence to show that you have demonstrated the required skills and competence.

Evidence can be collected in a number of different ways. For example, it can be in the form of a signed witness testimony from a colleague or line manager, a copy of any related emails or letters you have produced, or a verbal discussion with your assessor.

Speak to your assessor to identify the best methods to use in order to complete each portfolio task and remember to keep copies of all the evidence that you produce.

Be able to respect and support other people at work in an organisation

Portfolio Task 303.26

→ Links to **LO7**: assessment criteria 7.1, 7.2, 7.3 and 7.4

Gather evidence of your work to show your assessor that you have successfully carried out the tasks outlined in the table below. Check with your assessor on the best ways of gathering evidence for each of the tasks before you begin.

Task	Evidence

1 Complete work tasks with other people in a way that shows respect for
    a) backgrounds
    b) abilities
    c) values, customs and beliefs.	

A version of this table, ready for you to complete, is available to download from www.contentextra.com/businessadmin

Be able to maintain security and confidentiality

Portfolio task 303.27

→ Links to **LO8**: assessment criteria 8.1, 8.2 and 8.3

Gather evidence of your work to show your assessor that you have successfully carried out the tasks outlined in the table below. Check with your assessor on the best ways of gathering evidence for each of the tasks before you begin.

Task	Evidence
1 Keep property secure, following organisational procedures and legal requirements, as required.	

A version of this table, ready for you to complete, is available to download from www.contentextra.com/businessadmin

Be able to assess, manage and monitor risk

Portfolio task 303.28

→ Links to **LO9**: assessment criteria 9.1, 9.2, 9.3, 9.4, 9.5 and 9.6

Gather evidence of your work to show your assessor that you have successfully carried out the tasks outlined in the table below. Check with your assessor on the best ways of gathering evidence for each of the tasks before you begin.

Task	Evidence
1 Identify and agree possible sources of risk in own work.	

A version of this table, ready for you to complete, is available to download from www.contentextra.com/businessadmin

Be able to support the minimisation of waste in an organisation

Portfolio task 303.29

→ Links to **LO10**: assessment criteria 10.1 and 10.2

Gather evidence of your work to show your assessor that you have successfully carried out the tasks outlined in the table below. Check with your assessor on the best ways of gathering evidence for each of the tasks before you begin.

Task	Evidence
1 Complete work tasks, keeping waste to a minimum.	
2 Use technology in own work tasks in ways that minimise waste.	

A version of this table, ready for you to complete, is available to download from www.contentextra.com/businessadmin

Be able to follow procedures for the disposal of hazardous waste in an organisation

Portfolio task 303.30

→ Links to **LO11**: assessment criterion 11.1

Gather evidence of your work to show your assessor that you have successfully carried out the tasks outlined in the table below. Check with your assessor on the best ways of gathering evidence for each of the tasks before you begin.

Task	Evidence
1 Follow procedures for recycling and disposal of hazardous materials in own work tasks, as required.	

A version of this table, ready for you to complete, is available to download from www.contentextra.com/businessadmin

Be able to support sustainability in an organisation

Portfolio task 303.31

→ Links to **LO12**: assessment criteria 12.1, 12.2, 12.3 and 12.4

Gather evidence of your work to show your assessor that you have successfully carried out the tasks outlined in the table below. Check with your assessor on the best ways of gathering evidence for each of the tasks before you begin.

Task	Evidence
1 Follow procedures for the maintenance of equipment in own work.	

A version of this table, ready for you to complete, is available to download from www.contentextra.com/businessadmin

Check your knowledge

1 **What is a good method of supporting others at work?**

a) Standing over them and correcting their errors.

b) Emailing them once per hour to see if they need any help.

c) Providing them with a collection of help manuals for all of the office equipment.

d) Acting as a mentor to them, so that they can come to you for help and advice when they need it.

2 **Which of these statements best describes diversity at work?**

a) Those with management positions.

b) Staff with a wide variety of backgrounds, skills and age groups.

c) Staff with company vehicles.

d) Female employees who are between 25 and 35 years of age.

3 **What is meant by treating others with respect?**

a) Always saying yes to them.

b) Treating them in a way which values their contribution and opinions.

c) Treating them to dinner.

d) Treating them in a way which undermines them.

4 **Which of the following is a good method of securing your computer at work?**

a) Setting a user password and locking your screen when you step away from it.

b) Leaving a note of your password on your monitor.

c) Locking your computer away in a cupboard when you step away from your machine.

d) Removing the hard drive from your computer when you go home at night.

5 **What is the best way of dealing with a document that you need to type up, which is confidential?**

a) Go and work in the canteen.

b) Only type it up in the evening.

c) Use a very small font size so that nobody can read it over your shoulder.

d) Take care to keep the contents of the document out of sight and make sure you do not leave it lying around while you are away from your desk.

6 **In what way is the Data Protection Act 1998 related to security and confidentiality in an organisation?**

a) It outlines the types of locks and security systems that organisations must use.

b) It forbids employees from using the phone for personal calls.

c) It outlines the rules on sending personal emails during work time.

d) It outlines the legal requirements for organisations that process personal data.

7 **What is the main purpose of conducting a risk assessment in the workplace?**

a) To identify any risky business strategies.

b) To identify potential risks to the safety of employees and ways in which these risks can be minimised.

c) To outline how to lay cables under the floor.

d) To make sure there are no more than ten risks present at work.

8 **Which of these are the main causes of waste in a business environment?**

a) The staff canteen.

b) Packaging, energy and office consumables such as stationery.

c) The recycling bins.

d) Open windows.

9 **What are the main benefits of recycling?**

a) Cost savings to employees and customers.

b) Cost savings to the organisation and benefits to the environment.

c) High costs to society and the environment.

d) Higher costs of stationery.

10 **Which of these improves efficiency?**

a) Keeping your office desk clean and dust-free.

b) Delegating as much of your work as possible.

c) Completing tasks more quickly and to a very high standard.

d) Timing yourself on every task that you carry out.

Answers to the Check your knowledge questions can be found at www.contentextra.com/businessadmin

What your assessor is looking for

In order to prepare for and succeed in completing this unit, your assessor will require you to be able to demonstrate competence in all the performance criteria listed in the table below.

Your assessor will guide you through the assessment process, but it is likely that for this unit you will need to:

● complete short written narratives or personal statements explaining your answers

● take part in professional discussions with your assessor to explain your answers verbally

● complete observations with your assessor ensuring that they can observe you carrying out your work tasks

● produce any relevant work products to help demonstrate how you have completed the assessment criteria

● ask your manager, a colleague or a customer for witness testimonies explaining how you have completed the assessment criteria.

Please note that the evidence which you generate for the assessment criteria in this unit may also count towards your evidence collection for some of the other units in this qualification. Your assessor will provide support and guidance on this.

The table below outlines the portfolio tasks which you need to complete for this unit, mapped to their associated assessment criteria.

Unit Q303 Work in a business environment

Task and page reference	Mapping assessment criteria
Portfolio task 303.1 (page 50)	Assessment criterion: 1.1
Portfolio task 303.2 (page 51)	Assessment criterion: 1.2
Portfolio task 303.3 (page 52)	Assessment criterion: 1.3
Portfolio task 303.4 (page 53)	Assessment criterion: 1.4
Portfolio task 303.5 (page 53)	Assessment criterion: 1.5
Portfolio task 303.6 (page 54)	Assessment criterion: 1.6
Portfolio task 303.7 (page 54)	Assessment criterion: 1.7
Portfolio task 303.8 (page 56)	Assessment criterion: 2.1
Portfolio task 303.9 (page 56)	Assessment criterion: 2.2
Portfolio task 303.10 (page 57)	Assessment criterion: 2.3
Portfolio task 303.11 (page 57)	Assessment criterion: 2.4
Portfolio task 303.12 (page 58)	Assessment criterion: 3.1
Portfolio task 303.13 (page 60)	Assessment criterion: 3.2
Portfolio task 303.14 (page 61)	Assessment criterion: 3.3
Portfolio task 303.15 (page 62)	Assessment criterion: 4.1
Portfolio task 303.16 (page 63)	Assessment criterion: 4.2
Portfolio task 303.17 (page 64)	Assessment criterion: 4.3
Portfolio task 303.18 (page 64)	Assessment criterion: 4.4
Portfolio task 303.19 (page 65)	Assessment criterion: 4.5
Portfolio task 303.20 (page 65)	Assessment criterion: 4.6
Portfolio task 303.21 (page 66)	Assessment criterion: 5.1
Portfolio task 303.22 (page 67)	Assessment criterion: 5.2
Portfolio task 303.23 (page 68)	Assessment criterion: 6.1
Portfolio task 303.24 (page 69)	Assessment criterion: 6.2
Portfolio task 303.25 (page 70)	Assessment criterion: 6.3
Portfolio task 303.26 (page 71)	Assessment criteria: 7.1, 7.2, 7.3 and 7.4
Portfolio task 303.27 (page 71)	Assessment criteria: 8.1, 8.2 and 8.3
Portfolio task 303.28 (page 72)	Assessment criteria: 9.1, 9.2, 9.3, 9.4, 9.5 and 9.6
Portfolio task 303.29 (page 72)	Assessment criteria: 10.1 and 10.2
Portfolio task 303.30 (page 73)	Assessment criterion: 11.1
Portfolio task 303.31 (page 73)	Assessment criteria: 12.1, 12.2, 12.3 and 12.4

Unit Q305

Work with other people in a business environment

What you will learn

- Understand how to support an organisation's overall mission and purpose
- Understand how to work as a team to achieve goals and objectives
- Understand how to communicate as a team
- Understand the contribution of individuals within a team
- Understand how to deal with problems and disagreements
- Understand the purpose of feedback when working as a team
- Be able to work in a team to achieve goals and objectives
- Be able to deal with problems in a team
- Be able to share feedback on objectives in a team

Introduction

In this unit you will be looking at working with others in order to achieve important goals at work. Some tasks are too large and difficult for you to achieve on your own, and you need to be able to find the best ways of working alongside your colleagues to get the job done.

You will be looking at the importance of agreeing work plans and goals when working with others so that everyone knows what they are supposed to be doing and when.

Communicating effectively with your fellow team members is vital for successful team-working. You will be looking at the different ways in which you can communicate with your team members at work to achieve goals and targets.

As individuals we each have different strengths which we bring to a team. One person may be good at presenting to the group and leading team meetings. Another may be good at putting the plan of action together. Each of these team members' key strengths is vital to the team's overall success. You will be looking at the importance of these individual contributions to teams.

For a team to be truly successful at work, you need to value and respect others and the contribution that they make. You need to see how the work they do helps you in your role and how we can all support one another in order to achieve team goals.

Supporting an organisation's mission

After working through this section you will understand and be able to:

- explain how organisations work
- explain an organisation's mission and purpose
- compare how your organisation works with other types of organisations
- explain the relationship between your main responsibilities, the organisation's structure and mission
- define policies, procedures, systems and values of your organisation relevant to your role
- seek advice at work about objectives, policies, systems, procedures and values.

How organisations work

Have you ever wondered how all the different parts of your business come together to make it work? In this section, you are going to look at the way in which your own job role and associated responsibilities fit into the bigger picture of the company as a whole. You will examine the ways in which you contribute to the success of your business by carrying out the tasks which you do on a day-to-day basis.

You may not have thought about this before, but the business which you work for depends upon the hard work and daily contributions of each and every member of its staff for its success — and this includes you.

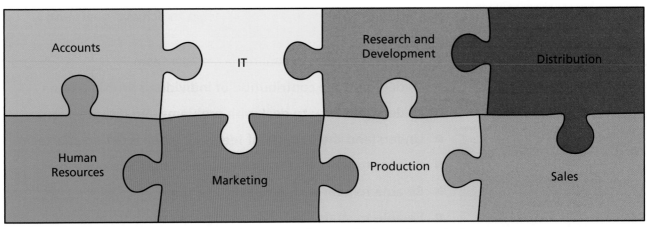

Figure 305.1: *Why is it important for all the different parts of an organisation to fit together?*

Portfolio task 305.1

→ Links to **LO1**: assessment criterion 1.1

Write a short report which explains how your organisation works. To complete this task you may wish to complete the table below in order to gather all the information you need for your answer. Remember that your final piece of work should be in the form of a written report.

What does your organisation do?	
How many departments are there? How many staff work in each department? Where are all the departments located?	
Does the company operate locally, nationally or internationally?	

A version of this table, ready for you to complete, is available to download from www.contentextra.com/businessadmin

An organisation's mission and purpose

An organisation's mission and purpose are achieved by goals and targets which employees work towards. The relationship between these terms can be illustrated as follows in Figure 305.2.

Key term

Mission statement – a short statement setting out the reason why an organisation exists.

Mission

An organisation's mission (sometimes also referred to as its vision) is, quite simply, the reason why it exists.

The mission is communicated in a **mission statement**, which you can usually find on the organisation's website. Mission statements are usually very short – one or two sentences at most – and set out the overall philosophy of the organisation. Metrosyst Technologies, a global producer of powerful computers for businesses has the following mission statement:

'Our mission is for businesses everywhere to achieve success by embracing the potential of our technologies.'

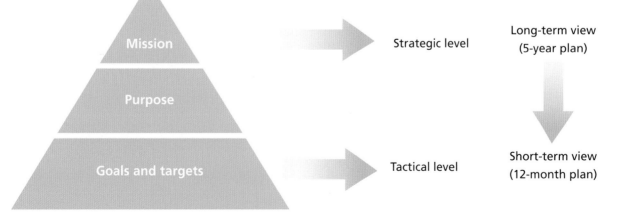

Figure 305.2: *Hierarchy of mission, purpose and goals in an organisation*

Metrosyst Technologies is in the **private sector**, that is, it exists to make a profit for its shareholders. The mission statement of a charity would be quite different. For example, the charity *No More Cruelty* has the following mission statement:

> '*No More Cruelty* exists to eradicate all cruelty to animals in the UK. We hold rallies and publicise our cause in the national press. We also investigate cases of animal cruelty and make sure the perpetrators are prosecuted.
>
> Our members are dedicated to rescuing animals from cruel treatment by their owners and re-homing them in caring environments.'

Purpose

The purpose of an organisation is a more detailed explanation of what the company actually does. For example, the purpose of the NSPCC is to stop cruelty to children, whereas the purpose of eBay is to allow people to buy and sell their products online for the best price.

Key terms

Private sector – the sector of the economy that consists of profit-making organisations.

Goals and targets – short-term plans for the achievement of specific aims.

Goals and targets

Goals and targets are the short-term plans that are put in place by teams and departments within the organisation in order to achieve its purpose and mission. Goals and targets should be detailed and are usually set out as in the following two examples:

> 'Our goal is to achieve sales of 10,000 pairs of trainers in the North of England sales territory in the next 12 months.'

> 'Our target is to generate £100,000 worth of sales of our new line of chilled pasta meals in the UK in the next 12 months. We will do this by employing direct sales staff, who will visit grocery retailers directly and offer wholesale discounts to them. We will also run in-store tasting promotions in 100 stores over this 12-month period.'

Activity 1

Read the mission statements for Metrosyst Technologies and *No More Cruelty* again. Which do you prefer and why? Which gives the better idea of what the company does?

You can use the following table to write up your answer.

The mission statement I prefer is ....
I prefer this one because ....
The mission statement that gives the better idea of what the company does is ....

A version of this form, ready for you to complete, is available to download from www.contentextra.com/businessadmin

Portfolio task 305.2

➡ Links to **LO1**: assessment criterion 1.2

In order to complete this portfolio task, you need to produce a written summary which explains your organisation's mission and purpose.

To do this you will need to carry out some research to locate your company's mission statement and purpose. You should be able to find this quite easily either by looking on your organisation's website or by looking through published company literature.

You will need to keep a copy of the original information that you used to find the mission statement as evidence for your assessment portfolio. This could be either a screenshot of the web page or a photocopy of a page from a company publication. Completing the following table will help you order your research.

Your organisation's mission statement: ....
....
....

What is the main purpose of your company? ....
....
....

A version of this table, ready for you to complete, is available to download from www.contentextra.com/businessadmin

Functional skills

English: Reading

If you carry out research involving the reading of texts including work-related documents as well as Internet research in order to complete your portfolio task, you may be able to count this as evidence towards Level 2 Functional English: Reading. Remember to keep records of all the documents, handbooks or guidelines which you study, along with the websites which you visited, as you will need to document any reading research you carry out.

✓ Checklist

Mission statement and purpose

Remember:

- An organisation's mission statement is a brief summary outlining the philosophy of the organisation.

- An organisation's purpose is a more detailed statement outlining, in simple terms, exactly what the organisation does.

Comparing how your organisation works with other types of organisations

Within the industry or sector in which your organisation operates, there will usually be a number of other organisations. These may be direct competitors to your organisation, as Asda and Tesco are to each other, or they may operate in a complementary way, such as the fire service and the police, which are both in the

public sector. Other examples of organisations that operate in complementary rather than competitive ways include suppliers — for example, auto-parts suppliers to garages and product suppliers to retailers.

Identifying how different organisations work involves looking at factors such as:

- the products or services which they provide
- the industry in which they operate
- the sector in which they operate
- the size, location and number of premises

- the distribution methods
- the type, number and geographical location of customers
- the number and type of employees.

Key term

Public sector – the sector of the economy run by the government. This includes schools, hospitals, the NHS, as well as local councils.

Portfolio task 305.3

→ Links to **LO1**: assessment criterion 1.3

In order to complete this portfolio task, you need to produce a short written summary which compares how your organisation works with two other different types of organisation.

- To begin this task, you will need to select two other organisations. It may help if you choose two organisations with which you are familiar. Ask your assessor if you are unsure of which ones to select.

- Carry out research on each of these organisations to find out key information about how they work.

- Next, look at the similarities and the differences between these and your own organisation.

It may help to complete the following table in order to gather all the necessary information for your portfolio task. Remember to keep copies of websites visited and documents you have looked at to gather this information.

	My organisation: _____	Other organisation 1: _____	Other organisation 2: _____
Products or services provided			
Industry in which the organisation operates			
Sector in which the organisation operates			

A version of this table, ready for you to complete, is available to download from www.contentextra.com/businessadmin

Relationship between your main responsibilities, the organisation's structure and mission

Identifying your main responsibilities

We each have our own role and associated responsibilities within the organisation. These are important because our responsibilities are the things that must be met in order to carry out our role effectively.

Below is an example of a job description and **person specification** for a customer service assistant position at Tesco.

Read over the job description section in the example (the last eight bullet points). It says that the job holder will need to perform eight key tasks. These are the responsibilities that are central to the job. As such, they are the key tasks against which the performance of the job holder will be measured.

Key term

Person specification – a list of the skills and abilities that the post-holder must possess.

Tesco Customer Service Assistant
Job Description and Person Specification

We are looking for someone who is:

- **passionate** about retail
- **focusing** on the customer and **striving** to understand them better than anyone
- **driven** to achieve results through determination and commitment
- **committed** to treating people in a fair and consistent way
- **willing** to roll their sleeves up to get things done
- **determined** to respond energetically to customer feedback
- **motivated** to work in partnership with others to achieve individual and team objectives
- **adaptable** and **flexible** to thrive in a 24/7 business
- **devoted** to seeking feedback on their performance and investing time in their own development.

Within your job you will need to perform the following tasks:

- Maintain excellent store standards.
- Achieve customer service target levels.
- Deal with customers in a friendly and positive manner.
- Ensure compliance with food safety standards.
- Deal with disputes and customer complaints in a constructive and positive way.
- Detect and prevent shoplifters.
- Carry out duties of a checkout assistant where applicable.
- Issue exchange and refunds brought to the CS desk.

Figure 305.3: *An example of a job description and person specification for a customer service assistant position at Tesco*

Activity 2

For this activity you will need to have a copy of your job description to hand. Look over it and pick out the key responsibilities which your job involves. Make notes of these in the left-hand column of the following table.

Next, you need to give an example of how you can meet each of your key responsibilities at work. List these in the right-hand column of the table below. For example, if you have responsibility for 'achieving customer service target levels', as in the Tesco job description (see Figure 305.3), you may achieve this by answering the phone within three rings, or by resolving 90 per cent of customer service queries immediately.

Key responsibility	How I can meet this at work

A version of this table, ready for you to complete, is available to download from www.contentextra.com/businessadmin

Key term

Reporting line – the line showing which position reports in to which manager.

How do responsibilities fit into the organisational structure?

The next section looks at how responsibilities at work fit into the organisation's structure. A business usually shows its structure in the form of a simple chart (see Figure 305.4). It gives a brief overview of all the different people or departments within the company, showing how they fit together and who reports to whom.

In Figure 305.4:

- there are ten production operators
- the production operators all work within the production department and they report in to the production manager
- there is one human resource assistant who reports in to the human resource manager
- there is also one accounts assistant who reports in to the accounts manager
- the accounts manager, the production manager and the human resource manager all report in to the managing director.

This is how all the various roles and responsibilities fit together within the overall structure of this particular organisation.

Organisational structure charts are very useful for seeing who reports in to whom. This is very important information for employees to know, and you will go on to look at **reporting lines** in your own organisation in the following portfolio task.

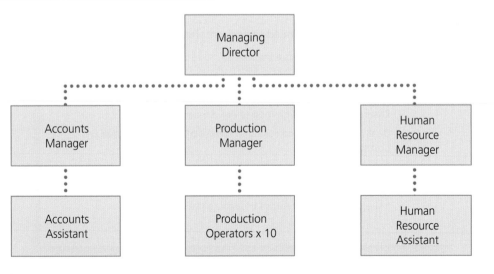

Figure 305.4: *An organisational structure chart*

How responsibilities contribute to the organisation's mission

The responsibilities of each and every member of staff feed into and contribute towards the achievement of the organisation's mission.

Let's suppose that you work for an electronics retailer as a sales assistant. How do your responsibilities contribute to the organisation's mission?

To find out, take a look at Figure 305.5.

Figure 305.5: *How responsibilities contribute towards the organisation's mission*

Portfolio task 305.4 → Links to **LO1**: assessment criterion 1.4

In order to complete this portfolio task, you need to write a brief summary which explains:

- your main responsibilities (you can include the work which you did for the activity on page 84 for this part of the task)

- how these fit into your organisation's structure

- how these contribute to achieving your organisation's mission.

It may help to begin by sketching out a simple structure chart for your organisation. Sketch your chart here.

> My organisational structure chart

A version of this form, ready for you to complete, is available to download from www.contentextra.com/businessadmin

It may also be helpful for you to answer the following questions.

Which department does your position in the organisation belong to?	
Who do you report in to? (This is usually your line manager.)	

A version of this form, ready for you to complete, is available to download from www.contentextra.com/businessadmin

Remember, your final piece of work for this task should be in the form of a well-presented written summary.

Policies, procedures, systems and values of your organisation relevant to your role

In this section you will examine which of your organisation's policies, procedures, systems and values are directly relevant to your role within the organisation.

Policies and procedures

Policies and procedures that are relevant to your role will certainly include the following:

- the health and safety policies of your organisation such as reporting of health hazards or incidents and accidents at work

- human resource policies; for example, on reporting your absence from work if you are sick

- IT policies, such as software to be used and restrictions on employee downloads

- organisational security and confidentiality policies covering things such as protection of sensitive data (which will include compliance with the Data Protection Act 1998)

- organisational procedures such as the fire drill procedure, the filing procedure, as well as the telephone call handling procedure.

Systems and values

Systems in organisations can be used for many aspects of work such as:

- workflow planning
- IT
- operations
- communications
- company intranets
- pay
- reviewing and rewarding performance.

The specific systems that relate to your position within your organisation will depend on the type of organisation you work for and the nature of the work that you do.

The values of an organisation often concern issues such as the treatment and development of staff and the ethical behaviour of the business (two well-known examples of ethical businesses are The Co-op and The Body Shop), as well as customer service excellence.

So, for example, an organisation which values customer service excellence might use phrases such as 'The customer is always right,' or 'Excellence is our standard.' Instilling the underlying values of the organisation into its employees has a tremendous effect on attitudes and behaviour. Over time, the organisation's values become part of the **culture** of the organisation.

Key term

Culture – many unspoken rules which develop in an organisation over time and which simply become the way things are done.

Activity 3

There may be other policies, procedures, systems and values that are specific to your organisation and which impact in some way on your job. Carry out some work-based research by asking your manager or mentor to go over with you all the relevant policies, procedures, systems and values which you need to be aware of.

This information will also be very useful in helping you to complete the next portfolio task.

Portfolio task 305.5

→ Links to **LO1**: assessment criterion 1.5

In order to complete this portfolio task, you need to write a short summary which defines the policies, procedures, systems and values of your organisation that are relevant to your role. You need to select three examples.

It may help you to use the table below to gather all the relevant information which you will need for your answer.

Policies, procedures, systems and values which are relevant to my job	How this relates to my job and why I must follow it

A version of this table, ready for you to complete, is available to download from www.contentextra.com/businessadmin

Functional skills

English: Reading

If you carry out research involving the reading of texts including work-related documents as well as Internet research in order to complete your portfolio task, you may be able to count this as evidence towards Level 2 Functional English: Reading. Remember to keep records of all of the documents, handbooks and guidelines which you study, along with the websites which you visit, as you will need to document any reading research you carry out.

Getting advice at work about objectives, policies, systems, procedures and values

If you are unsure about any aspect of your organisation's objectives, policies, systems, procedures and values, and this is directly affecting your work, holding you up from completing a work-related task or causing you any concern, then it is appropriate to seek guidance from others at work in order to get clarification.

The first point of contact is your line manager. They will have a good all-round knowledge of the company's policies and procedures and should be able to advise you on most general areas.

Alternatively, if you have a specific enquiry, for example, about pay, then the payroll department will be able to answer your query. If you have a specific query about your contract of employment, the human resource department would be well placed to provide you with the answers you need.

Portfolio task 305.6

→ Links to **LO1**: assessment criterion 1.6

In order to complete this portfolio task, you need to produce a written summary which describes when it is appropriate to seek guidance from others when unsure about objectives, policies, systems, procedures and values. You must include three examples. Give examples from your own experience, if possible, to show when you have asked others to help explain organisational issues to you.

Your assessor may wish to carry out a verbal discussion with you in order to assess this task. If so, make your own notes before the discussion in order to prepare yourself and to show the assessor that you have a professional approach.

You may, if you wish, use this table to help gather all the information you need for your answer. Remember, your finished task should be in the form of a well-presented written piece of work.

Issue	Do you have access to any documents at work containing this information?	Who is the person you think would be best to consult?	When do you think it is appropriate to seek guidance?
Objectives			
Policies			

A version of this table, ready for you to complete, is available to download from www.contentextra.com/businessadmin

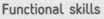

Functional skills

English: Speaking and listening

If your assessor asks you to take part in a discussion about this portfolio task as part of the assessment for this learning outcome, you may be able to count it as evidence towards Level 2 Functional English: Speaking and listening.

Working as a team to achieve goals and objectives

After working through this section you will understand and be able to:

● explain the purpose and benefits of working with other people to achieve agreed goals and objectives

● describe situations in which working with others can achieve positive results

● explain the purpose and benefits of sharing work goals and plans when working with others

● describe situations where team members might need support

● explain different ways of providing support to teams

● explain the purpose and benefits of agreeing quality measures with a team.

Working with others to achieve goals and objectives

Sometimes team-working is the most effective way to achieve the best results. This is especially true where there is a tight deadline or a large project which needs to be completed. You may have heard the phrase 'Many hands make light work.' There are many examples where this is the case. It is, in fact, good business practice to put together special teams of people who are the most highly skilled and qualified to achieve the targets needed by the organisation at specific times.

Purpose of working with others

Teams can achieve much more than individuals working alone. Think of it this way; one man on a production line can produce 1000 widgets per eight-hour shift. The managing director has promised an order of 20,000 widgets to a key customer by the end of the week.

The man working alone will manage to produce only 5000 widgets by the end of the week. The smartest business solution to this problem is to draft in a team of three additional people to help on the widget production line. With a total of four people producing widgets at a rate of 1000 per shift (so, 4000 per shift in total), they will achieve the 20,000 target which they need in order to fulfil the order for their customer by the end of the week.

Benefits of working with others

There are many benefits of teams working to achieve goals and objectives. Perhaps the key one is **synergy**. Synergy occurs where the total is greater than the sum of the parts.

In other words, you get more out than you put in. In business, this is a very valuable thing to have. It means that ten people working efficiently as a team will produce more than the same ten people if they were working alone.

Key term

Synergy – the total is greater than the sum of the parts.

Why would this be so? The answer lies in the relationships which develop within teams working towards a common goal or target:

- Motivation – team members often motivate each other much more effectively than a manager, as they have a more informal and closer relationship with each other.
- Support – they are more supportive to each other when one person needs a little help.

- Flexibility – they can also find ways of working flexibly together to meet changing needs.
- Mutual respect – team members develop a good sense of respect for each other which creates a very good working environment.
- Feeling of involvement – working as part of a team gives people a greater sense of involvement with the end goal, and this is a key reason why teams are so good at reaching targets.
- Increased sense of responsibility – being part of a team gives a better sense of responsibility, therefore team members are more likely to work harder to achieve their target.

Portfolio task 305.7 → Links to **LO2**: assessment criterion 2.1

Produce a short written piece of work which explains the purpose and three benefits of working with other people to achieve agreed goals and objectives. It may strengthen your answer if you include examples from your own experience of working with other people on a project. Describe what the project was and say what the benefits were of being part of a team.

Working with others to achieve positive results

Working with others as part of a team can bring about a range of positive results both for the individual team members and for the business. In particular, as we have seen, working in teams with a common goal or target achieves greater results than individuals working alone.

It allows the team members to develop new and better working relationships with people in the workplace. This may lead to even better and more productive team projects in the future.

Working with others in teams allows team members to develop new and important skills, maybe in team leadership, project planning and costing, or in motivating fellow team members. These are very important skills to acquire if you are planning on progressing into a management position later in your career.

Portfolio task 305.8 → Links to **LO2**: assessment criterion 2.2

Write a short summary which describes two situations where working with others can achieve positive results. Try to include examples from your own work experience in your answer and say what the positive results were.

Sharing work goals and plans

When working with others in a team it is very important to have clearly defined goals and plans which everyone in the team is familiar with. Without these, the team would achieve little, as no one would know what they were supposed to be doing at any given time.

Purpose of sharing work plans and goals

The main reason why teams must work to shared and agreed plans and goals is so that everyone knows what they need to do and by when. The team plan is the starting point of its activity. The plan sets out each step that needs to be carried out in order for the team to achieve its goals.

Clear plans help each team member to know exactly what is expected of them and when they must carry out each task. Each team member needs to be given a copy of the plan so that they can all see at a glance who is doing what and who is working with whom on a given task.

Goals are essential elements of teamwork because they set out the desired results for team members to aim for. For example, if each member of a sales team is given the goal of making 100 sales in a week, this sets out the rate at which they must work and also gives them something to aim towards. This can be broken down to a daily target of 20 sales, and the team members can easily monitor their own success against this figure each day.

Goals also encourage team members to work harder and to be more motivated to achieve results. If you are sitting alongside four colleagues who are also aiming to make 100 sales that week, there will be an element of friendly competition which will keep people motivated, as people aim to make the highest number of sales. This all has a great effect on team productivity. This is another example of synergy, which you looked at earlier in the unit.

Benefits of sharing work plans and goals

Setting out shared plans and goals has a number of benefits to team members:

- It sets out who is doing what and by when. It also ensures a smooth flow of work.
- It allows team members to monitor and track their own progress against goals so that they can see their achievements.
- It improves morale and makes for a positive work environment.

If you did not have shared plans and goals for the team, the team members would be unable to see the end goals to which they were working. This could cause loss of commitment and focus.

How can sharing plans and goals contribute to creating a successful team?

✓ Checklist

Plans and goals

Remember:

- From the manager's point of view, plans and goals are the tools by which they will evaluate a team's progress.
- The work of the team will be tied in to the larger goals of the department and the organisation.

Portfolio task 305.9 → Links to **LO2**: assessment criterion 2.3

Write a short summary report which explains the purpose and three benefits of sharing work goals and plans when working with others. It may help you to include examples from your own work experience which demonstrate the benefits of shared work goals.

Functional skills

English: Writing

If you take care to produce a professional and well-presented report for your answer to this portfolio task, you may be able to count it as evidence towards Level 2 Functional English: Writing. Remember to use headings and subheadings, check you have used correct spelling and grammar and then print out the final version of your report, once you have made all your corrections.

Support within teams

Perhaps one of the key benefits of team working is the readily available support which people can give each other as they work together. It is this support which is critical in keeping the team together and keeps it going during challenging times.

✓ Checklist

A team

Remember:

- A team is all about shared responsibility in achieving goals.

- All team members are dependent upon each other in order to work together successfully.

When do team members need support?

There are a few occasions when it is vital to support team members in their work. These include times when the team may have fallen behind agreed goals and **morale** is starting to suffer.

There may also be times when individual team members become overloaded with tasks assigned to them, and they need help to take stock, prioritise and maybe get someone else to help share the tasks.

Support is also needed when team members lose their motivation or even become upset or angry. If these issues are not dealt with, it will have a huge effect on the performance of the team as a whole. Teams work best when they are **unified** and when everyone is happy and pulling in the same direction. When one team member feels isolated, overworked or unhappy, the whole team may well suffer.

Portfolio task 305.10 → Links to **LO2**: assessment criterion 2.4

- Write a short report which describes three situations in which team members might need support from one another. You should try to include examples of situations from your own experience at work.

- Explain ways of providing support to teams. You can include here examples of support you have provided to other team members and how this was helpful to the team.

Ways of providing support to teams

There are a number of ways in which team members can show support for each other. For example:

- They can listen to problems – being a good and effective team listener is harder than you might think. It is important to let the other person get their point across without interrupting them or dismissing their opinion. Remember that each team member's opinion is important.

Key terms

Morale – enthusiasm and willingness of employees, or a measure of how happy they are at work.

Unified – working together towards a common purpose.

• They can show genuine concern for others – if you show that you really care about what the other person is saying, this will help build the team up. Teams are built on trust, so be tactful and show respect to your team members.

• They can be prepared to share the load – the best performing teams are those which share the work and don't allow one team member to become overloaded.

• They can be prepared to present a problem to the whole team – arranging a team meeting to air the issue means a quick and simple solution can be put in place.

• They can be positive – maintaining a positive approach is a very important team skill to develop.

Portfolio task 305.11 ➡ Links to **LO2**: assessment criterion 2.5

Write a short summary which explains three ways of providing support to teams. You can also include examples of support you have provided to other team members at work and how this was helpful to the team.

Agreeing quality measures within a team

Agreeing quality measures within a team is a good way of helping to focus team members on good performance and output. It also has a positive effect on the performance of the team because it focuses them on working towards improvements.

For example, a customer service team may agree a quality measure such as a 95 per cent customer satisfaction rate. Every team member is made aware of this rate and it makes them take that extra step to ensure high quality standards in their work.

A big factor here is the emphasis on positive outcomes by aiming for high quality, which is great for team-building. Because these measures are part of the team's brief, quality becomes central to

the working **ethos** of the team. An individual team member would not want to let down the rest of the team by being found to have let quality standards slip. So, in this way, quality measures help the team to be highly productive.

Key term

Ethos – character or spirit.

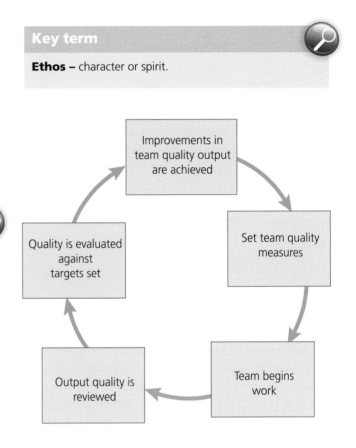

Figure 305.6: *How do quality measures improve team performance?*

Portfolio task 305.12 ➡ Links to **LO2**: assessment criterion 2.6

Write a brief report which explains the purpose of agreeing quality measures within a team. You should also include a section in your report which gives three benefits of agreeing quality measures. It may help you to include examples of team quality measures from your own work experience.

How to communicate as a team

After working through this section you will understand and be able to:

- explain when it is essential to communicate with the people working in a team
- compare and contrast different methods of communication and when to use them
- explain the benefits of effective communication within a team.

When team communication is essential

Good communication skills are essential in making a positive contribution to the team. Team communication is especially necessary when:

- giving information — keeping everyone up to date with the latest team information
- expressing ideas — allowing all team members to contribute their own individual ideas and opinions
- raising issues — asking the team for opinions and comments on issues or areas of concern (this opens up a forum for debate and an exchange of ideas)
- informing the team of progress against targets — it is very important to let everyone know how the team is doing and what they need to achieve to get to the next milestone
- asking for feedback — inviting contributions from all of the team
- raising morale — good communication is vital in raising morale and keeping the team spirit high.

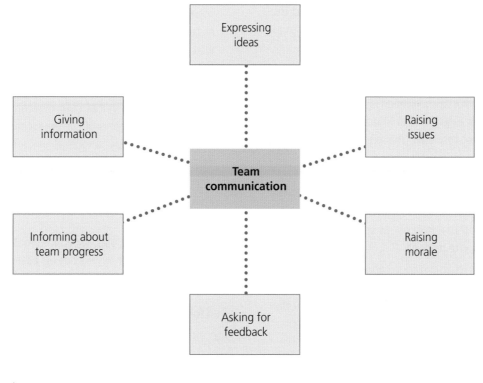

Figure 305.7: *Why is communication within a team essential?*

Portfolio task 305.13

→ Links to **LO3**: assessment criterion 3.1

Produce a short written report which explains when it is essential to communicate with people working within a team and give four examples. It may help you to include examples from your own work experience in your answer, and say why you think team communication was essential in these situations.

You could use the table below to help you gather the information for your answer.

Example of a team situation where communication is essential	Reasons why communication is essential in this situation

A version of this table, ready for you to complete, is available to download from www.contentextra.com/businessadmin

Methods of communication

There are a variety of communication methods and the best ones to use will depend on the situation and the issue to be communicated.

Communication takes many forms:

- Formal — formal communication is more likely to happen in large organisations where people do not know each other very well. This often takes the form of written letters and is suitable in situations where records need to be kept of such communication, in case they need to be referred back to at a later date. Large formal meetings are often used in bigger organisations. These are one-way communications, as you do not really have the chance to respond.

- Informal — informal communication is more likely in smaller organisations, or in fact in teams, where people know each other quite well, and can include face-to-face meetings as well as email and telephone conversations. They are quicker and more relaxed than formal methods and allow you the chance to respond immediately.

- Verbal — verbal communication means all methods of spoken communication including one-to-one meetings, group meetings, telephone (which can include conference calls to many people at once), as well as video calls and company broadcasts (these are calls from, say, the managing director to all company staff via the phone system).

- Non-verbal — non-verbal communication is one of the most important forms of communication. It includes such things as body language, posture and facial expressions.

- Written — written communication includes notes, emails and letters.

- Presentations — presentations are used to give information to a group of people. These have a wide range of uses from giving out necessary health and safety information to announcing good news to staff.

Portfolio task 305.14

→ Links to **LO3**: assessment criterion 3.2

Write a short summary which compares and contrasts different methods of communication and when to use them. You should include three methods of communication in your answer.

Large, formal meetings tend to be one-way communications – why is this?

Benefits of effective team communication

The frequency and quality of communications within a team are central to its successful working. Here are some key benefits of effective team communications:

● Everyone is kept fully up to date on progress so they can do their jobs effectively.

● Everyone feels involved and valued – effective communication means giving regular positive feedback to all of your team to show recognition for hard work and achievements to date.

● The whole team knows exactly what needs to be done next and by whom so that their work can progress efficiently and seamlessly.

Activity 4

Think of a time when you've been involved in a team project or event. Give one example each of effective and ineffective team communication which you have experienced. Say what the situation was and the communication method which was used in each case and why you think it was either effective or ineffective.

Portfolio task 305.15 → Links to **L03**: assessment criterion 3.3

To complete this portfolio task, you need to write a short summary which explains the benefits of effective communication within a team. Try to include examples from your own work experience in your summary.

The contribution of individuals within a team

After working through this section you will understand and be able to:

● explain the purpose and benefits of acknowledging the strengths of others

● explain the purpose and benefits of respecting individuals working within a team.

Acknowledging the strengths of others

Effective teams need to be made up of people with different skills and backgrounds. Just as these team members have different skills, they will also bring various different strengths to the group. It is a key task of the team leader to be able to get the best out of these different people and, to do this, they will need to assign tasks to them which allow them to play to their strengths.

Figure 305.8: *Elements of successful team-building*

For example, in any successful football team, the team manager will need people with different specialist abilities and strengths — some need to be good at attacking, while others need to be good at defending.

It is the same in business; a collection of different skills and abilities will make for the optimum team performance. People naturally play different team roles. One person may be naturally an ideas person but not good at implementing them, while another may be naturally very good at getting tasks completed, but not at coming up with the ideas in the first place.

Belbin's team roles

According to Dr Meredith Belbin, there are a number of different roles which team members can play, including:

● chair — coordinates the team

● shaper — sets priorities

● plant — the ideas person

● monitor — a shrewd evaluator of problems and progress

● resource investigator — good at networking and uses lots of contacts to help

● company worker — loyal to the task

● team worker — caring, with good communication skills, keeps the team together

● finisher — ensures the task gets done.

Look back over the list of team roles above and you may recognise some of your colleagues playing one or more of these roles in team situations. These roles are not necessarily all present in every team situation. However, it is also possible for one person to play more than one of these roles in a team setting.

A key benefit of team-working is to foster innovation and nurture new talent, and this can only be achieved by allowing people to play the roles to which they are best suited, thereby developing their strengths.

Activity 5

Think of a recent occasion where you were part of a team. Write down three different strengths which you noticed in other members of your team. For each, say why you think this is a valuable team skill to have.

Portfolio task 305.16 → Links to **LO4**: assessment criterion 4.1

Produce a brief report which explains the purpose and benefits of acknowledging the strengths of others in a team setting. For this task, it may help you to use an example of a recent team meeting or event which you attended.

Give a brief overview of the purpose of the team meeting or event. Make sure you talk about at least three benefits of acknowledging the strengths of other team members.

Portfolio task 305.17 → Links to **LO4**: assessment criterion 4.2

Write a short report which explains the purpose and three benefits of respecting individuals working within a team. In order to complete this task, you could give real examples from your own experience of team-working, where people have shown respect to others.

Respecting individuals working within a team

Teams are made up of individuals. These individuals play different team roles, come from different spheres of life and have different approaches to tasks. In fact, they will often have quite differing opinions on how things should be done.

It is perfectly acceptable to disagree with another individual's opinion in a team setting. However, the way in which these disagreements are voiced and subsequently dealt with is important. For example, you should:

● let the other person make the point which they want to get across without interrupting them

● acknowledge their point in a polite manner

● wait your turn to speak and put across your own point in a well-considered way, giving sound reasons for your thoughts

● display tact and be considerate of other people's feelings.

All of this is about showing respect to the other individuals within your team. Without this, conflict may manifest itself in a way which is detrimental to the team's spirit, and relationships between team members may well suffer. Under these circumstances, a team cannot perform well.

Dealing with problems and disagreements

After working through this section you will understand and be able to:

● explain the types of problems and disagreements that may occur when working with others

● evaluate ways of resolving problems and disagreements when working with others.

Types of problems and disagreements that may occur when working with others

Some of the typical problems that may occur between people at work include:

● clashes of personalities

● breakdown of trust

● disagreements on ways of working on a task

● loss of commitment

● loss of focus.

You may find some of these problems familiar from your own experience of working with others. Situations where deadlines are very tight and the stakes are high if the project fails to complete on time are more likely to be beset by problems and disagreements between members of staff. This is because of the high level of stress associated with the work. Other more routine working environments tend to be quieter and more harmonious.

Portfolio task 305.18

→ Links to **LO5**: assessment criterion 5.1

Write a short report which explains three types of problems and disagreements that may occur when working with others. You may like to use the table below to help you gather all the information you will need for your answer. Remember that your final piece of work should be in the form of a written report.

Type of problem or disagreement that may occur when working with others	Give an example of how this situation might arise

A version of this table, ready for you to complete, is available to download from www.contentextra.com/businessadmin

Resolving problems and disagreements with others

For every problem which you come across at work when working with others, there are usually several options available to you for resolving it and moving the team forward with their project or task. The option that you decide upon will depend on factors such as the time that you have available, the number, type and location of your team members, as well as the severity of the problem or disagreement.

Some issues will have a relatively straightforward solution, whereas others may be more complicated and require more time and **diligence** on your part in order to resolve them.

Key term

Diligence – a high degree of care and attention.

Clashes of personalities

Dealing with team members whose personalities clash and who are hampering the work of the team can be dealt with by:

- allocating tasks in a way that they only need have minimal contact
- reallocating one of them to another team.

Breakdown of trust

Breakdown of trust can be dealt with by:

- instigating trust-building initiatives in your team
- showing yourself to be trustworthy by being true to your word
- rewarding team-oriented behaviour.

Disagreements on ways of working on a task

This type of issue can be dealt with by:

- calling a working methods team meeting
- encouraging openness from team members in offering suggestions to arrive at a consensus
- monitoring team activity to ensure the correct approach is being adopted.

What are the aims of team-building activities?

Loss of commitment

Commitment can be regained in a team by:

- identifying the reasons for the loss of commitment and addressing these deeper issues
- keeping morale-boosting as a key part of team communications
- encouraging involvement from all the team
- making sure you are in regular communication with every individual in the team.

Loss of focus

Loss of focus of team members needs immediate attention and addressing by:

- using objective-setting in all team communications
- setting up a special re-focusing meeting
- following up with team members to monitor progress on meeting objectives.

Portfolio task 305.19

→ Links to **LO5**: assessment criterion 5.2

Produce a short written report which evaluates three ways of resolving problems and disagreements when working with others. Remember that to evaluate you should consider both the advantages and disadvantages of the different methods of problem resolution. You can use the three problems that you wrote about in portfolio task 305.18 to complete this task.

It may help you to use the table below to gather the information for your answer. Remember that your final piece of work should be in the form of a well-presented report.

Type of problem or disagreement that may occur when working with others	Way of resolving problems and disagreements when working with others	Advantages	Disadvantages
1			

A version of this table, ready for you to complete, is available to download from www.contentextra.com/businessadmin

Office life

Ben's story

My name is Ben Solis and I am 19 years old. I have been working as an account executive in a medium-sized advertising agency in London for six months. One of my first tasks was to get together a project team to come up with a winning pitch for a new celebrity perfume which was launching some months later. This was a key account for us and, if we won the pitch for the advertising campaign, it would be worth £5 million in business for the company.

So I put together the team and briefed them on the requirements of the pitch. We needed a show-stopping design concept, a superb storyboard for a TV advert and a promotional campaign to take the global fragrances market by storm.

A week later I got my team together to review their ideas. However, progress was not good. The team started arguing loudly amongst themselves and could not reach agreement on the storyboard for the TV ad campaign. It became clear to me that my team were not performing at all well. My business pitch was in danger and, with it, the £5 million of business for our company.

Ask the expert

Q I have a project team currently putting together a pitch for an advertising campaign. Although the team consists of the best creative minds in the company, there have been numerous incidents of disagreements and arguing amongst the team and progress on the project is not good.

A You need to consider the different individuals and their personalities and skills when you recruit your team. You need the team members to be able to cooperate with each other and also to maintain a focus on completing the required tasks in addition to coming up with good ideas.

Top tips

In order to get the best performance from a team, it is important that Ben gathers together people with different skills and personalities. This way, he will have a well-rounded mix of individuals who, together, can complete the project on time and to budget, as well as having an impact creatively.

This means that as well as recruiting the best creative minds and 'ideas' people, he will also need to consider the other aspects of the project. For example, he will also need team members whose focus will be on coordinating the project and getting the tasks completed on time.

The purpose of team feedback

After working through this section you will understand and be able to:

- explain the purpose and benefits of giving and receiving constructive feedback
- explain ways of using feedback to improve individual work, the work of others and of a team as a whole.

Constructive feedback

Let's begin by investigating the issue of **constructive feedback**.

What is constructive feedback?

Constructive feedback is given with the intention of having a positive effect. It is not designed to criticise or antagonise, but instead its aim is to give helpful advice on how to make improvements in certain areas of performance for the future.

Key term

Constructive feedback – feedback which is designed to focus on the positives, helping the employee to find ways of improving, while avoiding personal criticism.

The purpose of constructive feedback

The purpose of giving constructive feedback is to:

- make the receiver of the feedback aware of an area of their performance which can be improved and why this is needed
- give them specific help and advice on how to go about making this improvement
- be supportive, reminding the receiver of the overall positive nature of this feedback.

How to provide constructive feedback

One good method of providing constructive feedback is to use the following technique, which is sometimes called a feedback sandwich.

- Begin with a positive feedback point – 'your report was very informative'.
- Next, mention the issue which you would like to see improved upon – 'however, perhaps it would have been better if you had focused a little more on the spelling and grammar'.
- Finally, end with another positive – 'overall, a very good job and we will find this report very useful in our next management meeting'.

The benefits of constructive feedback

The benefits of constructive feedback are that:

- it is designed to focus on positives
- it avoids overt criticism or 'telling off'
- it makes the receiver of the feedback feel good about themselves and their performance.

Portfolio task 305.20 → Links to **L06**: assessment criterion 6.1

Write a brief report which explains the purpose and benefits of giving and receiving constructive feedback. Your answer should include three benefits of giving and receiving constructive feedback. Try to also mention examples from your own work experience in your report where you have either given and/or received feedback.

Using feedback to improve work

Feedback is somebody else's view or assessment of the quality of your performance, whether as an individual or a team. So, how can you best use this feedback to improve performance?

Checklist

You could use this checklist as a guide for making the most effective use of feedback

- Reflect over the feedback received.

- Consider the positives and negatives.

- Congratulate your team on the positives – make sure everyone who contributed hard work is recognised and thanked.

- Look back over the negative aspects and think about what can be done differently in future to improve performance in this area.

- Invite team members to come up with suggestions for new and improved ways of working.

- Instigate team initiatives which are based on the improvements needed, so that these become a focus for improving the performance of the team.

Be able to work in a team to achieve goals and objectives

Portfolio task 305.21 → Links to **L06**: assessment criterion 6.2

Write a short report which explains three ways in which you can use feedback to improve individual work, the work of others and that of a team as a whole. It may help you to include examples from your own work experience in your answer.

Evidence collection

In order for you to complete the remaining assessment criteria to successfully pass this unit, you will need to carry out various tasks at work and then produce evidence to show that you have demonstrated the required skills and competence.

Evidence can be collected in a number of different ways. For example, it can be in the form of a signed witness testimony from a colleague or line manager, a copy of any related emails or letters you have produced or a verbal discussion with your assessor.

Speak to your assessor to identify the best methods to use in order to complete each portfolio task and remember to keep copies of all the evidence that you produce.

Portfolio task 305.22

→ Links to **L07**: assessment criteria 7.1, 7.2, 7.3, 7.4, 7.5 and 7.6

Gather evidence of your work to show your assessor that you have successfully carried out the tasks outlined in the table below. Check with your assessor on the best ways of gathering evidence for each of the tasks before you begin.

Task	Evidence collected
1 Work in a way that supports your organisation's overall mission.	
2 Follow policies, systems and procedures relevant to your job.	

A version of this table, ready for you to complete, is available to download from www.contentextra.com/businessadmin

Portfolio task 305.23

Links to **LO7**: assessment criteria 7.7, 7.8, 7.9, 7.10, 7.11 and 7.12

Gather evidence of your work to show your assessor that you have successfully carried out the tasks outlined in the table below. Check with your assessor on the best ways of gathering evidence for each of the tasks before you begin.

Task	Evidence collected
1 Share work goals, priorities and responsibilities with a team.	
2 Agree work objectives and quality measures with a team, to achieve a positive outcome.	A version of this table, ready for you to complete, is available to download from www.contentextra.combusinessadmin

Be able to deal with problems in a team

Portfolio task 305.24

Links to **LO8**: assessment criteria 8.1 and 8.2

Gather evidence of your work to show your assessor that you have successfully carried out the tasks outlined in the table below. Check with your assessor on the best ways of gathering evidence for each of the tasks before you begin.

Task	Evidence collected
1 Identify problem(s) or disagreement(s) in a team.	
2 Resolve problem(s) or disagreement(s), referring if required.	A version of this table, ready for you to complete, is available to download from www.contentextra.com/businessadmin

Be able to share feedback on objectives in a team

Portfolio task 305.25

Links to **LO9**: assessment criteria 9.1, 9.2 and 9.3

Gather evidence of your work to show your assessor that you have successfully carried out the tasks outlined in the table below. Check with your assessor on the best ways of gathering evidence for each of the tasks before you begin.

Task	Evidence collected
1 Share constructive feedback on achievement of objectives with a team.	
2 Receive constructive feedback on own work.	A version of this table, ready for you to complete, is available to download from www.contentextra.com/businessadmin

Check your knowledge

1 **What is the main purpose of a mission statement?**

a) To tell people why they should invest in a business.

b) To tell staff what they should be doing each day.

c) To let people know what the business is all about and why it exists.

d) To keep competitors away.

2 **What are organisational goals and targets?**

a) They tell us the five-year business strategy.

b) They tell us the profit figures for the business.

c) They are short-term plans which usually focus on the next 12 months

d) They are long-term plans for selling the business.

3 **What is an organisational structure?**

a) It refers to the way in which all the people and departments are organised within the business.

b) It refers to the premises in which the business operates.

c) It refers to the way in which all the customers are organised.

d) It refers to the values of the organisation.

4 **What do company policies tell us?**

a) They tell us what must be done to get a promotion.

b) They tell us the rules and provide guidelines on how to act within an organisation.

c) They tell us how to put out a fire at work.

d) They tell us how to deal with customer complaints.

5 **One of the key benefits of working with others in a team is that 'synergy' is created. This means:**

a) People can take time off whenever they want.

b) The total is greater than the sum of the parts, so you get more out than you put in.

c) You get a free energy supply.

d) Morale will drop.

6 **Which of the following is not a valid reason to communicate with a team?**

a) To boost morale.

b) To raise issues.

c) To discuss the weather.

d) To give information.

7 **Which one of these statements is true?**

a) Formal communication is much more suitable in a small team.

b) Formal communication allows quick responses.

c) Formal presentations are a good forum for everyone to express their opinions.

d) Formal communication is usually used more in larger organisations where people do not know each other.

8 **Which one of these forms of communication is formal?**

a) Emails.

b) Company presentations.

c) Notes.

d) Phone messages.

9 **Why do people in teams perform different team roles?**

a) Because some people do not like to take part.

b) Because some people are more hard-working.

c) Because individuals bring different skills to the team and so it makes sense for them to be allocated tasks which relate to their strengths.

d) People in teams should always perform the same roles as each other.

10 **What is constructive feedback?**

a) It is feedback telling somebody why their performance is unacceptable.

b) It is feedback used in the construction industry.

c) It is feedback given in such a way as to focus on the positives as well as helping employees improve some aspect of their work performance.

d) It is usually destructive.

Answers to the Check your knowledge questions can be found at www.contentextra.com/businessadmin

What your assessor is looking for

In order to prepare for and succeed in completing this unit, your assessor will require you to be able to demonstrate competence in all of the performance criteria listed in the table below.

Your assessor will guide you through the assessment process, but it is likely that for this unit you will need to:

- complete short written narratives or personal statements explaining your answers

- take part in professional discussions with your assessor to explain your answers verbally

- complete observations with your assessor ensuring that they can observe you carrying out your work tasks

- produce any relevant work products to help demonstrate how you have completed the assessment criteria

- ask your manager, a colleague, or a customer for witness testimonies explaining how you have completed the assessment criteria.

Please note that the evidence which you generate for the assessment criteria in this unit may also count towards your evidence collection for some of the other units in this qualification. Your assessor will provide support and guidance on this.

The following table outlines the portfolio tasks which you need to complete for this unit, mapped to their associated assessment criteria.

Task and page reference	Mapping assessment criteria
Portfolio task 305.1 (page 79)	Assessment criterion: 1.1
Portfolio task 305.2 (page 81)	Assessment criterion: 1.2
Portfolio task 305.3 (page 82)	Assessment criterion: 1.3
Portfolio task 305.4 (page 85)	Assessment criterion: 1.4
Portfolio task 305.5 (page 87)	Assessment criterion: 1.5
Portfolio task 305.6 (page 88)	Assessment criterion: 1.6
Portfolio task 305.7 (page 89)	Assessment criterion: 2.1
Portfolio task 305.8 (page 90)	Assessment criterion: 2.2
Portfolio task 305.9 (page 91)	Assessment criterion: 2.3
Portfolio task 305.10 (page 91)	Assessment criterion: 2.4
Portfolio task 305.11 (page 92)	Assessment criterion: 2.5

continued

Unit Q305 Work with other people in a business environment

Task and page reference	Mapping assessment criteria
Portfolio task 305.12 (page 92)	Assessment criterion: 2.6
Portfolio task 305.13 (page 94)	Assessment criterion: 3.1
Portfolio task 305.14 (page 94)	Assessment criterion: 3.2
Portfolio task 305.15 (page 95)	Assessment criterion: 3.3
Portfolio task 305.16 (page 97)	Assessment criterion: 4.1
Portfolio task 305.17 (page 97)	Assessment criterion: 4.2
Portfolio task 305.18 (page 98)	Assessment criterion: 5.1
Portfolio task 305.19 (page 99)	Assessment criterion: 5.2
Portfolio task 305.20 (page 101)	Assessment criterion: 6.1
Portfolio task 305.21 (page 102)	Assessment criterion: 6.2
Portfolio task 305.22 (page 102)	Assessment criteria: 7.1, 7.2, 7.3, 7.4, 7.5 and 7.6
Portfolio task 305.23 (page 103)	Assessment criteria: 7.7, 7.8, 7.9, 7.10, 7.11 and 7.12
Portfolio task 305.24 (page 103)	Assessment criteria: 8.1 and 8.2
Portfolio task 305.25 (page 103)	Assessment criteria: 9.1, 9.2 and 9.3

Unit Q308

Supervise a team in a business environment

What you will learn

- Understand the purpose and benefits of team work
- Understand the purpose of communication in teams and how to communicate effectively
- Understand the purpose of planning work with teams and how to do this
- Understand the value of people in a team and learn how to respect and support them
- Understand the purpose and benefits of assessing and evaluating the work of a team and how to do so
- Be able to supervise a team
- Be able to assess, evaluate and improve the work of a team

Introduction

If you are responsible for managing a team, then this unit will assist you in developing your skills and knowledge to become a more effective team leader. The unit explains the principles and benefits of continuously improving your team's performance to help improve the overall efficiency of the organisation. It also explores the value of effective communication in your team.

By empowering, supporting and valuing your team, you will be able to motivate and encourage your team members to meet their own work objectives, which should in turn meet the overall objectives of the organisation. Effective teams can steer through challenges and difficulties and can normally manage any conflict before it becomes a problem.

The unit will also cover different leadership styles, various team behaviours and how to encourage and motivate your team. There will be some detailed practical guidance throughout the unit to assist you in managing your team effectively. Please note that there is some overlap in this unit with Unit Q302, 'Evaluate and improve own performance in a business environment'.

The purpose and benefits of teamwork

After working through this section you will understand and be able to:

- explain the purpose and benefits of working with other people to achieve goals and objectives
- describe situations in which supervision of others can achieve positive outcomes.

Purpose and benefits of working with other people to achieve goals and objectives

The work and outcomes produced by a team should link directly to the overall goals and objectives of the organisation. SMART objectives have already been discussed in Unit Q302, but to re-cap briefly, SMART means:

- **S**pecific – It says exactly what you intend to do.
- **M**easurable – You can measure progress and show that you have completed it.
- **A**chievable – The targets are not beyond your reach.
- **R**ealistic – The target is not too optimistic.
- **T**ime-bound – You have a specific deadline for completion.

Who sets SMART objectives:

- The organisation will set SMART objectives and these are likely to be shown in the mission statement and the overall objectives for the organisation.
- Different departments or divisions within the organisation will also set SMART objectives and these will feed into the overall objectives of the organisation.
- Different teams or team leaders will set SMART objectives or targets and these will feed into the departmental objectives.
- Individual members of staff will also set targets in conjunction with their team leader to feed into their team's targets or objectives. Figure 308.1 below shows how this would work in an organisation.

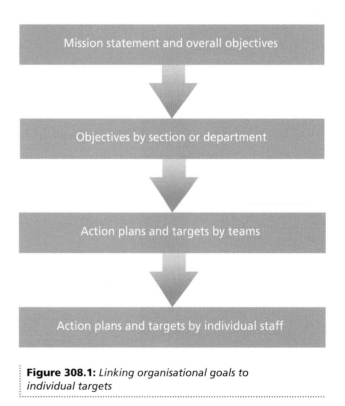

Mission statement and overall objectives

Objectives by section or department

Action plans and targets by teams

Action plans and targets by individual staff

Figure 308.1: *Linking organisational goals to individual targets*

You and your team may not always realise it, but what you do on a day-to-day basis will link directly into the organisation's overall mission and objectives. If what you are doing does not link into the mission, why are you doing it?

Once you know the targets for your team as a whole, the next stage of the process is to plan the activities in conjunction with your team members. This will involve team members agreeing targets and objectives with you. This may be done as part of the annual appraisal meeting. Once the individual targets are agreed, then the specific activities can be planned and the resources put in place. (Resources include the personnel available and the equipment/facilities to do the job).

Then, as the tasks are undertaken, it will be up to you to monitor and review the performance of individuals and the team as a whole. This is shown in Figure 308.2.

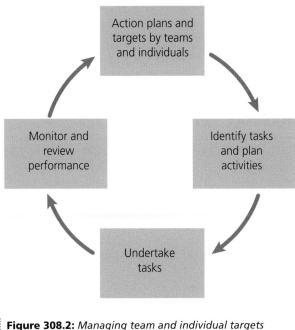

Figure 308.2: *Managing team and individual targets and performance*

Imagine that you work for a telecommunications company and the company's mission is to be the 'number one telecommunications provider in the UK'. Their main

objective for the forthcoming year is to increase sales by five per cent. Other objectives include updating the existing customer database by the end of the year.

Imagine that you manage part of the customer service team and one of your responsibilities is the customer database for your geographical region, the eastern region. You have been assigned some objectives from your manager, one of which is to update the customer database. You now need to involve your team in the process and set sub-objectives for your team members to achieve which should link into your objective as follows:

- The overall organisational objective is to update the customer database by 31 December 2011.
- The date for completion of the update for your region, the eastern region, is 30 November 2011.
- You need to work with your team and set sub-objectives for some or all of your team members. You may formulate a mini project plan to set out what you need to achieve by some agreed dates (**milestones**).
- Once you have agreed a plan with your team then you need to manage and monitor their performance to ensure that they are making good progress and can meet your agreed deadline.

Key term

Milestones – scheduled events signifying the completion of a task.

Bear in mind that other teams from different regions will also be working on their customer databases to ensure that the whole customer database is updated by the agreed date.

This is just one example and it is likely that you will have several objectives to achieve both as an individual and as a team as a whole, so careful planning is needed to ensure that you keep track of what you and your team are achieving.

What benefits are these work colleagues accruing by working together?

In addition to the team leader being competent, the team also needs to work together collectively to ensure that

- everyone is encouraged to share in the decision-making process
- staff are learning continuously in order to achieve the organisation's objectives
- effective communication is in place between all staff
- everyone is proud of the organisation and its achievements
- there is a strong emphasis on product quality and customer service.

Portfolio task 308.2 → Links to **LO1**: assessment criterion 1.2

Describe how you or your manager achieve positive outcomes in your team.

Portfolio task 308.1 → Links to **LO1**: assessment criterion 1.1

Collect examples of any objectives that you and your team need to achieve. Explain the purpose and benefits of ensuring that the team achieve their agreed goals and objectives.

How supervision of others can achieve positive outcomes

Effective supervision of a team can achieve positive outcomes as long as the team is managed effectively. For the team to be managed effectively, the team leader needs to be able to demonstrate certain competencies as follows:

- have a positive attitude
- be an effective communicator
- be competent in their role as a team leader
- be respected by their team
- be able to motivate, influence and encourage the team
- be able to harness and develop the skills and knowledge within the team
- know and understand individual team members' strengths and weaknesses
- be able to link the team goals to the overall objectives of the organisation.

Communicating within a team: its purpose and how to do it

After working through this section you will understand and be able to:

- explain the purpose and benefits of different methods of communication with and within teams and when to use them
- explain when it is essential to communicate with others in a team.

The purpose and benefits of different methods of communication within teams

Effective teams have effective communication channels in place. In order to communicate effectively with your team members, it will be necessary to communicate through a variety of methods. You will need to use the most appropriate method to ensure that the information being communicated is timely, is sent to the right people and has the right level of detail. This has the benefit of ensuring that everyone knows what is going on, all the time.

Unit Q309 covers communication in greater detail. However, in the context of managing people, it is important to reiterate a number of elements. You may be familiar with the acronym KISS which stands for 'keep it short and simple'. This is an essential requirement in a business environment, both in terms of verbal and written communication. The basic principle of this approach is to:

- use fewer words
- use shorter words
- use pictures, graphs or charts if possible.

Key term

KISS – Keep **I**t **S**hort and **S**imple – a useful acronym to remember in verbal and written communication.

The 'kiss' approach can be linked to more general principles to ensure that you communicate effectively. Use the following as a checklist to remind you.

✓ Checklist

Communicating effectively

- Use the right language to fit the occasion.
- Use the right medium – emails, letter, verbal feedback, etc.
- Get the attention of the people you are communicating with.
- Get your message across as you want it to be received – reduce the potential for misinterpretation or confusion.
- Maintain eye contact and observe body language.
- Allow people to respond.
- Listen to what is being said to you.
- Be prepared to discuss issues.

Portfolio task 308.3 → Links to **LO2**: assessment criterion 2.1

Collect examples of all the ways that you communicate with your team; for example, through formal methods such as appraisals or target setting and through more day-to-day methods like emails and team-meeting minutes. These will provide useful evidence for your portfolio.

Functional skills

English: Reading

If you carry out research involving reading texts including work-related documents as well as Internet research in order to complete your portfolio task, you may be able to count this as evidence towards Level 2 Functional English: Reading. Remember to keep records of all the documents, handbooks or guidelines which you study, along with the websites which you visit, as you will need to document any reading research you carry out.

When it is essential to communicate with others in a team

Always communicate important information as soon as practicable and do this face to face, if possible. This will avoid any uncertainty and should ensure clarity.

Always discuss any issues that are important, sensitive or potentially contentious. Other forms of communication are not appropriate when it is a matter of an important nature. For example, being told in a team meeting by your manager about a potential change to the organisational structure of the company is much better than receiving an email or letter about the change.

Communication is also about agreeing things together. You may need to admit defeat when you are outvoted by your team. Collective decisions that the whole team is on board with are more powerful and more likely to work than those decisions imposed by the team leader.

A meeting between three members of a team. Do they look as though they are listening to each other?

When communicating, actively listen to what is being said to you. This is not easy and needs concentration and practice. Try to make sense of the information being communicated and listen with intent. Then apply the information to the situation and context of the discussion to reach a more detailed understanding of the issues being raised.

Collaboration means working together. By working together, team members can share their values and the vision of the organisation, develop a team spirit and absorb the information that they need to work well with each other. Trust, mutual respect and honesty between all team members is vital.

As discussed, the principles of effective communication are:

- making sure that it is a two-way process
- making sure information is clear, concise and at the right level of detail for the recipient
- ensuring that everyone is clear about what is being communicated
- listening actively to what is being said
- keeping people informed on a regular basis, both in relation to general issues and their individual performance.

Portfolio task 308.4 → Links to **LO2**: assessment criterion 2.2

Explain when it is essential to communicate with others in a team and support this with relevant workplace evidence.

Planning work with teams and how to do so

After working through this section you will understand and be able to:

- explain the purpose and benefits of recognising the strengths of the individuals in a team and of balancing abilities in a team
- describe ways of giving work to teams so the best use is made of strengths and abilities
- explain the benefits of diversity in teams
- explain the purpose and benefits of respecting others
- describe situations in which team members might need support and how to provide this
- describe the types of problems and disagreements that may occur when working with a team and how to resolve them.

Purpose and benefits of agreeing work goals and plans with a team

As part of your job, you will need to plan your own work and the team's work. For regular and routine jobs, you might prepare a 'to do' list of things that you need to do that day or that week. By prioritising your tasks you will be able to plan your work more effectively.

However, as a team leader you will also need to plan resources in more detail for the whole team by identifying the work to be undertaken and then planning how you are going to achieve this with the resources that you have in place.

✓ Checklist

Planning

The following list should help you to plan your tasks more effectively.

- Write down all your team's objectives and targets and when you need to achieve them by.

- Highlight any specific deadline dates and try to achieve them ideally one week ahead of the deadline.

- For larger jobs, break down the tasks into more manageable elements if required or form a small project team.

- Classify your tasks by deciding how important they are and when they need to be completed by. You can use a system to help prioritise them.

- Identify at the outset any targets that may be difficult to achieve and try to negotiate extra time or resources if required.

- Manage your objectives, resources and the performance of your team through regular consultation and communication with team members including team meetings and one-to-one meetings.

- Don't worry if a more urgent objective comes up; just slot it into your list and plan the resources required to complete it.

- Always review your plan at the end of each week.

Portfolio task 308.5 → Links to **LO3**: assessment criterion 3.1

Explain the purpose and benefits of agreeing workplace goals and objectives and gather some examples of how you plan your tasks.

Scheduling activities and resources for a team

In order to schedule the activities for your team, you need to allocate the tasks based on the resources available.

✓ Checklist

Scheduling activities effectively

To ensure that you manage your resources effectively, you need to:

- focus on the organisation's mission and objectives

- be clear on your own and your team's objectives and targets and agree these objectives with your team

- identify the resources that you have in place – personnel, equipment, budgets, etc.

- schedule your activities and prioritise the objectives

- agree processes and procedures to undertake the activities

- manage performance and budgets.

Portfolio task 308.6 → Links to **LO3**: assessment criterion 3.2

Explain how you schedule activities and resources for the team. Also gather any relevant workplace evidence that demonstrates how you plan resources. An example could be a rota or timesheet.

Purpose and benefits of agreeing quality measures and timescales with a team

Teams need a common purpose to ensure that they can link into the overall objectives of the organisation. Individual team members need to be committed to their own job but at the same time be aware and understand that what they do ensures that their team meets its objective, which in turn ensures that the whole organisation meets its objectives.

Most organisations have an agreed working culture. This means 'this is how we do things round here'. At work, you will notice how people and teams communicate and interact with each other and how people plan their work.

It is also likely that there will be some performance standards in place which you and your team will need to meet. These may include some specific targets and behaviours that you need to achieve on an on-going basis and also may include some general standards. For example:

- dealing with customers and colleagues quickly, courteously and efficiently
- treating everyone equally and fairly.

Some specific standards that you may set for your team may be on an individual basis dependent on their current level of knowledge and ability, and these are likely to be linked to their targets/objectives.

It is worth remembering that not all standards will be written down or communicated and there may often be an assumption that the behaviour of the staff will meet the standard anyway.

Portfolio task 308.7 → Links to **LO3**: assessment criterion 3.3

Explain the purpose and benefits of having quality measures in place and investigate if your organisation has any. If it does, take a copy as this will provide useful information for your portfolio.

Respecting, valuing and supporting the people in a team

After working through this section you will understand and be able to:

- explain the purpose and benefits of recognising the strengths of individuals in a team and of balancing abilities in a team
- describe ways of giving work to teams so the best use is made of strengths and abilities
- explain the benefits of diversity in teams
- explain the purpose and benefits of respecting others
- describe situations in which team members might need support and how to provide this
- describe the types of problems and disagreements that may occur when working with a team and how to resolve them.

The purpose and benefits of recognising the strengths of members of a team and balancing abilities

Members of a team have two distinct roles. Firstly, they have to achieve the goals of the team and secondly, they have to maintain an effective working relationship with each other. These two elements are interlinked: if the goals of the team are not met, then it will inevitably put pressure on the day-to-day working relationships.

Through his extensive research in the late 1970s, Dr Meredith Belbin devised a world-recognised model for team preferences which can help us to understand why team members can behave in certain ways. He identified the following specific roles as shown in Figure 308.3:

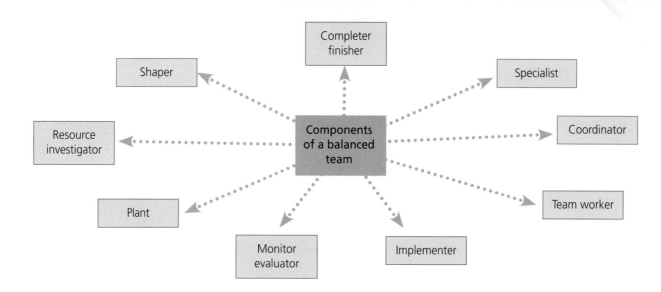

Figure 308.3: *Team model devised by Dr Meredith Belbin*

In most teams, some people can take on several characteristics. Belbin argued that 'although one person can't be perfect, a team can be'.

The essential characteristics of each team role are as follows:

- The *Completer finisher* ensures that nothing is overlooked and provides thorough attention to detail.
- The *Specialist* will be able to support the team on specialist issues and may sometimes work within a separate team.
- The *Coordinator* controls the activities of the team and is able to get the team working together as a complete unit.
- The *Team worker* promotes team spirit and encourages other team members through their supportive approach.
- The *Implementer* translates ideas into plans and breaks things down into tasks and actions.
- The *Monitor evaluator* is a critical thinker, who is objective in their approach and can analyse ideas and suggestions.
- The *Plant* concentrates on the big issues, can be a source of innovation and ideas for the team, and can be single-minded.
- The *Resource investigator* harnesses resources for the team and networks with other teams and organisations.
- The *Shaper* makes things happen by injecting energy and strong direction.

As you can imagine, not all teams will have all these types of people in place, and some team members will have more than one attribute. However, hopefully you will see from the list that these characteristics are all useful elements for a team to become fully effective.

There have been more recent studies by other experts who suggest similar personality types within teams as follows: an action person, a caring person, a detail person, a coordinator and a creative thinker. Again, some team members will have some or all of these attributes, and don't forget – you are a member of the team as well.

For a team to be effective the team leader should recognise how each person's individual skills and abilities can help the team achieve its tasks/objectives.

Portfolio task 308.8 → Links to **LO4**: assessment criterion 4.1

Consider your own team and check to see if you have any specific gaps in behaviours and then try to think of a solution to resolve this. For example, if you don't think that you have many people in your team who can think creatively, then how can you resolve this? Maybe you could have a brief creative session in your team meeting from time to time and ask the team to come up with any potential new and innovative ways of working.

Ways of giving work to teams so the best use is made of strengths and abilities

As you plan your team's work schedule for the week, month or year you will need to identify members of your team who are able to undertake specific tasks. By **delegating** tasks, you are giving team members responsibility for an element of their job. This can be a motivating factor as they will enjoy the control and the opportunity to make decisions.

Key term

Delegating – giving authority or responsibility to another person to carry out a task.

Unfortunately, not all managers are good delegators and some managers are unable or unwilling to delegate tasks. Also, some team members do not enjoy having additional responsibilities placed on them when a task is delegated to them. These team members may need additional support and reassurance as they learn to take on new tasks and responsibilities.

When you delegate, you need to be aware that it may take your team member longer to undertake the task than it would take you. Also they may not perform the task to as high a standard and mistakes may occur. However, you need to be supportive and build in additional time for your team member by guiding them through the process, particularly if they are doing something new for the first time. Think back to when you were learning something new.

An easy option is to think, 'I can do that job much more quickly, so I'll just get it done.' This is not the best option. It is likely that as a team leader you will have a high workload and will not have enough hours in the day to get the work completed. If you do not delegate, the problem will be compounded and you will become busier and busier and your team will be less and less effective as you try to control all the tasks.

By implementing the elements in Figure 308.4, you are more likely to become an effective delegator.

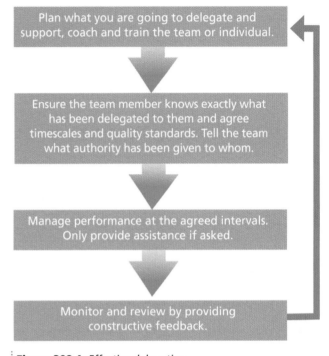

Figure 308.4: *Effective delegation*

A workplace example

The scenario

Imagine that you have a presentation to deliver to the management team next week. You have known about it for a while, but because you have been so busy, you have been putting off formulating the presentation. You have been asked for it by the end of the week so that it can be loaded up onto a laptop ahead of the meeting next Monday. You really don't have time to do it and you are going to stay late tonight or do it when you get home. You had thought about asking your colleague Jack (who is not that busy at the moment) to help you with it, but you know that he does not have that much experience of computer-based presentations, so you think it is quicker to do it yourself.

The solution

It might be too late this time to ask for Jack's assistance, but the key learning point here is planning. If you know about something in advance, plan the time to either do it yourself or delegate it to a colleague and provide them with the relevant support.

Don't put things off as they will come back to bite you!

Option 1 – If you have known about this for some time, then you should have planned time in your diary to formulate the presentation.

Option 2 (preferred option) – Plan some time with your colleague Jack (again, well in advance) to show him how the computer-based presentation software works. Give him some support and instruction and also allow him some time to work through the software in a bit more detail. Meet up with him the following week and work through your presentation with him, asking him to have a go at pulling it together. This will take longer than it would take you to do it and you will have to check for mistakes, but it is a better solution in the long term. Most people only need to be shown how to do something once, and they are often a lot more resourceful than you might think.

The outcome

Maybe you might need to spend a considerable amount of time planning the presentation with Jack, but once he is up to speed, he will probably be able to formulate future presentations in a fraction of the time. This will in turn release some of your time and also ensure that Jack's role is more varied. As a result he is likely to be more motivated and it will build up his confidence, skills and knowledge.

Which tasks to delegate?

Always remember that, as a team leader, you can delegate specific one-off ad hoc tasks as well as regular tasks. Ask yourself, 'Am I the most suitable person to be undertaking this task?' Also bear in mind that it is not appropriate to delegate some tasks. For example, if you had some interviews planned and it was important for you to make the appointment yourself, you would not normally delegate this type of task.

Remember to always utilise the diverse skills and knowledge of your team.

✅ Checklist

Delegation

Delegation gives a person:

- the freedom and authority to undertake certain tasks or elements of their own job without the need to constantly refer issues back to their manager for a decision

- the ability to make certain decisions and become empowered

- the ability to work on their own initiative

- the motivation to work effectively and more productively.

Portfolio task 308.9

➡️ Links to **L04**: assessment criterion 4.2

How good at delegating are you? Complete the following short questionnaire. This will provide useful evidence for your portfolio and might highlight some development needs that you can also include in your development plan.

Table 308.1: *Do I delegate enough or is this an area for development?*

Issues in my team	Agree	Disagree
Some of my team members are not motivated and find their roles mundane		
Some of my team members say that they are not always that busy		

A version of this table, ready for you to complete, is available to download from www.contentextra.com/businessadmin

Empowering and motivating your team

By motivating, supporting and empowering your team members, you will be allowing them to take an active role in shaping your team. It is worth remembering that a team is like a living thing; you will be able to control most elements but not all, and whilst you will be able to manage the team to some extent, there are other dynamics in place that you may not have control over. Ultimately, the way the team operates on a day-to-day basis is based on a number of factors including:

● your own management style

● the pace that the team is developing at

● the dynamics of the team members including the skills, knowledge and motivations of individual team members

● your interaction with other teams and the interaction that takes place with your customers

● the resources in place and the objectives that you need to achieve with these resources

● your ability to manage performance and to link it to organisational objectives

● an individual understanding their job role.

Empowerment is the process of allowing your team members to take control over their work and also become involved in the decision-making process.

By trusting and supporting your colleagues, they can become more and more efficient and should begin to strive towards achieving excellence. By working closely with your team you will develop their skills, knowledge and career aspirations. You can do this by:

● providing training which will develop their knowledge, skills and competencies

● providing positive and constructive feedback on their performance

● involving team members in the decision-making process and agreeing objectives collectively

● coaching team members on a one-to-one basis and supporting their individual development

● creating a friendly environment in which team members feel that their input is valued and welcomed

● creating an 'open door' policy, making yourself available to all staff at all times

● communicating effectively with your team, by making sure that all team members know what is happening all the time.

Once you have all these practical elements in place, it is very likely that your team will be empowered and motivated on a day-to-day basis.

Motivating your team does not have to cost much. You may be able to offer flexible working or incentive schemes. Discuss ideas with your manager and your team. It is sometimes difficult to give monetary rewards, but think of alternative ways to reward your staff.

Your team members don't just need rewards, they also need recognition. You should put time aside to speak with each team member on a one-to-one basis to see how you might improve the scope of their role or provide them with additional development opportunities. And remember, give praise to your team and thank them when they do a good job.

The benefits of diversity in teams

A diverse team is a team that is able to discuss ideas and proposals openly and is happy to work collaboratively to ensure that their objectives are met. The benefits of diversity in a team mean that you can encourage creativity and innovation. As a result, you will be creating an environment where people look at their role and the organisation differently and explore all aspects by not just accepting the 'status quo' as the most appropriate solution.

You can encourage creativity and innovation by organising group sessions. If you get everyone involved in the process, it should ensure that the whole team is on board and no one feels intimidated or uncomfortable. If you hold these types of team events once or twice a year, your colleagues can come up with new ideas, suggestions and creative ways of working that could potentially improve efficiency and productivity. All ideas should be considered and explored further where appropriate.

As your team develops, innovation and creativity should be more prevalent.

Checklist

How to encourage creativity and innovation

- Your team members will only respond to requests for new ideas and initiatives as long as they are always appreciated and never mocked.

- New ideas can involve risk-taking and you need to be ready to take on some risks where appropriate.

- Allow team members time to think about creative ideas; for example, organise some team events.

- Set up groups to explore ideas in greater detail.

- If an idea is approved and implemented, always make sure that you thank your team member and put in place any new resources, training or support required to undertake the new or revised process.

Portfolio task 308.10 → Links to **LO4**: assessment criterion 4.3

Innovative ways of working should also be encouraged during normal day-to-day operations. Ask your colleagues if they can think of any ways to improve their job and write this up as a personal statement to include in your portfolio.

The purpose and benefits of respecting others

Do you agree with the following statements?

- As a team leader, the way that you manage your team will determine how effective you are at your job.

- By achieving the team's goals and objectives you will be a good team leader and be well respected by the whole team.

Exploring these statements in a little more detail will tease out some further discussion points. In relation to the first statement, most people would generally accept this viewpoint. However, the statement is not result-focused and does not explain whether or not you and your team will achieve your objectives. The second statement is more explicit in stating the intention to achieve goals and objectives, but it does not explain how this will be undertaken.

Both statements are partially true, but the key element is how to manage people effectively. For example, you

may well achieve your goals as a team, but if you as the team leader have been totally driven by results and less focused on your team's abilities and behaviours, then it may be that the goals have been achieved at the expense of the goodwill and the respect of your staff.

Clearly, there is a balance to be made to ensure that the team is nurtured and managed well, whilst at the same time achieving the required results. Effective teams need careful management and can take long periods to build and grow, but the trust and goodwill that may have been built up over many years can be destroyed very quickly. Take care to manage your team 'firmly but fairly' and treat all team members equally and with respect.

Some detailed studies have been undertaken over the past few years which conclude that the effectiveness of people to work well is not solely determined by their individual competence to do the job, but more importantly the ability of their manager to manage, coach, develop, support and motivate them. In principle, most people will be helpful and cooperate with you as long as they are asked in the right way. This may even include tasks that the person has never done before, tasks that they don't have the resources to complete or tasks that are out of their comfort zone. It is human nature to please other people, and your colleagues will normally be really pleased to be asked to do something — just ask them in the right way.

Take a look at the following verbal communications:

- 'Get that job done by five o'clock today.'

- 'I have a presentation to prepare for the board meeting next week, but I'm going to struggle to get it all finished on time. Would you be able to help me with it, please? It will involve importing some pictures into the presentation, which I can help you do.'

The first statement is inappropriate, and it is unfair as a manager to be that abrupt with your team members. Always respect your colleagues and be courteous, polite and say please and thank you. The second example of a verbal communication shown above clearly demonstrates the correct polite and courteous way to communicate with your staff.

Portfolio task 308.11 → Links to **LO4**: assessment criterion 4.4

Explain the purpose and benefits of respecting your colleague's roles and opinions.

When and how to provide support to team members

As a team leader, you will need to be able to provide moral support; for example, if someone has some personal difficulties that they may need assistance with. You will also be required to provide practical support; for example, if a colleague is struggling to meet a specific deadline.

The level of support required will vary significantly from team to team and also individually. Some team members will require little or no support, whereas other team members may require regular assistance, advice and support. Care needs to be taken as you need to be clear in your own mind what represents a reasonable level of support. For example, if a person needs regular support in relation to a routine task, it is likely that they may not be competent in their role, and it may be appropriate in these circumstances to review their capabilities through a formal procedure. However, if a team member needs supporting in relation to a new task or change in circumstance, then that is perfectly acceptable. Also remember that your colleagues can provide support to each other, as specific staff with specialist knowledge may be better placed than you to provide any relevant support.

The types of support and advice that your team may need will depend on a number of factors including:

- the type of organisation that you work for and the policies and culture in place
- the rewards and benefits available to staff
- the ability of your team to meet its objectives
- the mix of personalities in your team and the degree of competitiveness within the team
- the personal circumstances of your team members.

Don't just think about individual support; you can support the whole team through team-building sessions, specific problem-solving meetings, team briefings and by clarifying the overall objectives and planning the work to be undertaken.

Portfolio task 308.12 → Links to **LO4**: assessment criterion 4.5

Think of some recent examples of when you have given support to individual team members or the whole team. This could be through a team briefing or maybe during a one-to-one meeting. If you collect this information, it will provide useful evidence for your portfolio.

Functional skills

English: Reading

If you carry out research involving reading texts including work-related documents as well as Internet research in order to complete your portfolio task, you may be able to count this as evidence towards Level 2 Functional English: Reading. Remember to keep records of all the documents, handbooks or guidelines which you study, along with the websites which you visit, as you will need to document any reading research you carry out.

The problems and disagreements that might occur in a team and how to resolve them

It is inevitable that you will from time to time have to deal with disagreements and/or conflicts, either within your own team or between your team and other groups. Generally speaking, these disagreements can be classified into either task-based challenges or people-based challenges.

- Task-based difficulties are normally easier to solve than people-based problems as they are less complex. Task-based problems relate to 'doing the job' and examples would include meeting tight deadlines, lack of skills, equipment or resource breakdown or staff absences.
- Examples of people-based difficulties can include personality clashes, problems over the allocation of roles, lack of support between team members, team members blaming each other or staff deliberately being disruptive.

What potential disagreements could occur between these work colleagues? How could disagreements be avoided?

✓ Checklist

Steering your team through difficulties and challenges

- Recognise that difficulties and challenges will naturally occur within any team.

- Identify the simple task-based issues first, e.g. lack of resources or time, and then propose a solution to resolve these issues.

- Try to encourage the team to be proactive and look for solutions to problems rather than focusing on the problems.

- Destructive conflict, which involves people insulting or criticising each other, or refusing to communicate, must not be tolerated.

- Insist on open negotiations between the various parties and try to achieve a 'win-win' solution for all parties.

- Be able to think of a completely different solution or idea in order to diffuse the situation if required.

- Check that all parties agree with the outcome and any agreed action at the end of the discussion.

Difficulties can also arise during times of uncertainty; for example, during periods of economic downturn or the reorganisation of a team. During these times, staff may be worried about the security of their jobs and it will be up to you to keep them informed at all times and provide relevant support and advice as required.

You may need to steer your team successfully through these challenges, but you also need to recognise that you cannot control everything. As discussed earlier, teams are influenced by individual personalities, beliefs, personal feelings and attitudes. You can do your bit, but some things may be outside your control and may sometimes go wrong.

Sometimes, you may need to impose a decision or introduce a new system or process that may prove to be unpopular. Again, the best way to undertake this is to have an open and frank discussion with all members of the team and explain the reasons for the proposed changes. Listen to the concerns of your team members and take on board any relevant issues. If people know why something is happening and it is explained to them in person, they are more likely to accept the changes even if they do not agree with them entirely.

Remember to communicate effectively at all times. You do not want your team members saying, 'We're always the last people to know' or 'We never get to know about anything'.

Kurt Lewin (1890-1947) developed a change model which shows a more autocratic approach to leadership. He described a three-step process to create change. In the first step, named 'unfreeze', the motive for the change is defined and the need identified. Next comes 'change', where new behaviours are communicated and behavioural change is encouraged. In the final step comes 'refreeze' as new behaviours are consolidated.

When change is needed it is possible to facilitate this by explaining the reasons behind the change and communicating the new proposals.

Unit Q308 Supervise a team in a business environment

What follows is team training and development in order for the change to be embraced and implemented. Once the new processes have been in place for a while, then the new behaviours are consolidated into the day-to-day operation and are accepted as the 'norm'. In other words, as time moves forward people accept what was once new as now being the way it has always been done.

Portfolio task 308.13 → Links to **LO4**: assessment criterion 4.6

Describe the types of problems and disagreements that you have experienced in your team. You may want to record this as part of a professional discussion with your assessor.

The purpose and benefits of assessing and evaluating the work of a team and how to do it

After working through this section you will understand and be able to:

- describe the purpose of work assessment

- explain how to assess the work of teams and team members

- explain the purpose and benefits of giving opportunities to team members to assess their own work

- explain the purpose and benefits of giving and receiving constructive feedback and how to do so

- explain how to make use of feedback to improve the work of others and the work of the team as a whole.

Work assessment

As a team leader an important part of your role will be to assess your team's performance on an on-going basis, both collectively as a team and also on an individual level. Clearly it is essential to meet your own and the team's objectives in order to meet the overall objectives of the organisation and remain efficient and competitive.

It is likely that you will have some internal performance management processes to track and manage performance, and you may also undertake a formal annual review of performance through an appraisal meeting.

By managing your team's performance effectively and gaining the respect of your colleagues, you are also more likely to build a positive working relationship with your team and you should see:

- less resistance to change

- improved commitment, cooperation and enjoyment of their roles

- increased output, productivity and efficiency

- improved supportive working within the team and across other team boundaries.

Portfolio task 308.14 → Links to **LO5**: assessment criterion 5.1

Describe how work is assessed in your team and provide relevant examples of how performance is managed as this will provide useful evidence for your portfolio.

Assessing the work of teams and team members

One of the key elements for improving performance is to make sure that you and your team members are self-motivated and enjoy their job. Being self-motivated means that you are able to come into work each day in a positive frame of mind and you are able to complete the tasks by taking ownership of your job. This will improve your job satisfaction and should get you thinking about how you might be able to improve your job role and associated processes and become more efficient.

All team members should be accountable for their job and take responsibility for their actions. By following these principles all team members will be able to plan their work and achieve their objectives.

✓ Checklist

How to manage performance in your team

Read through the following list and challenge yourself and your own team. If you think that you can improve in some or all of these areas, plan to do so.

- **Ensure achievement of personal and team objectives.** All team members should know what is required of them and you should know how to manage this, through regular reviews, one-to-one meetings or team meetings. You also need to know what to do when things go wrong; for example, when team members are not meeting the agreed standards of performance and/or achieving their targets/objectives.

- **How effective is your team?** Do team members trust each other? Are you all open and honest with each other? Do team members support each other? Have any recent changes affected performance?

- **Do you have the right resources in place?** You may encounter problems if you do not have the correct resources in place: time, personnel, equipment, systems, etc. You may need to resolve some issues and you need to question whether any new technology can be used to improve the efficiency of your team.

- **Knowledge and skills.** Are your team members competent in their roles? Do they have adequate skills and knowledge? Do they need further additional support? Are there any skills that the whole team lacks? Is your team ready for any future challenges?

Remember to always try to plan effectively. If you plan well, there is less chance of things going wrong.

Portfolio task 308.15 → Links to **LO5**: assessment criterion 5.2

Think about you and your team's performance over the last 12 months and ask yourself the following questions:

- Did we achieve our targets and objectives and, if so, how well did we do?

- What would we do differently next time?

- If we failed to achieve our targets and objectives, what went wrong?

- Did we spend enough time planning and securing the resources to achieve our objectives?

- Did we plan the activities well, and did I manage performance effectively?

Record your responses.

Purpose and benefits of giving opportunities to team members to assess own work

As already stated, teams can be very powerful, and as teams grow stronger and more effective, they can begin to transform the whole organisation. As a manager, you will need to utilise the strengths and expertise of individual team members, which will in turn make your whole team more efficient and effective. Some team members are likely to have very detailed specialist skills. Encourage and utilise these skills to best effect.

You will need to be able to 'let go' of some aspects of your work to allow your team to develop and grow. This could involve supporting and coaching individuals to further develop their skills and knowledge. You must harness all positive energy in your team and encourage team members to take the lead on certain things. By doing this, you will be:

- developing the skills, knowledge and confidence of your team

- empowering and delegating by allowing team members to control some aspects of their own work

- encouraging team members to undertake other jobs (multitasking) by sharing their skills and experiences with other team members

- encouraging each team member to take responsibility for their own role.

Portfolio task 308.16 → Links to **LO5**: assessment criterion 5.3

Describe the ways in which you allow your team members to manage and assess their own work on a day-to-day basis. You could do this by either writing up a personal statement or by completing a professional discussion with your assessor.

Purpose and benefits of giving and receiving feedback

Generally speaking, feedback of any type is useful and it should always be constructive. Constructive feedback should be meaningful, acceptable and of value. Giving feedback to your team members and accepting feedback from your team members should help you to improve the team's overall performance.

The most common formal feedback that you are likely to give to your team members is through reviews or appraisal meetings. Most organisations have a process in place to allow for meetings between individual employees or teams and their managers to review performance and capability. At these meetings, you can discuss with your team members:

- their achievements for the previous year

- their specific goals or objectives for the forthcoming year

- their training and development needs.

Always think of feedback as positive. Try to be objective in your evaluation of any feedback that you give or receive and try to learn from your mistakes.

Feedback should occur on a regular basis and it is good practice to give frequent feedback to your team members.

✓ Checklist

Feedback

How to give feedback to your colleagues:

- Feedback has more impact when it is immediate – don't wait to feed back at a later time, as you will forget the detail.

- In order to motivate your team, you need to be positive. You may have some issues to address, but be positive and tactful.

- Always give praise openly and freely when it is due.

- Get to the point quickly and focus on the issues not the person.

- Give clear specific examples to support what you are saying.

- Be objective, don't 'judge' the person – look at the specific issues and then feed back.

- Don't expect your colleague to agree with everything you say but actively listen to their response and work out a way forward.

- Check that you both agree with the outcome and any agreed action at the end of the discussion.

- Treat all colleagues equally and fairly by giving them an equal amount of feedback and support.

- Give feedback at the right time and avoid feedback overload.

Portfolio task 308.17 → Links to **LO5**: assessment criterion 5.4

Think of some recent examples of when you have given feedback to any of your team members. This could be feedback through a formal process, for example at an appraisal meeting, or it could be some feedback that you have given in an email. Also, bear in mind that if you have given some verbal feedback, you can record this as part of a personal statement. Alternatively, you could plan with your assessor for them to observe you giving feedback to a colleague. This will be useful evidence for your portfolio.

How to use feedback to improve the work of the team as a whole

As mentioned earlier in the unit, always think of feedback as positive. You may receive some feedback about yourself, the team or a team member. Try to be objective in your evaluation of any feedback and try to ensure that you action the feedback and put plans in place to make sure that you get it right next time.

If you have received some feedback, consider:

● Is the team still learning the system/process? If so, it may take time to be fully competent.

● Is it possible to ask for support or advice if the same situation occurs again?

● Was there enough time given and were there the correct resources available to manage the activities efficiently?

● Is a procedure note required for the team to make sure that the task is done correctly the next time?

● Has the feedback resulted in any specific development needs? Is training required?

● Was the problem outside my control?

By working through these questions, you will start to identify how you can improve and make changes to the team's working methods to become more effective in the future.

Sometimes, particularly if you are doing something for the first time, it is useful to review your experience to ensure that you do even better next time. You can do this by:

● making a note of everything that went well

● making a note of any problems you had and identifying solutions to deal with those issues next time

● analysing the problems and checking if they were preventable or if they were outside your control

● learning from your experiences and doing it better next time.

Portfolio task 308.18 → Links to **LO5**: assessment criterion 5.5

Think of some recent examples of when you have received some feedback and explain what action you have taken to improve your personal and your team's working processes/performance.

Evidence collection

In order for you to complete the remaining assessment criteria to successfully pass this unit, you will need to carry out various tasks at work and then produce evidence to show that you have demonstrated the required skills and competence.

Evidence can be collected in a number of different ways. For example, it can be in the form of a signed witness testimony from a colleague or line manager, a copy of any related emails or letters you have produced or a verbal discussion with your assessor.

Speak to your assessor to identify the best methods to use in order to complete each portfolio task and remember to keep copies of all the evidence that you produce.

Be able to supervise a team

Portfolio task 308.19 → Links to **LO6**: assessment criterion 6.1, 6.2, 6.3, 6.4, 6.5, 6.6, 6.7, 6.8, 6.9 and 6.10

Gather evidence of your work to show your assessor that you have successfully carried out the tasks outlined in the table below. Check with your assessor on the best ways of gathering evidence for each of the tasks before you begin.

Task	Evidence collected
1 Communicate with people in a team during work activities.	
2 Supervise work goals and plan work objectives, priorities and responsibilities for a team and individuals.	
3 Identify, agree and supervise opportunities for others to work to achieve agreed outcomes.	

A version of this table, ready for you to complete, is available to download from www.contentextra.com/businessadmin

Be able to assess, evaluate and improve the work of a team

Portfolio task 308.20 → Links to **LO7**: assessment criterion 7.1, 7.2, 7.3, 7.4 and 7.5

Gather evidence of your work to show your assessor that you have successfully carried out the tasks outlined in the table below. Check with your assessor on the best ways of gathering evidence for each of the tasks before you begin.

Task	Evidence collected
1 Assess and evaluate the work of a team and individuals to identify strengths and areas for improvement.	
2 Make sure team members have opportunities to assess their own work for strengths and areas for improvement.	

A version of this table, ready for you to complete, is available to download from www.contentextra.com/businessadmin

Office life

Suzie's story

My name is Suzie and I'm employed as a team leader in a bank in central London and I manage a team of eight part-time staff. I've only recently joined the company and it is the first time that I have managed a team.

Part of my role is to set and agree objectives with my team and to manage their performance. I agree specific targets with each team member as part of their annual appraisal meeting, but this is something that I have not done before, so I was a little unsure what I needed to do.

I decided to arrange a meeting with my manager to ask her exactly what performance targets we were working towards achieving and how I could manage the process effectively. I knew about some of our performance targets and standards, but I needed everything to be clarified. Before the meeting, I wrote out a list of the things I needed to be clear about as follows:

- the exact corporate performance standards that were in place
- the specific targets that were in place for my team to achieve
- when I needed to complete the appraisals by
- how the company dealt with any training requests.

My manager was pleased that I had taken the time to prepare for the meeting and she explained everything to me in detail. I learned a lot of new things about the company and as a result I was able to structure the appraisal meetings well and I set and agreed a number of objectives/targets for my team members. I also agreed a process to have a quick thirty-minute 'one-to-one' meeting with each member of my team on a monthly basis to help me manage their performance.

Ask the expert

Q I have to formulate a series of SMART objectives for my team. What do I need to do?

A Begin by clarifying the team's objectives with your manager and then start to prepare a list of objectives by considering how:

- your objectives will link to the organisation's overall mission/objectives
- to prioritise the objectives
- to plan your resources (can you complete the objectives alone or do you need any specialist support?)
- to agree dates for completing the objectives
- to consult with your team and finalise the objectives
- to agree the objectives with the team
- to manage the process to ensure that you complete the objectives within the agreed timeframe.

Top tips

Suzie could have researched the performance targets and objectives in a bit more detail before she met with her manager. By doing this, she would have had more of an overview of the performance standards and objectives that were already in place.

Suzie did well to write down a list of all the issues. This demonstrated that she had thought about everything and, by preparing a list, she was starting a structured process towards setting and agreeing the objectives and managing the team's performance.

Can you think of anything else that Suzie could have done better?

Unit Q308

Supervise a team in a business environment

Check your knowledge

1 How can you demonstrate effectiveness?

a) By providing the service as cheaply as possible.

b) By doing things more quickly at a reduced cost.

c) By increasing the turnover.

d) By getting the job done as quickly as possible.

2 What is the culture of an organisation?

a) 'This is how we do things round here.'

b) Being the cheapest provider of a service/product.

c) Asking the staff to work extra hours to help out.

d) When an organisation is able to secure profits above the average gained by its competitors.

3 What does the term 'milestone' mean?

a) Making your product more competitive.

b) Increasing your turnover.

c) The overall cost of something.

d) A scheduled event signifying when you need to do something by.

4 By empowering your team members, what are you allowing them to do?

a) Work extra hours.

b) Take control over their work and also become involved in the decision-making process.

c) Take work home.

d) Be released to work within another team.

5 In relation to communication, what does 'kiss' mean?

a) Keep it short and simple.

b) Keep it short and sweet.

c) Keep it steady and safe.

d) Keep it softly spoken.

6 Which of the following are resources within an organisation?

a) Staff/personnel.

b) Computer equipment.

c) The organisation's office building.

d) All of the above.

7 What does collaboration mean?

a) Sharing resources.

b) Helping out your competitors.

c) Planning a new product or service.

d) Working together.

8 What does delegation mean?

a) Helping out with tasks in your team.

b) Working with another team to gain additional skills.

c) Giving authority or responsibility to another person to carry out a task.

d) Shadowing a team member to learn about their job.

9 When might you need to provide moral support to a team member?

a) If they are encountering some personal difficulties.

b) If they are struggling to complete their tasks on time.

c) If they are unhappy in their job.

d) All of the above.

10 What is a good method for managing the performance of your team?

a) Meeting up with your colleagues when things go wrong.

b) Meeting up with your colleagues when they ask for a meeting.

c) Meeting up with your colleagues on a regular basis.

d) Meeting up with your colleagues once a year.

Answers to the Check your knowledge questions can be found at www.contentextra.com/businessadmin

What your assessor is looking for

In order to prepare for and succeed in completing this unit, your assessor will require you to be able to demonstrate competence in:

- understanding and being able to describe the purpose and benefits of teamwork

- understanding and being able to describe the purpose of communication in teams and how to communicate effectively

- understanding the purpose of planning work with teams and being able to demonstrate how you supervise your team

- valuing a team and being able to demonstrate how to respect and support them

- assessing and evaluating the work of a team and being able to demonstrate improvement.

You will demonstrate your skills, knowledge and competence through the seven learning outcomes in this unit. Evidence generated in this unit will also cross-reference to the other units in this qualification.

Please bear in mind that there are significant cross-referencing opportunities throughout this qualification, and you may have already generated some relevant work to meet certain criteria in this unit. Your assessor will provide you with the exact requirements to meet the standards of this unit. However, as a guide it is likely that for this unit you will need to be assessed through the following methods:

- one observation of relevant workplace activities to cover the whole unit

- at least one witness testimony to be produced

- a written narrative, reflective account or professional discussion

- any relevant work products to be produced as evidence.

The work products for this unit could include:

- your objectives or targets

- your team's objectives or targets

- relevant research that you have undertaken

- emails or other communication methods that you have used in your team

- copies of any team-meeting agendas and minutes

- your organisational structure

- any feedback that you have received on your performance

- your appraisal document

- examples of any creative or innovative working methods.

Your assessor will guide you through the assessment process as detailed in the candidate logbook. The detailed assessment criteria are shown in the logbook, and by working through these questions, combined with providing the relevant evidence, you will meet the learning outcomes required to complete this unit.

Unit Q308 Supervise a team in a business environment

Task and page reference	Mapping assessment criteria
Portfolio task 308.1 (page 110)	Assessment criterion: 1.1
Portfolio task 308.2 (page 110)	Assessment criterion: 1.2
Portfolio task 308.3 (page 111)	Assessment criterion: 2.1
Portfolio task 308.4 (page 112)	Assessment criterion: 2.2
Portfolio task 308.5 (page 113)	Assessment criterion: 3.1
Portfolio task 308.6 (page 113)	Assessment criterion: 3.2
Portfolio task 308.7 (page 114)	Assessment criterion: 3.3
Portfolio task 308.8 (page 115)	Assessment criterion: 4.1
Portfolio task 308.9 (page 117)	Assessment criterion: 4.2
Portfolio task 308.10 (page 119)	Assessment criterion: 4.3
Portfolio task 308.11 (page 119)	Assessment criterion: 4.4
Portfolio task 308.12 (page 120)	Assessment criterion: 4.5
Portfolio task 308.13 (page 122)	Assessment criterion: 4.6
Portfolio task 308.14 (page 122)	Assessment criterion: 5.1
Portfolio task 308.15 (page 123)	Assessment criterion: 5.2
Portfolio task 308.16 (page 124)	Assessment criterion: 5.3
Portfolio task 308.17 (page 124)	Assessment criterion: 5.4
Portfolio task 308.18 (page 125)	Assessment criterion: 5.5
Portfolio task 308.19 (page 126)	Assessment criteria: 6.1, 6.2, 6.3, 6.4, 6.5, 6.6, 6.7, 6.8, 6.9 and 6.10
Portfolio task 308.20 (page 126)	Assessment criteria: 7.1, 7.2, 7.3, 7.4 and 7.5

Unit Q309

Communicate in a business environment

What you will learn

- Understand the purpose of planning communication
- Understand how to communicate in writing
- Understand how to communicate verbally
- Understand the purpose and value of feedback in developing communication skills
- Be able to plan communication
- Be able to communicate in writing
- Be able to communicate verbally
- Be able to identify and agree ways of further developing communication skills

Introduction

At work, you will be communicating with different people all the time. This unit explains the principles and benefits of continuously improving your own communication skills, which should in turn help to improve the overall efficiency of the organisation.

By being **proactive** in your approach towards achieving effective communication and by supporting and valuing your colleague's opinions, you will be able to present information in the relevant format, layout and house style and deliver communications that meet the audience's needs.

It is important to plan communication and be sure that you know what your intended **outcomes** are and also be sure that you know what the audience's needs and requirements are. Different methods of communication can be used in different circumstances, and these methods will be explored in greater detail to help you learn how to communicate in the most appropriate and effective way.

The final section of the unit will explore the principles and benefits of receiving feedback on your performance at work. By receiving feedback from your colleagues, manager or perhaps your customers, you will be able to further develop your communication skills.

The principles and purpose of planning communication

After working through this section you will understand and be able to:

- describe the various benefits of knowing and understanding the purpose of communication
- explain the reasons for knowing the audience's needs
- explain the importance of knowing the intended outcomes of what is being communicated
- describe the different methods of communication and when to use them.

The benefits of knowing the purpose of communication

In a business environment you will be communicating both formally and informally using different methods that are verbal or in written form. You will also be communicating in more subtle ways; for example, by **body language**.

Key terms

Proactive – acting in anticipation and dealing with any potential problems.

Outcomes – the end results of activities which can also be measured or quantified.

Body language – the gestures, postures or facial expressions of a person.

What are the advantages/disadvantages of communicating by phone?

Communication in organisations can be complex as there are some specific factors to consider, including:

- the flow of information within the organisation
- the culture of the organisation
- the systems and processes that are in place
- the degree of complexity of the information
- any organisational policies that may be in place.

Communication involves the transfer of information between people. The level of understanding and interpretation of what is being communicated will depend significantly on some or all of these factors listed:

- Is the information being communicated easy to understand or complex?
- Are the parties involved in the communication known to each other?
- Is the communication formal or informal?
- Is the information that is being communicated specific or general?
- Are there any barriers in respect of the information that is being communicated?

All these issues will be explored in greater detail later in the unit. The principles of effective communication are to:

- ensure that communication is a two-way process
- ensure that the information is clear, concise and at the right level of detail for the recipient
- ensure that all parties are clear about what is being communicated
- listen actively to what is being said.

As a result of applying these principles, you and your organisation should reap the benefits and be able to work more productively. By building positive working relationships, the organisation should see:

- less resistance to change
- improved commitment, cooperation and enjoyment by staff of their roles
- increased output, productivity and efficiency
- improved supportive working within teams and across other team boundaries.

Portfolio task 309.1 → Links to **LO1**: assessment criterion 1.1

In order to complete this portfolio task, you need to write a short summary describing the principles of effective communication.

The reasons for knowing the audience that you are communicating with

When you are communicating with someone, you need to ensure that you meet the specific needs of that person or group. You can achieve this more effectively by planning what you are going to say and by asking yourself what the audience's (recipient's) requirements are. By working through this process you can identify the correct communication method and be sure to meet the audience's needs and achieve your intended outcome.

If you do not know what the audience's requirements are, you will not be able to provide them with the relevant information that they need in the most suitable format.

Portfolio task 309.2 → Links to **LO1**: assessment criterion 1.2

Collect three examples of how you have communicated with someone recently. This could be a customer or a colleague. For each example, explain what the recipient's (audience's) needs were.

Functional skills

English: Reading

If you carry out research involving reading texts including work-related documents as well as Internet research in order to complete your portfolio task, you may be able to count this as evidence towards Level 2 Functional English: Reading. Remember to keep records of all of the documents, handbooks and guidelines which you study, along with the websites which you visit, as you will need to document any reading research you carry out.

Purpose of knowing the intended outcomes of communications

To ensure that what you want to communicate meets both your intended outcomes and also meets the audience's needs, you need to communicate in the right format, at the right time and with the right level of detail. By doing this you will meeting both your own needs and the needs of the person you are communicating with. The most effective method is to plan what you are going to communicate. Following the checklist will help you.

There are various types of communication methods and these will be explored in more detail throughout this unit. However, it is important to bear in mind that some methods of communication give the opportunity to provide feedback and receive feedback.

When you are communicating with someone, you can give and receive feedback for a number of reasons:

- to ensure that the information is clear, concise and at the right level of detail and that you can clarify any issues that you are unsure about

✓ Checklist

Planning communication

- WHO is the communication with?

- WHY am I communicating with this person – what are my intended outcomes?

- WHAT am I communicating? Be very clear and specific.

- WHEN is the best right time to communicate with them?

- HOW much detail should I use and what is the most appropriate format?

- to ensure that you and the other person are clear about what is being communicated and what has been agreed

- to give you the opportunity to make suggestions to the other person on some improvements in how the information might be communicated more effectively to you and others in the future.

What are the preferred outcomes for the giver of feedback and the recipient of feedback?

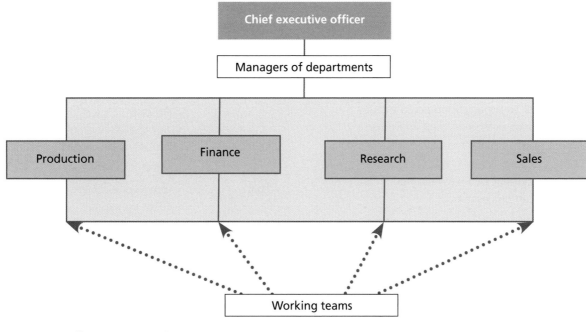

Figure 309.1: *A 'flat' organisational structure*

Some communication methods are more of a one-way process and provide little or no opportunity to give feedback. An example of this scenario is a voice or data recording. This will involve information that is communicated to you and you will be able to listen to it, but you will have no opportunity to feed back, make suggestions or clarify the information being communicated to you. Examples of communication methods where you will have an opportunity to feed back and interact there and then include email correspondence, one-to-one verbal communications and appraisal meetings.

Remember you should ensure that you have the opportunity to clarify issues – 'Can I just check that you want me to do this?' – and you should also have the opportunity to feed back to the other person (where appropriate) suggestions or improvements for future communications; for example, 'Would it be better if we sent the information by email in the future as opposed to sending a letter?'

Portfolio task 309.3 → Links to **LO1**: assessment criterion 1.3

Think about something that you intend to communicate to a customer or a colleague in the near future and write down how you are going to undertake this. Consider your needs and outcomes, the recipient's requirements and how and when you are going to undertake the communication. You could write this up as a personal statement to include in your portfolio.

The different methods of communication and when to use them

To aid communication, companies have tended to reduce the number of tiers in their organisation. Most companies have three or four tiers, as shown in Figure 309.1. This allows for communication to flow more effectively throughout the organisation.

By having fewer tiers and larger teams in place, communication should be more effective and working practices can be standardised more easily.

Communication and information can flow upwards, downwards or horizontally throughout an organisation as follows.

- 'Top-down' communication – for example, from managers to other employees. Examples of this type of communication could include briefing sessions or newsletters. Top-down communication is much less prevalent today as there has been a significant shift in recent years to implement two-way and horizontal communication processes.

- Two-way communication – this is the most common method of communication within organisations. On a day-to-day level, this will occur naturally as you interact with your colleagues and your manager. It should also occur when you communicate in a slightly more formal environment; for example, in team meetings. Other examples of when two-way communications could take place include appraisal meetings, suggestion schemes or employer surveys.

- Horizontal communication – this is similar to two-way communication, but it also allows for teams as well as individuals to work collectively across team boundaries. For example, teams may work together within an organisation to develop business improvements, including total quality management and customer care systems.

Some of the main methods of communication are shown in Table 309.1.

Portfolio task 309.4 ➡ Links to **LO1**: assessment criterion 1.4

Examples of pure top-down communication in modern business today are few and far between. Briefing sessions should be a two-way process and newsletters or company magazines often have input from staff also. Can you think of any top-down communication processes in your organisation?

Table 309.1: *Types of communication*

Type of communication	Method
Written	Emails Letters Reports Newsletters/journals Posters/notice board Suggestion schemes
Verbal	One-to-one communication Team meetings Appraisal meetings Team 'away day' meetings Small group presentations Large formal presentations Project/improvement groups
Other methods	Body language Telephone/mobile phone Data/voice recordings DVD/television communication Video/telephone conferencing Internet Intranet

How to communicate in writing

After working through this section you will understand and be able to:

- identify relevant sources of information that may be used when preparing written communication

- explain the communication principles for using electronic forms of written communication in a business environment

- explain different styles and tones of language and situations when they may be used for written communications

- explain the reasons for selecting and using language that suits the purpose of written communication

- communicate in a way that meets the audience's needs
- describe ways of checking written information for accuracy of content
- explain the purpose of accurate grammar, spelling and punctuation
- explain what is meant by plain English and why it is used
- explain the purpose of proofreading and checking work
- explain the purpose of and be able to confirm methods of recognising work that is important and urgent
- understand and be able to use organisational methods for storing, saving and filing written communications.

Identifying relevant sources of information to prepare written communication

When you are communicating verbally, you don't always have the time to plan how you are about to communicate. When you are communicating in written form, you have the opportunity to be more effective, as you can plan your communication. You can decide the most suitable format, the style of communication (formal or informal) and the urgency of the communication. After you have done this, you will then select the most appropriate format for the communication.

For some communications, there may be a standard letter or email that you may send out in a specific circumstance. For example, if you are welcoming a new customer to your organisation, then you may send a standard email or letter out to them. If you work in human resources and you are sending out an appointment letter to a person who has successfully secured a job with your company, there is likely to be a standard letter format in place for you to follow.

However, if you are communicating something new or specific, you need to be clear about your requirements from the communication and also the receiver's requirements and expectations.

The following checklist should help you to plan your written communications.

> ### ✓ Checklist
>
> **Planning written communication**
>
> - WHO is going to read this communication — customer or colleague?
> - WHY am I communicating to this person — what are my intended outcomes and how will I also meet their needs?
> - WHAT language should I use — formal or informal?
> - HOW much does the reader know already — should the communication be technical, specific or general?
> - HOW can I be clear that they have read and understood my communication?
> - GIVE the person enough time to respond.
> - DON'T communicate too far ahead.

Once you have worked through these elements, you should have a framework to help you decide how and when you are going to communicate. It may be that once you have thought through the process, you might decide that it is more appropriate to telephone or speak to the person face to face rather than communicate by a written method.

Portfolio task 309.5 → Links to **LO2**: assessment criterion 2.1

Collect three examples of how you have planned a communication with someone recently. This could be a customer or a colleague. For each example, explain how you planned the communication and why you chose that particular method and format.

Using electronic forms of written communication in a business environment

Traditionally, emails were used to transmit short informal communications. There has been a significant shift in recent years and emails are now used as a more formal method of communication in business environments. Remember to take care when writing and sending emails. Emails are a proper and accepted form of communication and in that respect they are no different to communicating via letter or verbally.

Would you write anything in a letter to a customer that may cause offence? Would you say anything offensive or inappropriate to your manager?

Emails are the same as any other form of communication and they must be professional, meaningful and accurate. If you send an inappropriate email or forward an inappropriate email to other people, then there may be serious consequences and you could be disciplined. Most organisations have an 'acceptable use policy' to cover email and Internet use in the workplace. Check if your organisation has one and make yourself familiar with the contents. Ask for advice or support from a colleague or your manager if you are unsure about what type of information you can communicate.

Emails are a fast and inexpensive way of delivering communications and information. Emails can be sent globally and, once you click the send button, an email will be delivered in seconds either to another person sitting right next to you or to another organisation thousands of miles away. Emails also have the advantage of being able to distribute information to large groups of people quickly, and the recipients then have the opportunity to respond, print, save or forward information in their own time. When communicating by email, plan what you are going to say and apply a common-sense approach.

There is a generally accepted etiquette for communicating by email in a business environment and this is explained in the following checklist.

✓ Checklist

Communicating by email

- Start the email with the name of the person you are communicating with. 'Hi' is acceptable for informal emails.

- Set up and use your email 'signature' box with your job role and contact details.

- Plan what you are going to communicate in the same way as you would if you were writing a letter.

- Write a subject line or title at the top of the email.

- Use a polite and professional tone.

- Use short sentences, paragraphs and bullet points, as this will make it much easier for the recipient to understand.

- Remember that specific legislation and internal policies cover what you send by email. Do not send anything that may cause offence or breach any other type of legislation.

- Be aware that you must protect any personal information about yourself, colleagues or customers and do not forward any information to third-party organisations without the express consent of the relevant person. Do not share your user ID or password with anyone.

- Don't forget to lock your computer when you are away from your desk.

- Don't forget to put your 'out of office' reply on when you are away from work.

- Don't write in capitals or red typeface as it is the equivalent to shouting.

- Don't forward chain emails to other people.

- Don't send sensitive or confidential information by email.

- Don't write aggressive emails or say something that you might later regret.

Portfolio task 309.6 → Links to **LO2**: assessment criterion 2.2

Collect two examples of emails that you have sent to someone recently. This could be a customer or a colleague. For each example, explain how you have communicated in a polite and professional manner and demonstrate the email communication etiquette that you have used.

Styles and tones of language in written communication

Letters are not as common now as they were but they are still fairly widely used throughout most business sectors. Letters are a formal way of communicating and can be used to communicate within organisations as well as outside the organisation to a customer, client or partner organisation.

The method of writing letters shown below is recognised as a standard approach and, by preparing your letter in this way, the recipient will be comfortable with the format and should be able to understand what the letter is asking or telling them to do and what action they may need to take. Pay particular attention to the middle part of the letter and structure it carefully to ensure that both you and the recipient understand what the letter is saying. If you have prepared a draft letter, but are unsure if it is correct, ask a colleague or your manager to check it for you and give you some feedback.

Portfolio task 309.7 → Links to **LO2**: assessment criterion 2.3

Collect two examples of letters that you have sent out recently; for example, to a customer or a contractor. In both cases show evidence of how you have communicated in a polite and professional manner and have used the 'house style' where appropriate.

Functional skills

English: Reading

If you carry out research involving reading texts including work-related documents in order to complete your portfolio task, you may be able to count this as evidence towards Level 2 Functional English: Reading. Remember to keep records of all the documents, as you will need to document any reading research you carry out.

✓ Checklist

Writing a letter

A letter should have a beginning, middle and end and there is a standard format that is used, which is generally accepted, as follows:

Examples of opening lines:

*   Thank you for your letter dated 25 September...

*   In reply to your letter, I would like to...

*   I wrote to you recently in relation to...

The main content of the letter should include:

*   the points that you want to get across in a structured and logical order

*   subheadings or bullet points, if suitable

*   short paragraphs using a maximum of three to four sentences for each paragraph.

Examples of how to close the letter:

*   If you require any further information, please do not hesitate to contact me.

*   I look forward to hearing from you.

*   I look forward to meeting you on...

Always remember that if you began your letter with 'Dear Sir', then you need to end your letter with 'Yours faithfully', whereas if you started your letter with the person's name, you should end it with 'Yours sincerely'.

Selecting and using language and images that suit the purpose of written communication

All organisations produce reports. These will vary significantly from organisation to organisation and may also vary from department to department. A report is a written document that presents information for a specific purpose or audience. Reports can be formal or informal and can be short or very detailed. Examples of reports that you may see in your organisation could include:

- a report produced by the sales team showing the sales achieved during last year

- a report produced by the human resource manager showing the staff absences and sickness statistics for the month

- a detailed financial report produced by the finance director showing the profit and loss forecasts for the next few years

- a report produced by the health and safety officer showing the accidents for the last 12 months

- a report produced by your manager showing your team's productivity for the month

You may come across some of these reports if you attend team or departmental meetings.

You may already produce some reports in your day-to-day job. If it is not something that you already do, it may be something that your manager may ask you to do in the future. If so, don't panic and use the following checklist with a few simple rules that should help you.

Images can portray a powerful message. An advertising or marketing campaign may use a sensitive situation or a vulnerable person to get a powerful message across. As with words, images can be interpreted in different ways by different people.

In a business environment, care is needed to ensure that any images, which may include graphs, charts or brand logos, are understood by the audience. For example, it would be appropriate during a presentation by a sales manager to show a graph or pie chart detailing the sales targets by sector or region to the rest of the sales team, as the information would be understood by all the people present. However, detailed or complicated information should not be presented to people if they are unable to understand the information or put it into the context of the organisation.

Graphs and charts can provide really useful information in innovative ways. Good examples include graphs which show a 'headline' trend, such as a bar chart, please see Figure 309.3. In this example, it clearly shows a dip in the second column and then an upward trend. This type of bar chart is in a standard format showing the timeline (years 1–7) across the bottom of the chart (the horizontal line) and the data line on the vertical axis (number of customers). The information or data to be shown could show anything from customer numbers, purchase costs or sales targets. Charts and graphs (as long as they are not too complicated or specialist) can provide a really useful way to present information.

✓ Checklist

Writing a report

- It should have a beginning, middle and end.

- It should introduce the issue by describing the purpose of the report and any background information.

- The main body of the report will detail the issues and a proposal incorporating any wider issues including any requirements for additional resources or potential risks that may occur.

- It should contain a formal recommendation.

- Additional information should be presented in an appendix.

- Use a standard 'house style' format for all reports in your organisation.

An example of a formal report is shown in Figure 309.2.

XYZ LIMITED – MANAGEMENT TEAM

TITLE	**Health and safety training budget**
Item Number	009
Date of Meeting	17 May 2011
Author of Report	Alberto Rossi – Business Support Manager

Mission statement:

Example: To be accountable and meet the needs of our customers and partner organisations.

1.0   Purpose of report:

1.1   Example: To provide an update in respect of the health and safety training completed in 2010 and to propose a way ahead and request additional funding for the next two years.

2.0   Background:

2.1   Explain the background/history.

2.2   Link to any strategic aims or objectives.

3.0   Proposal:

3.1   Detail the proposal or solution. Use bullet points to help present the information in a clear and concise way.

4.0   Resources:

4.1   Detail any resource implications, e.g. human or financial. Will the proposal incur extra costs?

5.0   Partnership-working, risks, equality and diversity

Detail any specific implications and explain how the proposal fits with the organisation's requirements to work with other organisations if applicable and also identify any potential risks to the business if your proposal is implemented.

6.0   Recommendation:

6.1   That the management team ...

Attach any supporting information as appendices.

Figure 309.2: *An example of a formal report*

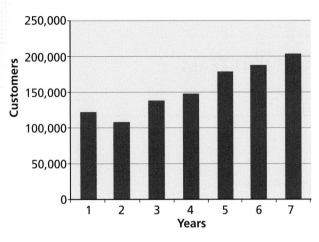

Figure 309.3: *A bar chart is a good visual way of communicating information*

If this type of chart were to be shown in a formal presentation, it is much more likely that in, say, a week's time you would remember the trend of what the chart told you as opposed to what the presenter actually said.

Charts and diagrams can also be used quite successfully within organisations that either employ multi-language staff or sell their products or services to a multi-language customer base. Many organisations use charts and graphs in their annual report documents.

Portfolio task 309.8 → Links to **LO2**: assessment criterion 2.4

Collect two examples of any reports that you have had some input in or that are relevant to the section that you work in. Have a professional discussion with your assessor to explain how you are able to present different information in different formats using relevant language to meet the specific requirements of the audience.

Organise, structure and present written information to meet the needs of different audiences

When you present information, you should ensure that it is in the right format and layout and also presented in your organisation's house style. Make sure you:

- write the letter or report in a way that meets the needs of the audience
- write the letter or report in the standard house style
- write letters in the correct format; for example, a formal letter is needed for an external customer
- use the relevant letter-headed paper or report format
- send the letter out within the agreed standards and timescales that you work to
- use your signature box if you are communicating by email (ask someone to help you if you don't know how to set it up).

Portfolio task 309.9 → Links to **LO2**: assessment criterion 2.5

Collect three different examples of written information that you have sent to different audiences. For each example, explain why you used this type of communication method and how you met the audience's needs. Note that the evidence that you have collected for performance criteria 2.1, 2.2, 2.3 and 2.4 may cover this assessment criteria.

Checking written communication for accuracy

In your role, you will be producing work all the time and you will need to ensure that it is accurate and correct. Checking your work needs to be ongoing and systematic. When using a software package to prepare written communication you will be able to use certain tools to assist you, for example 'spell check'. Make sure that you check grammar, spelling, name, address and date in all your documents.

Some letters are generated from computer databases and you may not have time to check all the information, but for specific individual communications, whether it is a letter or an email, you should spend a couple of minutes checking the information before you send it out. When there is a large mailshot being generated, some organisations have systems in place to undertake a sample check of, for example, ten per cent of the documents.

It is sometimes useful to print out the document you are checking and then ask a colleague to read it to you whilst you check it. You may not always be able to do this, but it is quite an effective method.

Portfolio task 309.10 ➡ Links to **LO2**: assessment criterion 2.6

Ask your assessor to assess how well you have checked a written piece of communication. Print out the document you are about to check and then, before you check the document on screen, turn on the 'track changes' feature on your computer software. This will show any changes that you make to the document. Print out the checked document and, with your assessor, compare the unchecked and checked documents. Is there any room for improvement? Is there anything you missed?

The purpose of accurate use of grammar, punctuation and spelling in written communication

When you are communicating it is important to use accurate grammar, spelling and punctuation. You should understand the principles of how to formulate meaningful sentences that will be understood correctly by the recipient. Poorly constructed letters and reports with grammatical errors and spelling mistakes can create a negative image of you and your organisation. English may not be your first language or you may struggle with punctuation, spelling and grammar, but it is important to communicate in a professional way that the reader will be able to understand.

Use **plain English** and do not overcomplicate communications with technical words or words that may be difficult to understand. Do not use abbreviations unless you are sure that the other person will know what they mean.

If you are going to use abbreviations, explain them in the communication the first time that you use them and then you can use the abbreviation throughout the remainder of the document. For example, if you had sent a letter to a client and had referred to the CBI, you would need to state that this meant the Confederation of British Industry. It would then be acceptable to refer to the CBI in its abbreviated form throughout the remainder of the correspondence.

Portfolio task 309.11 ➡ Links to **LO2**: assessment criterion 2.7

Explain the importance of using accurate grammar, spelling and punctuation in written communications in your organisation. You may want to undertake this by writing a short narrative.

Plain English

In order to meet the audience's needs, you need to use plain English with simple short sentences and words that people will understand. Avoid using long sentences, use lists or bullet points to break up the text and try to present the information in a positive and professional way.

The plain English campaign was established in 1979 and campaigns against the use of jargon and misleading information. They state that they have helped many government departments and other official organisations with their documents, reports and publications.

Key term

Plain English – language that the intended audience can read and act upon the first time they read it.

Unit Q309 Communicate in a business environment

For communications, the campaign also promotes:

- the use of active verbs
- the use of 'you' and 'we'
- short sentences
- using words as appropriate for the reader
- using instructions where appropriate.

These pointers are useful practical solutions that you can adopt into your written communications.

Portfolio task 309.12 → Links to **LO2**: assessment criterion 2.8

After carrying out further research on plain English, explain what it is and why it is used.

Functional skills

English: Reading

If you carry out research involving reading texts including work-related documents as well as Internet research in order to complete your portfolio task, you may be able to count this as evidence towards Level 2 Functional English: Reading. Remember to keep records of all of the documents, handbooks and guidelines which you study, along with the websites which you visit, as you will need to document any reading research you carry out.

The purpose of checking and proofreading work

The work that you produce will need to be accurate and correct. You will need to check your work to ensure that there are no errors and that you get it right first time every time. By checking your work you will be able to identify any errors and correct them before the information is processed further. By doing this you will be performing in a professional manner and you will be producing meaningful and accurate information. The reputation of your organisation can be damaged if incorrect information is sent out to your customers. You can ask a colleague to help or support you with checking work. Many people 'double-check' their work with another person.

Sending out well-structured and well-written communications is vital for all organisations but some organisations may spend more time checking correspondence/published papers than others. For example, publishing companies, educational establishments, government bodies, television companies and the press, all have a responsibility to present themselves in the best possible light; communication is their business and any written communication needs to be accurate, well-written and accessible.

Portfolio task 309.13 → Links to **LO2**: assessment criterion 2.9

Explain the importance of checking and proofreading your work. You may want to undertake this by writing a short narrative. Annotate your narrative with some examples of information that you might check as part of your job.

Important and urgent communications

In your job, you will come across 'important' and 'urgent' tasks that you need to complete on a day-to-day basis, and it is important to classify and plan your work. Urgent tasks will always take priority as they will have a specific deadline that you will need to meet. All tasks are important – if they are not important then why are you doing them?

An important task need not necessarily be done by you, but could be completed by a colleague in your team. If you pass this task on to another person, you will be **delegating** the work. For example, it may be important to phone a number of customers by the end of the day, but if you have a specific urgent task that you also need to complete, you may be able to agree with your colleagues that they phone the customers. By doing this, you are working effectively as a team and sharing the resources that you have. Confirm regularly throughout the day with your colleagues and manager exactly what is urgent. Communicate actively and agree with your colleagues who is doing what.

Key term

Delegating – giving authority or responsibility to another person to carry out a task.

The following checklist should help you to plan your tasks and communications more effectively.

> ### ✅ Checklist
>
> **Planning tasks**
>
> Remember to:
>
> - write down all your tasks and communications and when you need to achieve them by
>
> - highlight any specific deadline dates and try to achieve them by, for example, one day ahead of the deadline
>
> - classify your tasks by deciding how important they are and when they need to be completed by. Then use a rating system, such as 1, 2, 3 or A, B, C, to help prioritise them.
>
> - think about what you *must* do, *should* do, and *could* do
>
> - check your list each day and work through your tasks in the order that you have rated them in
>
> - always review your plan at the end of each day and reschedule any new targets into the plan
>
> - keep your manager informed of your progress.

By preparing a list of all your tasks and classifying them in terms of importance and target dates, you will be planning your communications and other tasks effectively.

Remember also to consider:

- Delegation — it is likely that you are not the only person in the office who can carry out a particular task. Can you delegate a particular task to a colleague?

- Must, should, could — try to prioritise your work into these three areas: work that I must complete this week; work that I should complete this week; and work that I could complete if I get some spare time.

> **Portfolio task 309.14** → Links to **LO2**: assessment criterion 2.10
>
> Prepare a 'to do' list of things that you need to do that day or that week or use a 'task manager' system on your computer. By prioritising your tasks you will be able to plan your work more effectively. Put a copy of a recent 'to do' list in your portfolio.

Storing, saving, filing and confidentiality

By keeping copies of written communications, you will always have a record that you can refer back to if you need to at any date in the future. Some organisations keep documents for a specific 'retention period' and this is often seven years from the date of the original record. Some documents are kept for longer than that and may be retained indefinitely.

Finding storage space for old documents can prove to be expensive and, unless they are filed in a logical order, it is sometimes difficult to retrieve information once it has been stored. It is likely that you will have a system in place to file information which will include correspondence, letters and other information. Many organisations adopt an alphabetical approach for customer files and then also file the information in date order on each individual file. Files must be stored in a clean safe environment and all confidential files must be kept in a locked cupboard with restricted access.

Documents can also be 'scanned' electronically and then stored on a disc or hard drive. This is a very effective way of storing files as huge amounts of data can be stored onto a single hard drive and then retained in a safe place; for example, a fireproof safe. It is important to have a detailed index of what is on the hard drive or disc.

Where live files are being stored electronically, for example, if there is a computer database containing customer details, then it is likely that all computer files will be 'backed up' each day by your IT team. The same will apply to your own work and emails on your own computer. Most people also find it useful to arrange their computer files in folders. If you are unsure how to do this, ask your colleagues for some assistance or check out the help facility on your computer. Also, make yourself familiar with your 'in-house' filing systems.

You should ensure that your computer is password-protected and that you lock your screen when you are not at your desk. This will make sure that no one can gain unauthorised access to your computer files.

Why is it important to lock your computer screen when you are away from your desk?

Portfolio task 309.15 ➡ Links to **LO2**: assessment criterion 2.11

Arrange your computer files in a systematic way and formulate your work folders to contain work relating to a specific subject. Then complete a screen print of your file configurations. Your assessor may also want to observe you storing, retrieving and filing information, but the screen print will provide useful evidence for your portfolio.

How to communicate verbally

After working through this section you will understand and be able to:

- describe ways of verbally presenting information and ideas clearly
- make verbal contributions to discussions
- describe ways of adapting verbal contributions to suit different audiences, purposes and situations
- explain how to use and interpret body language and voice tone
- describe and be able to demonstrate the techniques associated with active listening
- explain the purpose and importance of summarising verbal communication.

Ways of verbally presenting information and ideas

Verbal communication occurs all the time in any type of business. Verbal communication is not a luxury, it is essential. Verbal communication can take several different forms and can include:

- one-to-one verbal communication in person
- one-to-one verbal communication through a device, such as communicating by telephone or video-conferencing
- informal verbal communication between small groups of people; for example, a conversation between two or three people in the office
- more formalised verbal communication in small to medium-sized groups; for example, at a team meeting
- formalised verbal communication between one or more people; for example, at a committee meeting or a formal presentation.

Verbal communication is a two-way process. Information is sent from one person to another person who interprets the information and continues the conversation by responding. The communication is then in a perpetual loop until one or both parties agree to end the discussion.

Ineffective communication can be costly to a business. Barriers to effective verbal communication do exist (see Table 309.2), but if you plan your communication well, you can avoid these issues.

Table 309.2: *Barriers to effective verbal communication*

Barrier	Specific examples
Environmental factors	Background noise in the office making it difficult for both parties to hear.
Psychological factors	The receiver may have limited perception of the issues or have selective hearing.
Physiological factors	The receiver may have disabilities or poor memory retention.
Barriers to understanding	The information being communicated is taking too long or it is too complicated for the receiver.
Barriers to acceptance	The receiver does not respect the other person and has a poor attitude.

What barriers to communication might this person (and the person they are communicating with) be experiencing?

Effective verbal communication can be achieved in the following way:

- Make strong eye contact
- Ensure that your tone of voice reflects interest
- Have a good posture and positive body language

↓

- Know what you are trying to achieve
- Ask yourself – what are my intended outcomes?
- Communicate in a clear and concise way

↓

- Be tactful, polite and professional
- Separate the facts from the opinion
- Determine what the other person's needs are
- Ask open-ended questions

↓

- Actively listen to the other person
- Clarify/reflect back on what is being said
- Summarise what has been agreed

Figure 309.4: *A flow diagram showing how effective verbal communication can be achieved*

Delivering verbal presentations

Get used to talking to people in a group on a semi-formal basis, such as explaining an issue at a team meeting. By doing this regularly you will build up your confidence to potentially deliver a more formal presentation to a larger group of people.

Formal oral presentations can be daunting if you have never done them before. However, don't panic if you have been asked to deliver a presentation to a large group of people. Prepare well and you will succeed. The following checklist will help you to prepare and deliver a presentation.

Unit Q309 Communicate in a business environment

✓ Checklist

How to plan and deliver successful presentations

Before the presentation:

- Check the presentation brief — what is the purpose of the presentation, what do I need to cover?
- Check the practicalities — format, timings, resources and equipment to be used, etc.
- Decide on what you are going to say and complement the presentation with pictures, graphs, video clips or hand-outs, as appropriate.
- Decide how you will learn the presentation and prepare some notes to assist you.
- Practise the presentation on your own or with a colleague and ask for some feedback.

During the presentation:

- Make sure that you are well-prepared and are ready.
- Wear smart clothes and have a good positive posture, don't be static, but don't move around too much either.
- Stay calm, relaxed and confident.
- Before you begin, take a couple of deep breaths and start slowly with your opening line — and SMILE — that will relax you and the audience.

- At the start, communicate the housekeeping arrangements, e.g. fire exit, break times.
- Create an opener that will get everyone's attention, such as a fact, quote or question; for example, 'Did you know that...'
- After your opener, you should explain the aim of the presentation, e.g. 'At the session today, we will...'
- Work closely with the audience and be aware that you will need to make transitions between different topics or issues. Changing the pace of the presentation can help to grab the audience's attention back. Pausing for a few seconds can help you to achieve this.
- End the presentation well by summarising all the issues and linking them back to the aim of the presentation that you outlined at the beginning.
- Be ready to answer any questions at the end of the presentation.

After the presentation:

- Ask your colleagues for some feedback — 'How did I do?'
- Evaluate the feedback and identify any improvements for next time.

What will make this verbal presentation successful?

148

Ways of making contributions to discussions which help to achieve objectives

When you are in a group situation, try to contribute to discussions in a positive way. Examples of discussions could be an informal chat with some colleagues in the office or a discussion during a team meeting. Try to be confident and make useful contributions and suggestions. This is not always easy to start with, especially if you are new to the organisation, but as your confidence grows and you get more of a detailed understanding of your own job role and the organisation's processes and procedures, you will soon be able to make positive contributions and suggestions to your colleagues. Listen carefully to what other people are saying and then make your contributions.

If you are nervous about speaking in a group environment, a good way to break the ice is to ask your manager if you can update your colleagues on an issue at one of your team meetings. Prepare what you are going to say in advance and also write out a few of the main points that you want to cover in a hand-out that you can give to your colleagues.

Portfolio task 309.16 → Links to **LO3**: assessment criteria 3.1 and 3.2

Ask your manager if you can present some information at your next team meeting. Either ask your assessor to attend to observe you or ask your manager to write up a witness testimony explaining how you contributed to the discussion and interacted with your colleagues. You may also want to write a personal statement to reflect on the experience and explain what things you can improve for next time.

How to adapt verbal contributions to suit different audiences, purposes and situations

Generally, in order to meet the audience's needs, speak in plain English and avoid speaking in long sentences which listeners might find difficult or confusing. Always present verbal information in a positive and professional way.

When you are presenting information verbally, you should ensure that you are using the right communication method and utilising any resources to make the communication more effective. For example, if you are communicating with a customer, you will be speaking on a one-to-one basis in a formal manner, either face to face or over the telephone, and you will be contributing to the discussion by meeting the customer's needs. However, when you are communicating with your team members on a particular issue, for example, at a team meeting, you are likely to be communicating more informally and your purpose will be to meet the needs and objectives of the team.

Sometimes, it may be appropriate to communicate using specific technical language. This is perfectly acceptable and is the proper way to communicate when the situation requires it. However, remember that when you are communicating to a general audience or your customers, you should avoid the use of complicated or technical language as some listeners may not understand fully what you are saying to them.

Portfolio task 309.17 → Links to **LO3**: assessment criterion 3.3

Describe ways of communicating to two different audiences and explain why you would use each communication method and the specific language you would use, whether it be formal, informal or technical. Also, for each example, explain the recipient's (audience's) needs.

Functional skills

English: Reading

If you carry out research involving reading texts including work-related documents as well as Internet research in order to complete your portfolio task, you may be able to count this as evidence towards Level 2 Functional English: Reading. Remember to keep records of all of the documents, handbooks and guidelines which you study, along with the websites which you visit, as you will need to document any reading research you carry out.

How to use and interpret body language and tone of voice

Verbal communication is not just concerned with actually speaking and listening; there are other more subtle factors to consider, as follows:

● Eye contact – positive eye contact is a good thing, but don't stare as this can feel threatening to some people.

● Negative body language – negative body language traits include a blank stare, crossed arms, avoiding eye contact, looking at your watch and leaning back in your chair.

● Positive body language – good eye contact, smiling and taking interest, nodding encouragement where relevant, open arms/stance and leaning forward.

● Physical gestures – can include using your arms to explain an issue or simply putting your 'thumbs up'.

If you think that the person you are communicating with is showing signs of negative body language or an inappropriate or sarcastic tone of voice, you need to diffuse the situation by continuing the conversation in a professional way and clarifying that they are happy with what has been communicated to them. It is perfectly acceptable for you to clarify that the person is:

● clear about what is being communicated

● clear about what they need to do.

In addition to this, you need to allow the person to respond and listen to what they are saying to you. The best course of action is to engage the person in conversation and discuss the issues further. By doing this, you are likely to reduce their resistance and you can engage them by getting them involved in the process.

Portfolio task 309.18 → Links to **LO3**: assessment criteria 3.4 and 3.5

Think about a situation you have experienced recently at work where you have experienced some negative body language or resistance to an issue/change. Explain how you dealt with this and reflect on how you can deal with these types of issues in the future. You may want to have a professional discussion with your assessor to discuss this in more detail.

The methods and benefits of active listening

Listening might sound straightforward, but it is not that easy and needs practice. It is easy to 'hear' what is being said, but is something completely different to understand, interpret and then act upon what has been said to you. Also, it is easy to listen to someone speaking and to either finish off their sentence for them or think in your own mind what you want them to say rather than actually listening to what they are saying.

Always actively listen to what is being said to you. This is not easy and needs concentration and practice. Try to make sense of the information being communicated and listen with intent. Then apply the information to the situation and context of the discussion to reach a more detailed understanding of the issues being discussed.

Active listening is essential if you are going to communicate successfully and it is an often overlooked communication skill.

Portfolio task 309.19 → Links to **LO3**: assessment criteria 3.6 and 3.7

Practise and develop your listening skills. Ask a colleague to write up a witness testimony to explain how you actively listen and interpret information that is being communicated to you. Also, you may want to write up a personal statement to explain how you actively listen to your colleagues in the workplace.

Summarising verbal communication

When you are communicating verbally, it is important to clarify the conversation at various points as necessary. This could involve questioning or challenging a particular point if you are unsure what the other person meant. When you are asking for clarification, be very specific and ask exactly what you want to find out so that it is clear in your own mind what has been said and what you need to do, if anything. Not all people are effective verbal communicators and some people 'talk around' issues and then they interpret that as having asked you to do something, whereas you may well interpret what was said completely differently. Some people find it difficult to ask people outright to do something for them.

An example scenario

Your manager approaches you in the corridor explaining how busy she is and how your colleague Janet has just gone off on long-term sick leave and may not be back to work for a few weeks. Your manager ends the conversation by saying that your colleague has a lot of urgent work that is beginning to stack up.

From the conversation, nothing has been agreed between you and your manager. Your manager was hinting that she needed some help or support from you, but this was not expressly stated. Ideally you would approach your manager the following day with a suggestion as to how you might help out and enable the issue to be resolved. If you decide to do nothing, however, your manager might ask in a couple of weeks whether you have been able to help out with Janet's urgent work. This would put you in an awkward situation – you know that your manager did not ask you to do the work, but on the other hand you knew that she was implying that the work needed doing.

Either situation could have been avoided if there had been a summary of action points at the end of the initial conversation.

The following checklist should help your verbal communications to be more effective in the future:

Portfolio task 309.20 → Links to **LO3**: assessment criterion 3.8

Write up a personal statement to explain how you plan your communications and provide some relevant evidence to support this. An example could be an email that you have recently sent to a colleague.

The principles and value of feedback

After working through this section you will be able to:

- describe ways of obtaining feedback
- explain the purpose and benefits of using feedback to further develop communication skills.

Ways of obtaining feedback on success of verbal communication

Feedback of any type is useful, but it needs to be constructive. Constructive means meaningful feedback of some value that you can understand, accept and action in the future to improve your performance. You may receive some positive feedback and there may not be any action

---

✓ Checklist

Communicating verbally

- Identify who you are communicating to – it could be a client, your manager, your colleagues or a group of people.

- Identify any potential barriers.

- Is your audience shy, nervous, aggressive or receptive towards you?

- What method should you use – face to face, telephone or formal presentation?

- Would it be more appropriate to communicate in writing either by letter or email?

- You should be tactful, polite and professional at all times.

- Actively listen to what is being said to you.

- Clarify what is being said and question any elements that you are unsure about.

- Summarise at the end of the conversation and agree who is doing what.

required from you as a result of such feedback, but the important thing is to ensure that you understand what all feedback means and how to put this into context in relation to your whole job. If you receive some feedback from a customer or a colleague and you are not sure what it means, then ask them to clarify what they are saying in a bit more detail.

Accepting feedback from your colleagues and customers should help you to improve your own performance. By improving your performance, you should become more efficient in your role. If all your colleagues are also doing the same, then the whole organisation should improve and become more efficient.

Also remember that some people never give verbal feedback, but you will usually instinctively know if they are happy with your performance or not. Finally, don't forget that you can always ask someone for some feedback on your performance – 'How did I do?'

✓ Checklist

How to accept and value feedback

- Listen to what people have to say about you.

- Avoid overreacting and let people have their say; don't let your emotions get in the way.

- Pay attention to what is being said; clarify what the issue is or what you need to do to improve in the future.

- Be prepared to respond and explain what action you might take.

- Take the feedback on board and if it is valid and constructive, follow it up with some positive action.

- Make sure that you feed back to the person at a future date to let them know what you have done.

Methods for receiving feedback

Feedback can be formal or informal. An example of informal feedback might be a customer saying to you, 'You dealt with my problem really well, thank you.' This is obviously positive information and if you are doing something well, just carry on doing the same.

Sometimes, you will get more formal feedback. This may come from your line manager or a colleague that you work closely with. Other sources of feedback are from customers or from other organisations that you work with. If you have received some positive feedback from a customer, for example an email thanking you for assisting them, print this out as it will be a valuable piece of evidence for your portfolio.

Table 309.2 shows some examples of feedback and how you might respond appropriately.

Table 309.3: *Types of feedback and follow-up*

Type of feedback	Action to be taken/ follow-up
Written formal: customer email – 'Thank you for contacting me so quickly and sorting out my problem.'	Keep up the good work and continue to deal with all customers politely and efficiently.
Verbal informal: colleague in another section – 'Thank you for sending those urgent documents through to me.'	Keep up the good work and ask your colleagues if there is a quicker or more effective way to send the documents through in future; for example, electronically.
Verbal formal: you have gone past a deadline for a piece of work and the director has asked you to ensure that you meet the agreed timescales next time.	Check what went wrong and identify why you did not meet your deadline. Make sure that you address any issues ready for next time. If you need any further support, training or additional support then agree these with your manager and implement them as soon as possible.

A version of this table, ready for you to complete, is available to download from www.contentextra.com/businessadmin

Portfolio task 309.21 → Links to **LO4**: assessment criterion 4.1

Complete the table with two more examples of your own. Include the feedback you received and the follow-up action you took.

The purpose and benefits of using feedback to further develop communication skills

Remember that feedback is a two-way process as you can give feedback and you will receive feedback.

The most common formal feedback that you are likely to receive is from your manager through your review or appraisal meeting. Most organisations have a process in place to allow for meetings between individual employees or teams and their managers to review performance and capability. At these meetings you are likely to discuss and agree the following elements:

- your achievements for the previous year
- setting some specific goals or objectives for the forthcoming year
- your training and development needs.

This appraisal meeting would normally take place once a year, with perhaps a quarterly- or six-monthly review meeting to track progress. Some organisations have a less structured approach in place, but it is still likely that you will discuss issues with your manager from time to time and they will give you relevant feedback, even though this might not be written down.

Developing your communication skills

Always think of feedback as positive. Try to be objective in your evaluation of any feedback and try to learn from any mistakes that you have made.

Put plans in place to make sure that you improve your communication skills next time. If you have received some negative feedback, consider:

- Am I still learning the systems, processes and ways that the organisation communicates? If so, it may take time to be fully competent. What targets can I set myself?
- Can I ask for support or advice if the same situation occurs again?
- Perhaps I was not given enough time or the correct resources were not in place to allow me to communicate effectively.
- Do I need to write a procedure or note for myself to make sure that I remember how to communicate more effectively next time?
- Have I got a specific development need or do I need some training?
- Was the problem/issue outside my control?

By working through these questions, you will start to identify how you can improve in the future and possibly make changes to your working methods to become a more effective communicator.

Improvements and reflections

The business world is constantly changing and all organisations need to think up new and innovative ways of working. An example of this is technological change: it is important for organisations to update relevant processes and procedures to utilise any new technology that may be available. The benefits of introducing new ways of working are that they could make the organisation more efficient, more profitable and provide a better service to customers.

For any activity that you undertake in an office environment, including communication, it is a good idea to reflect on your experiences and try to improve for next time. Also, ask your colleagues for feedback: 'How did I do?' 'What could I do that would make it better for next time?'

Figure 309.5 provides a checklist to ensure that any communication problems are resolved for the future. Take time to reflect on what went well and what needs improving for next time.

Before the communication

- Did I plan the communication well?
- Did I communicate with the right level of detail using the right style of language?

During the communication

- Did I communicate in the right format?
- Did the recipient understand the communication?

Feedback/after the communication

- Did the person respond in the correct/expected way?
- Can I improve any aspects for next time?
- Can I undertake communication in a more effective way?

Figure 309.5: *A flowchart showing how a checklist can resolve any communication problems*

Portfolio task 309.22 → Links to **LO4**: assessment criterion 4.2

Specifically in relation to how you communicate and interact with people, make a list of any feedback that you have recently received from any source. If you have any written feedback, for example, an email, print it out for use as evidence in your portfolio.

Evidence collection

In order for you to complete the remaining assessment criteria to successfully pass this unit, you will need to carry out various tasks at work and then produce evidence to show that you have demonstrated the required skills and competence.

Evidence can be collected in a number of different ways. For example, it can be in the form of a signed witness testimony from a colleague or line manager, a copy of any related emails or letters you have produced or a verbal discussion with your assessor.

Speak to your assessor to identify the best methods to use in order to complete each portfolio task and remember to keep copies of all the evidence that you produce.

Plan communication

→ Links to **LO5**: assessment criteria 5.1, 5.2 and 5.3

Portfolio task 309.23

Gather evidence of your work to show your assessor that you have successfully carried out the tasks outlined in the table below. Check with your assessor on the best ways of gathering evidence for each of the tasks before you begin.

Task	Evidence collected
1 Identify the purpose of communication and the audience.	
2 Select methods of communication to be used.	

A version of this table, ready for you to complete, is available to download from www.contentextra.com/businessadmin

Communicate in writing

Portfolio task 309.24

→ Links to **LO6**: assessment criteria 6.1, 6.2, 6.3, 6.4, 6.5, 6.6, 6.7, 6.8 and 6.9

Gather evidence of your work to show your assessor that you have successfully carried out the tasks outlined in the table below. Check with your assessor on the best ways of gathering evidence for each of the tasks before you begin.

Task	Evidence collected
1 Find and select information that supports the purpose of written communications.	
2 Present information using a format, layout, style and house style suited to the purpose and method of written communications.	

A version of this table, ready for you to complete, is available to download from www.contentextra.com/businessadmin

Communicate verbally

Portfolio task 309.25

→ Links to **LO7**: assessment criteria 7.1, 7.2, 7.3, 7.4, 7.5 and 7.6

Gather evidence of your work to show your assessor that you have successfully carried out the tasks outlined in the table below. Check with your assessor on the best ways of gathering evidence for each of the tasks before you begin.

Task	Evidence collected
1 Verbally present information and ideas to others clearly and accurately.	
2 Make verbal contributions to discussions that suit the audience, purpose and situation.	

A version of this table, ready for you to complete, is available to download from www.contentextra.com/businessadmin

Identify and agree ways of further developing communication skills

Portfolio task 309.26

→ Links to **LO8**: assessment criteria 8.1 and 8.2

Gather evidence of your work to show your assessor that you have successfully carried out the tasks outlined in the table below. Check with your assessor on the best ways of gathering evidence for each of the tasks before you begin.

Task	Evidence collected
1 Get feedback to confirm whether communication has achieved its purpose.	
2 Use feedback to identify and agree ways of further developing own communication skills.	

A version of this table, ready for you to complete, is available to download from www.contentextra.com/businessadmin

Office life

Samira's story

My name is Samira, I'm 26 and I'm employed as a team leader in a company making waterproof clothing in North Yorkshire. I manage a team of four full-time staff and three part-time staff. One of my main tasks is making sure we have a process for rectifying any quality issues on the product before it is sent to the retailers.

Recently we have had a significant increase in reports of faulty stitching and loose threads on the clothing. We have several new members of staff and have also experienced some faults with new parts used to repair machines in the workshop. My manager, Paul, is aware of the quality problems and has asked me to prepare a report to present at the next directors' meeting.

Well before the meeting I prepared a detailed list of all the issues and then wrote my report, structured as follows:

- an explanation of the issues
- options to solve the issues
- recommendations.

Based on my findings I suggested replacing the faulty machine parts and delivering training to the new staff operating the equipment.

I presented my report at the meeting. I was quite nervous at first but I had prepared very thoroughly and the directors seemed pleased with my solutions, which they then agreed to.

Ask the expert

Q I have to formulate a report for a meeting. What do I need to do?

A Gather as much information as you can and make sure that you understand exactly what is being asked of you so that you can plan you report:
- Consider what the objectives are for the report – what outcomes do I want to achieve?
- Gather all the information and facts.
- Prepare the report in a format to meet the audience's needs, with the right language (formal or informal) and with right level of detail.
- Prepare the report in a format that everyone will understand and in the house style if required.
- Agree a specific date for completion.
- Make sure that there are no barriers to your communication method. If producing a written report is not the most appropriate method, then think of an alternative solution.
- The report should have a beginning, a middle and an end which includes a proposal or a recommendation.

Top tips

Samira could also have spoken to her colleagues to ask for their input or opinions. By doing this she would have discovered if there were any other quality issues.

Samira did well to write down a list of all the issues before starting her report. It was successful because she structured it well.

Can you think of anything else that Samira could have done better?

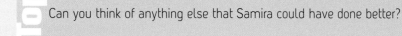

Check your knowledge

1 What does being proactive mean?

a) Taking an interest in things and looking for solutions to problems and also looking at how you can improve things.

b) Being reactive and sorting out problems when they arise.

c) Doing things quicker at a reduced cost.

d) Increasing the turnover of the organisation.

2 Which of the following demonstrate negative body language?

a) Crossing your arms.

b) Blank stares.

c) Slouching or leaning back in your chair.

d) All of the above.

3 What does the term constructive feedback mean?

a) It means allowing team members to take control of their work and be involved in decision-making.

b) It means increasing knowledge and skills in a particular area.

c) In means allowing a person to be released to work in another team.

d) It means meaningful feedback of some value that you can understand, accept and action in the future to improve your performance.

4 What is a flat organisational structure?

a) An organisation with no formal structure in place.

b) An organisation with a maximum of four tiers in place.

c) An organisation with at least five different tiers in place.

d) An organisation with teams managing tasks.

5 What does active listening mean?

a) Active listening is making a written note of what is being said to you.

b) Active listening is remembering what has been said to you.

c) Active listening is listening intently to what is being said to you and then interpreting the information.

d) Active listening is preparing what you are going to say at a meeting.

6 If you are planning a formal verbal presentation, what things do you need to agree and check before the presentation takes place?

a) The venue for the presentation.

b) The audience's needs.

c) The timings for the presentation.

d) All of the above.

7 The following are all examples of verbal communication apart from which odd one out?

a) One-to-one discussion.

b) A team meeting.

c) An appraisal meeting.

d) An email.

8 The following are all examples of written communication apart from which odd one out?

a) A letter to a customer.

b) A discussion at a team away day.

c) A report that you have written.

d) A staff newsletter.

9 What is an example of an environmental factor that could cause a barrier to communication?

a) Background noise in the office, making it difficult to hear what is being said.

b) The recipient has a lack of understanding of what is being said.

c) The recipient has a bad attitude and does not want to listen to what is being said.

d) There is a problem with the email system and the information cannot be sent through to the recipient.

10 What would be the normal frequency for regular structured team meetings?

a) Once a year.

b) When something goes wrong.

c) Once a month.

d) On an ad hoc basis.

Answers to the Check your knowledge questions can be found at www.contentextra.com/businessadmin

What your assessor is looking for

In order to prepare for and succeed in completing this unit, your assessor will require you to be able to demonstrate competence by:

● describing the purpose and benefits of effective communication

● describing the various methods, structures and processes used to communicate both in writing and verbally

● contributing to discussions and listening actively

● planning communication and presenting information in the most suitable format and with the right level of detail

● demonstrating effective communication in both written and verbal form

● demonstrating how to use feedback to further develop your competence.

You will demonstrate your skills, knowledge and competence through the eight learning outcomes in this unit. Evidence generated in this unit will also cross-reference to the other units in this qualification.

Please bear in mind that there are significant cross-referencing opportunities throughout this qualification, and you may have already generated some relevant work to meet certain criteria in this unit. Your assessor will provide you with the exact requirements to meet the standards of this unit. However, as a guide it is likely that for this unit you will need to be assessed through the following methods:

● one observation of relevant workplace communication to cover the whole unit

● at least one witness testimony to be produced

● a written narrative, reflective account or professional discussion

● any relevant work products to be produced as evidence.

The work products for this unit could include:

● emails, letters or other communication methods that you have used

● copies of any team meeting agendas and minutes

● any feedback that you have received on your performance; for example, your appraisal

● any formal communication that you have completed; for example, a presentation.

Your assessor will guide you through the assessment process as detailed in the candidate logbook. The detailed assessment criteria are shown in the logbook, and by working through these questions, combined with providing the relevant evidence, you will meet the learning outcomes required to complete this unit.

Unit Q309 Communicate in a business environment

Task and page reference	Mapping assessment criteria
Portfolio task 309.1 (page 133)	Assessment criterion: 1.1
Portfolio task 309.2 (page 133)	Assessment criterion: 1.2
Portfolio task 309.3 (page 135)	Assessment criterion: 1.3
Portfolio task 309.4 (page 136)	Assessment criterion: 1.4
Portfolio task 309.5 (page 137)	Assessment criterion: 2.1
Portfolio task 309.6 (page 139)	Assessment criterion: 2.2
Portfolio task 309.7 (page 139)	Assessment criterion: 2.3
Portfolio task 309.8 (page 142)	Assessment criterion: 2.4
Portfolio task 309.9 (page 142)	Assessment criterion: 2.5
Portfolio task 309.10 (page 143)	Assessment criterion: 2.6
Portfolio task 309.11 (page 143)	Assessment criterion: 2.7
Portfolio task 309.12 (page 144)	Assessment criterion: 2.8
Portfolio task 309.13 (page 144)	Assessment criterion: 2.9
Portfolio task 309.14 (page 145)	Assessment criterion: 2.10
Portfolio task 309.15 (page 146)	Assessment criterion: 2.11
Portfolio task 309.16 (page 149)	Assessment criteria: 3.1 and 3.2
Portfolio task 309.17 (page 149)	Assessment criterion: 3.3
Portfolio task 309.18 (page 150)	Assessment criteria: 3.4 and 3.5
Portfolio task 309.19 (page 150)	Assessment criteria: 3.6 and 3.7
Portfolio task 309.20 (page 151)	Assessment criterion: 3.8
Portfolio task 309.21 (page 153)	Assessment criterion: 4.1
Portfolio task 309.22 (page 154)	Assessment criterion: 4.2
Portfolio task 309.23 (page 155)	Assessment criteria: 5.1, 5.2 and 5.3
Portfolio task 309.24 (page 155)	Assessment criteria: 6.1, 6.2, 6.3, 6.4, 6.5, 6.6, 6.7, 6.8 and 6.9
Portfolio task 309.25 (page 156)	Assessment criteria: 7.1, 7.2, 7.3, 7.4, 7.5 and 7.6
Portfolio task 309.26 (page 156)	Assessment criteria: 8.1 and 8.2

Design and produce documents in a business environment

What you will learn

- Understand the purpose and value of designing and producing high quality and attractive documents
- Know the resources available to design and produce documents and how to use them
- Understand the purpose and value of following procedures when designing and producing documents
- Be able to design and produce documents to agreed specifications

Introduction

Documents are essential for the effective flow of information between employees and between departments within an organisation. They are also used to communicate information to suppliers and customers of a business. Well-presented documents play an essential part in the effectiveness of an organisation.

In this unit you will look at the skills and resources required in order to be able to design and produce attractive and professional business documents for a variety of purposes.

When designing and producing documents it is important to follow the organisation's guidelines to ensure that documents are produced to a consistently high standard.

Documents circulated within the organisation may contain important and possibly sensitive data and, as such, require careful and secure handling and storage.

You will investigate the relevant procedures and processes – including security and confidentiality – which may affect production of documents in your organisation.

Designing and producing high quality documents

After working through this section you will understand and be able to:

● describe different types of documents that may be designed and produced and the different styles that could be used

● describe different formats in which text may be presented

● explain the purpose and benefits of designing and producing high quality and attractive documents.

Different types of documents that may be designed and produced

Types of documents that may be needed in business

There are many different types of documents that need to be produced in businesses in order for activities to be carried out effectively. Different types of business documents can include:

● meeting agendas and minutes

● departmental reports
(for example, from accounts, marketing, sales)

● letters

● faxes

● emails

● published annual company reports.

Internal and external documents

Internal documents are only intended for the staff within an organisation. Some types of internal documents may also be confidential. External documents may potentially be viewed by a much larger group of people, including customers, clients and the general public.

Both types of document must be accurate and well presented; however, documents for external use must also be presented in such a way as to maintain the professional image of the organisation.

Things that may need to be included in public business documents include:

● the company logo

● correct corporate colours and fonts

● corporate contact information

● any other relevant branding design elements associated with the company's image.

Formal and informal business documents

Some business documents are formal in order to underline the importance of a situation. These can include documents relating to the annual shareholders' meeting, published corporate performance reports, letters and reports to clients.

Informal documents are used internally within an organisation to communicate the more routine **operational** information which is needed day to day by staff. An email is a good example of an informal business document.

Different styles of documents

The style which is applied to a particular document will depend on its purpose and its intended audience. Style can encompass many elements, such as:

- applying different fonts, sizes and colours in text
- printing on different types and qualities of paper – including letterhead
- inclusion of electronic media such as sound and videos to make presentations more dynamic and exciting for the audience
- professional finishing of reports such as binding and hard covering
- laminating
- production of documents via the web.

Let's take a look at some examples of the typical styles that are usually applied to business documents.

Agendas

Agendas are used for all business meetings. An agenda is a list of the main topics to be covered in a business meeting. Agendas are normally emailed round to all attendees prior to the meeting, so that they can take a look at the topics for discussion and prepare anything that they wish to contribute.

Agendas can vary in their level of detail and style, depending on the type of meeting which is being held. But the core information that is always required is a running order of what is to be discussed. For example, an internal monthly team meeting will be simpler and contain less detail than an international conference meeting agenda with 5000 attendees from all over the world.

Activity 1

Look at the list in the table below which shows some of the different types of documents that may be needed in business. Decide which of these types of documents are formal and informal and then use this information to complete the table. Remember that some types of business documents can be both formal and informal. The first one has been completed for you.

Type of business document	Formal, informal or both?	Reason
Emails	Both	Sent internally and externally, usually to communicate brief, practical information between colleagues, suppliers and clients.
Meeting agendas and minutes		

A version of this table, ready for you to complete, is available to download from www.contentextra.com/businessadmin

Sales Team Meeting Agenda

Time: 9.00 – 10.00 a.m.
Date: 24 January
Location: Main board room
Meeting called by: Josh Grainer
Attendees: Josh Grainer, Sally Owen, June Harper, Molly Isaac

Item	Owner
Old business and approval of last meeting's minutes	Josh
Review of this month's sales figures	Sally
Forecast for rest of year	Sally
Proposed new training to be introduced	June
Recruitment drive to increase number of sales personnel	Josh
Any other business	All

Figure 312.1: *A typical agenda for an internal business meeting*

The different styles which can be applied to agendas consist mainly of the many different agenda templates that you can apply – adding colour, professional formatting and even design elements. You could even include illustrations of location maps and conference venue floor plans for large formal meetings involving business clients.

Take a look at the example of a simple agenda in Figure 312.1.

It is likely that you will come across agendas in your job, as most employees attend meetings of some type on a regular basis. If you have not yet seen a meeting agenda in your organisation, ask your manager to show you an example of one.

Activity 2

1 In the example of an agenda in Figure 312.1, why do you think each item has an owner?

2 Think of one other detail which is not listed on the agenda, but which may be useful for attendees to know. Say what this detail is and why you think it would be useful for attendees to know it.

Emails

Emails can also vary in their style – being either formal or informal, depending on the subject and intended recipients. Informal emails (see Figure 312.2 for an example) usually contain only very brief and limited information which is straight to the point.

Formal emails may be used in situations such as company-wide announcements. For example, the managing director of an organisation may send an 'all-company' email to staff to convey some important information which will affect everyone. This could be good news about a new client which the company has won, a special bonus payment to staff, or it could relate to imminent cutbacks.

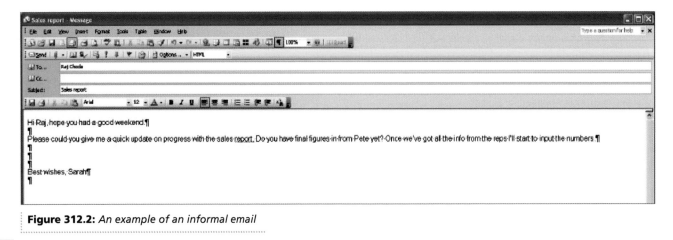

Figure 312.2: *An example of an informal email*

Reports

Reports can vary enormously in their style. This is because they can be used for so many different purposes, from small, informal documents intended for only a few employees to review, to 300-page financial accounts reports.

A small internal report may contain limited styling elements such as:

● stapled or paper-clipped pages
● single-sided printing
● black and white text and illustrations.

Larger, more formal reports may contain more elaborate styling features including:

● double-sided printing
● spiral or wire-bound
● hard cover
● full-colour illustrations.

Why do reports vary in style and format?

The style of the report must be in accordance with the intended audience and purpose. For example, there is very little point spending a whole week producing a full-colour glossy brochure for your weekly team meeting. On the other hand, launching a new international promotion via the Internet using only a word-processed A4 memo would be equally unsuitable.

Activity 3

Carry out some research in your organisation to locate two examples of different types of reports. If you are not familiar with the company reports used in your organisation, ask your manager to help you.

Once you have found two reports, spend ten minutes or so reviewing each of them and identify:

- the purpose and audience of each report
- any similarities or differences between the two
- any particular style issues which you notice about each of them.

You can use the table below to collect the information which you find.

	Report 1	Report 2
Purpose and audience		
Key similarities and/or differences		
Style of report (formal, informal, colour or black and white, stapled or spiral-bound, professionally finished with a plastic cover)		

A version of this table, ready for you to complete, is available to download from www.contentextra.com/businessadmin

Letters

Most organisations need to send out letters for a variety of reasons. A few examples are: to provide information and advice to customers; to inform people of business terms and arrangements; and to request further information from customers.

Activity 4

Carry out some research in your organisation to identify a selection of the different types of letters that the business sends out. Keep a note of your findings and try to get copies of at least three different types of letters.

Letters are external documents and are usually formal in nature. They are official communication channels for the business and, as such, they need to be set out and presented in an appropriate way. This includes:

- using a formal business letter format (see Figure 312.3)
- good formatting of text – including making the best use of the space available on the page to avoid text looking cramped; for example, inserting double spaces between paragraphs.
- using professional businesslike language
- presenting the letter on good quality A4 letterhead paper.

✓ Checklist

Remember, when formatting a business letter:

- Check that the language and tone of the letter are businesslike (avoid the use of slang!).

- Make sure that the formatting makes best use of the space on the page.

- Use paragraphs to split up sections of text and use double spacing between paragraphs.

- Check – and double-check – spelling and grammar on the finished letter before it is sent out.

Portfolio task 312.1 → Links to **LO1**: assessment criterion 1.1

Produce a short report which could be used to train new members of staff in an organisation and which describes three different types of documents that may be designed and produced. For each type of document which you identify, state the different styles that can be used. You may like to use examples of documents from your own organisation on which to base your answer.

Functional skills

English: Speaking and listening

If your assessor asks you to take part in a discussion about this portfolio task as part of the assessment for this learning outcome, you may be able to count it as evidence towards Level 2 Functional English: Speaking and listening.

Different formats for presenting text

There are a huge variety of ways in which text can be formatted to create a professional and attractive document. Text-formatting options are available within word-processing software, such as Microsoft Word, and you can try out many different effects to see which ones best suit your particular document.

Text-formatting options

Here are just some of the aspects of text which can be altered by using the various formatting options available to you:

- Font type – changing the font can have a dramatic effect on your finished document.
- Font size – increase font size to emphasise headings and subheadings in your document and to make the text in your document easier to read.
- Colour – use colour throughout your document to make it attractive and eye-catching to the reader and to complement the organisation's branding.

Standrite · Technologies ⓢ
The Business Park
Hightown
CS1 IJK
www.standritetechnologies.com

Mr Brown
1 High Street
Lowtown
SA1 1KP   3 March 2011

Dear Mr Brown

As a valued customer of our business, we are offering you a unique
opportunity to make huge savings on your orders with us over the next month.
Simply type in the code VALUEDCUSTOMER01 whenever you place an
order with us, either over the phone, in person or via the website.

We will discount all your orders over the value of £50 by 5% and, furthermore,
we will increase this discount to 10% on all orders over £100. So, what are you
waiting for? To take advantage of this very special offer, simply call in to one of
our branches, phone us or visit our website today to start saving!

We hope you enjoy taking advantage of this special offer – remember, the offer
closes at the end of the month, so hurry to make the most of the savings on
offer!

Yours sincerely

John White
Standrite Technologies

Figure 312. 3: *An example of a typical formatting style which is used in business letters*

- Lists – break up large sections of text with either bullet or number lists.
- Line spacing – adjust the space between lines of text to make the document more readable.
- Columns – change your document's layout to a two-column format to create a newsletter style.
- Headings and subheadings – good use of headings and subheadings can break up a large document into easily readable sections.
- Paragraphs – separating out the key points of a document into three or four paragraphs makes it easier to read and understand, especially if there is very important information included.

- Alignment of text – text can be aligned left, right or centred, depending on the document and the emphasis required.
- Margins and borders can be used to create professional-looking layouts for your documents.
- The **orientation** of documents can be altered to accommodate different types of content. For example, tables containing a large amount of information are often better presented as landscape rather than portrait, whereas letters and reports are more usually presented in portrait orientation.

By taking some time to study the different options for formatting your text, you can become skilled in creating a variety of different styles and formats which will suit the different types of documents which you need to produce at work including:

- letters
- meeting agendas
- reports
- newsletters.

Portfolio task 312.2 → Links to **LO1**: assessment criterion 1.2

Write a short report which describes different formats in which text may be presented. Use two examples of different business documents in your answer and, for each one, describe the specific formatting which has been applied. If possible, include two contrasting business documents from your own organisation.

Designing high-quality documents

The documents that are produced by an organisation are good indicators of the professionalism and credibility of that organisation. Whether they are for internal use or for publication externally, it is important that care and preparation has gone into their development.

Protecting the organisation's reputation

High-quality and attractive documents portray a professional image both within the organisation and externally to customers and potential customers.

Having high-quality internal documents allows for the efficient and accurate communication of information which is needed by staff to carry out their jobs effectively.

Poor **internal communication** is a major source of lost productivity in business. Lost productivity is lost profit – and so there is a clear business reason for maintaining the highest standards of document design and production in order to maximise business efficiency.

In the public domain, having professional and attractive documents reinforces the image of the organisation as one which is dependable, solid and trustworthy. It underlines the credibility and integrity of the business and ensures that all external communications from the organisation are of a **consistently** high standard. Consistency is important in business, as it engenders trust and familiarity among the public, giving your organisation an advantage over – and helping it to **differentiate** itself from – its competitors.

Promoting the organisation's brand name

High-quality external communications are a key source of promotion for an organisation and its **brand**. Making a brand name known and trusted by customers can cost a business millions in **paid advertising** and can take a long time. Brands such as Nike, Coca-Cola and Cadbury are all famous for producing multimillion-pound advertising campaigns

Key terms

Orientation – the way round a document is presented: either portrait or landscape.

Internal communication – communication (face to face, emails, memos) between staff in an organisation.

Consistently – always the same.

Differentiate – to find a way of making a company or product different from its competitors.

Brand – a brand is an identifiable trade name, product or logo.

Paid advertising – advertising which has to be paid for, such as TV adverts, and adverts in magazines and newspapers.

to promote their brand name to the public in a bid to increase business and make their organisation the leader in their field.

Having the highest-quality and most eye-catching documentation for all communications about your organisation will further enhance and promote the brand image to the public.

Generating good publicity

Eye-catching materials are more likely to be noticed – and read – by your customers and potential customers. This is why it pays to take the time and effort in finding as many opportunities as possible to produce attractive and eye-catching business materials. In most large organisations there are departments devoted to doing just this, highlighting the enormous value to be gained by producing business documents of the highest calibre.

Business materials will be particularly important at conferences, industry meetings, annual awards ceremonies and any other high-profile events where the organisation is being represented. Branding and design themes can be carried through from brochures and promotional literature to speaker presentation slides, corporate give-away items and business cards.

Portfolio task 312.3 → Links to **LO1**: assessment criterion 1.3

Write a short summary which explains the purpose and benefits of designing and producing high-quality and attractive documents. In order to complete this portfolio task, you need to select three examples of business documents and, for each one, describe the factors that need to be considered in making sure the document is of high quality and attractive. Make sure you include examples of both internal and external business documents in your answer.

Activity 5

Carry out Internet research by visiting www.interbrand.com to find out what the top five global brand names are for this year. Make a note of which companies produce each brand. (Sometimes the brand is quite different to the company.)

Are you familiar with all of these businesses? Visit their websites to discover what it is that their businesses do.

Use the information which you have found to complete the table below.

Top five global brands	Website	Main business areas

A version of this table, ready for you to complete, is available to download from www.contentextra.com/businessadmin

Resources for producing documents

After working through this section you will understand and be able to:

- describe the types of resources needed to design and produce high-quality and attractive documents
- explain the purpose and benefits of using different types of resources to design and produce high-quality and attractive documents
- describe different types of technology available for inputting, formatting and editing text, and their main features.

Types of resources needed

The design and production of high-quality business documents involves using a variety of resources. The specific resource requirements will depend on the exact document that is needed. However, some typical resources which are needed for almost all documents include:

- word-processing software, such as Microsoft Word
- graphic design software, such as Adobe Photoshop and Adobe Illustrator
- high-quality printers capable of double-sided and colour printing as well as collating
- binders, laminators and covers.

Employing the services of professional graphic designers can provide the organisation with a bank of excellent high-quality resources

Despite the resources mentioned, nothing will be possible without people skilled in researching, writing, checking and proofreading text, as well as skilled graphic designers to create logos and branding designs and to set out the content professionally on the page to gain maximum impact.

Activity 6

Carry out some research at work to locate three different types of business documents. If your organisation produces an internal staff newsletter, this would be a very good example of a document for this activity. Ask colleagues or your manager to explain to you the steps involved in designing and producing each document and the resources that were needed to create them. Make sure you keep detailed notes of your findings as these will help you to complete the portfolio task which follows.

Portfolio task 312.4 → Links to **LO2**: assessment criterion 2.1

Write a short report which describes the types of resources needed to design and produce high-quality and attractive documents. Use the three different examples of documents which you researched for the activity above and, for each one, say what resources were required in order to design and produce it. Include copies of the finished documents with your answer.

It may help you to use the table below to compile the information needed for your answer.

Document	Resources required to design and produce it

A version of this table, ready for you to complete, is available to download from www.contentextra.com/businessadmin

Using different resources to produce high-quality documents

You need to make use of the different types of resources at your disposal at work and combine them to create an end product that is professional and has the necessary impact.

These resources might be:

- word-processing software – ensures all of the text is produced to the highest standards
- design software – ensures you benefit from the latest cutting-edge design techniques in your materials
- presentation software – ensures the text and design elements which you have created can be transferred seamlessly into all your electronic slide presentations.

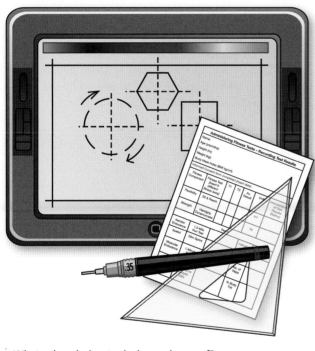

What other design tools do you know of?

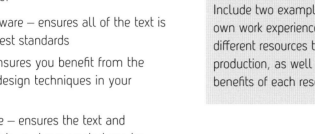

Portfolio task 312.5 → Links to **LO2**: assessment criterion 2.2

Write a short report which can be used to train new staff in your organisation and which explains the purpose and benefits of using different types of resource to design and produce high-quality and attractive documents.

Include two examples of such documents from your own work experience and, for each one, state the different resources that were used in its design and production, as well as describing the purpose and benefits of each resource.

Using technology for inputting, formatting and editing text

Word-processing software allows you to enter, format and then edit text in order to produce professional, high-quality finished documents including:

- letters
- agendas
- faxes
- reports.

Using templates

A good starting point if you are new to creating these types of documents is to take a look through the templates that are built in to the software you are using. For example, if you want to create a new memo, you can simply navigate to the templates and browse through the pre-installed template designs until you find one which you like. If you do not like any of the existing templates, there will be more choices available to you from the software provider's online help facility.

Entering text

Text can be entered into word-processing software by:

- typing it in manually
- copying and pasting it in from another electronic source, such as another document or from a website
- scanning a paper original into the computer and converting it to electronic format
- speaking into a microphone attached to the computer using voice-recognition software.

Formatting text

Formatting text means making changes to the way in which it appears on the page to improve its presentation (see Figure 312.4 on page 173). Formatting can involve changing:

- fonts
- colours
- size of type
- line-spacing
- alignment of text
- paragraph styles
- number of columns.

Formatting can also include the addition of photos, illustrations and charts to further improve the appearance of the finished document.

Have you ever used voice-recognition software?

Formatting can be carried out using word-processing and graphic design software packages.

Editing text

Editing text means making alterations to it and can involve adding further content, deleting content and changing the way in which the content is organised. All of these techniques are used in order to improve the text and to improve clarity for the reader.

Text can be edited using the many editing tools which are contained within word-processing software packages including:

- spelling and grammar check
- thesaurus and research facilities
- global search and replace (CTRL + H), which allows you to change all mentions of a particular term instead of having to change each mention of it manually (take care when using this facility, as errors can occur if you do not check each change individually)
- track changes facility, which allows you to view the changes which a user makes in a document (each change can then be accepted or rejected by the reviewer).

Portfolio task 312.6 → Links to **LO2**: assessment criterion 2.3

Write a short guide which can be used to train new staff in your organisation and which describes different types of technology available for inputting, formatting and editing text, and their main features.

Functional skills

English: Reading

If you carry out research involving reading texts including work-related documents as well as Internet research in order to complete your portfolio task, you may be able to count this as evidence towards Level 2 Functional English: Reading. Remember to keep records of all of the documents, handbooks and guidelines which you study, along with the websites which you visit, as you will need to document any reading research you carry out.

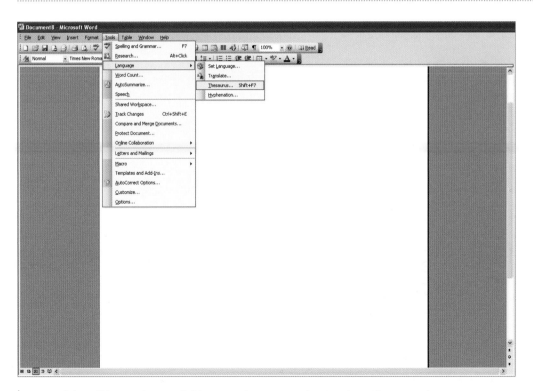

Some of the formatting options available to you in most word-processing software packages

Some of the editing options available to you in most word-processing software packages

Figure 312.4: *Formatting and editing options*

Office life

Sajid's story

My name is Sajid Hussain and I am 19 years old. I have been working as an administrative assistant for six months since completing my Business and Administration course at college. My job involves typing a lot of letters and memos and occasionally sending round all-company emails to staff on behalf of my manager. I really enjoy this aspect of my work along with the opportunity to develop my skills in this area.

Recently I have been asked to start up a new monthly staff newsletter. This is to contain topical stories on company events and achievements which will be provided for me by various members of staff. I have not produced anything like this before and am unsure of the best way to go about designing and producing such a document. I am also concerned that it will be very time-consuming to create a newsletter document from scratch.

Ask the expert

Q I need some advice on how to go about designing and producing a staff newsletter. Will it be sufficient to create it using a word-processing package or do I need additional software?

A Your word-processing software package should provide you with ample resources to be able to create a professional newsletter. You can even save yourself a large amount of time by using one of the many newsletter templates which are available to select from your word-processing package. These allow you to place your own articles and images in the pre-defined areas in order to quickly put together a very well-designed and professional-looking newsletter.

Top tips

Word-processing packages, such as Microsoft Word, contain templates for a huge variety of different types of documents, from letters, memos and faxes to blog posts, meeting minutes, time sheets and even newsletters. Sajid should find out if there is an existing template available in his organisation for him to work from; if there isn't, he should take a look at the templates section in his word-processing package and select a suitable template to use in his newsletter. If he does not want to use one of the available templates, he can always create one of his own. However, spending a little time browsing through the template versions will certainly help him to get a good idea of the sort of design elements required for a newsletter.

Following procedures when producing documents

After working through this section you will understand and be able to:

- explain the value and benefits of agreeing the purpose, content, style and deadlines for the design and production of documents
- describe ways of researching and organising content needed for documents
- describe ways of integrating and laying out text and non-text
- describe ways of checking finished documents for accuracy – including spelling, grammar and punctuation – and correctness, and the purpose of doing so
- explain the purpose of storing documents safely and securely, and ways of doing so
- explain the purpose of confidentiality and data protection when preparing documents
- explain the purpose and benefits of meeting deadlines.

Agreeing the purpose, content, style and deadlines

Agreeing the purpose, content, style and deadlines for the design and production of documents will set out the framework within which you will work to produce a document which meets all of its specified requirements.

- Agreeing the purpose underlines the rationale for the document – why it is needed.
- The content needs to be agreed to ensure correct coverage of certain key points of information. It may also involve elements such as inclusion of illustrations and word count, as well as other features which will contribute to the quality of the finished document.
- Agreeing on the style of the document will ensure that it is appropriate to the content and to its intended audience. Style encompasses the level of

formality as well as the tone of the writing. It also encompasses the use of colour, illustrations, charts, photos and the general look and feel of the finished document.

- Deadlines are critical factors in the production of finished documents. This is because the documents may be needed for a live event, such as a conference or other important corporate event. Being late with a document needed for a live event could be potentially disastrous for a business. So, it stands to reason that deadlines must be the key driving factor in the document production process.

Portfolio task 312.7 → Links to **LO3**: assessment criterion 3.1

Produce a short report which can be used to train new members of staff and which explains the value and benefits of agreeing the purpose, content, style and deadlines for the design and production of documents.

It may be helpful to base your answer on an example of a document which you have experience of producing at work. Remember to include four headings in your answer to make sure that you cover all the necessary information in your report. These are:

- purpose
- content
- style
- deadlines.

Ways of researching and organising content

Taking an organised and **systematic** approach to researching and organising the content for your document will be key to the quality of the finished product. Therefore, care and preparation are needed in order to make sure that you allow sufficient time for adequate research.

Key term

Systematic – organised and consistent.

Methods of researching content

Depending upon the nature of the content which you need for your particular document, you can carry out research by the following methods:

- **primary research** – also called field research, usually in the form of interviews and questionnaires
- **secondary research** – also called desk research; involves researching through information which already exists. Secondary research can be either:
  - internal – using information from within the company itself (sales figures, customer feedback, staff data); or
  - external – information in the public domain such as government statistics, or information which can be purchased from specialist market research organisations.

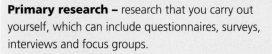

Key terms

Primary research – research that you carry out yourself, which can include questionnaires, surveys, interviews and focus groups.

Secondary research – research which already exists in some form.

Activity 7

Carry out some secondary research of your own by visiting the UK government's website for the Office for National Statistics. Go to www.pearsonhotlinks.co.uk, search for this title and click on the relevant unit. Look through the information available on the website and try to find out what the UK population was first in 1984 and then in 2009. By how much did the population increase over this 25-year period?

Methods of organising content

Depending on the type of document that you are producing, you may choose to organise the content by:

- date
- topic
- department

- deadline for completion
- priority for the business.

For example, if it were a staff newsletter, the most logical way to organise content would be by topic. That way, you could create an interesting and easy-to-read document for the staff. You could further enhance the document with the use of illustrations and photos (we will look at this aspect more closely in the following section on page 177).

If, however, you were producing a meeting agenda for your team or department, you would be more likely to organise the relevant content by business priority, so that the most important issues are scheduled on the agenda ahead of less critical items for discussion. This is done so that, if the meeting overruns, the key issues will have been addressed while the less important issues can wait until the next meeting.

Portfolio task 312.8 → Links to **LO3**: assessment criterion 3.2

Produce a report which describes ways of researching and organising content needed for two different types of business documents. Remember that the research requirements and methods of organising your content need to be tailored to each specific type of document. It may help you to base your answer on two different business documents which you have access to at work. If possible, include copies of each of them with your written answer.

Functional skills

English: Reading

If you carry out research involving reading texts including work-related documents as well as Internet research in order to complete your portfolio task, you may be able to count this as evidence towards Level 2 Functional English: Reading. Remember to keep records of all of the documents, handbooks and guidelines which you study, along with the websites which you visit, as you will need to document any reading research you carry out.

Integrating text with charts, photos and illustrations

Many business documents can be enhanced by the inclusion of non-text elements such as photos and illustrations, as well as graphs, charts and other graphics such as logos.

The reason why non-text elements improve the presentation of the finished document is that they break up what would otherwise be long sections of text and they also add interest, colour and variety – all of which make the document look much more appealing to the reader. In addition, the inclusion of elements such as charts gives the reader an easily understandable visual summary of any figures discussed in the text. Without the inclusion of charts, the information may be more difficult for the reader to interpret.

Laying out text

The main options available to you for laying out your text on the page include the use of:

- font styles and sizes – changing fonts can have a dramatic effect on the look of a document
- styles of headings and subheadings – creative use of heading styles adds emphasis and impact to your document
- paragraphs – breaking up long sections of text into short paragraphs makes your document much easier to read
- columns – altering the number of columns in your document to two or even three creates a different look for the finished document.

Integrating photos and illustrations

Once you have finalised all the text needed for your document (in this instance, a company newsletter), print

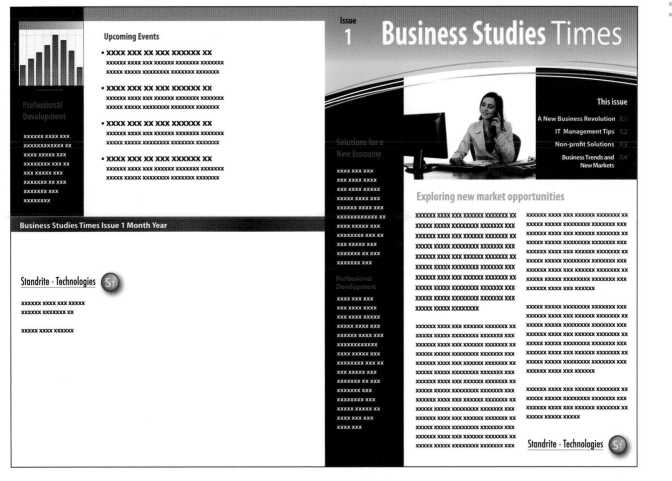

Templates are a useful starting point for company newsletters and can be adapted to include photos and many different design elements

out a draft copy. From this, you can work out where the best positions would be within the document to place photos and illustrations.

For example, if one of your articles was about recent activities within the administration department, a group photo of the administration team would complement the article and would add interest for the reader, as they could then see the staff members on which the article was based. Using one photo or illustration per article is a good rule of thumb for newsletters.

✓ Checklist

Remember, when integrating photos and illustrations into your text:

- First, print out the document.
- Next, look at the text to identify the most appropriate places to insert artwork.
- Finally, print out a draft complete with the artwork and adjust the size and position of photos and illustrations to make sure they fit in with your document's text.

Using word-processing packages to help integrate photos and art

Your word-processing software package comes with features especially designed to help with inserting images and other graphical features directly into your document. Depending on the version and brand of software which you use for word-processing, these may be found in the 'Insert' menu at the top of the screen. From this menu, you can insert:

- photos
- illustrations
- graphs and charts
- text boxes
- links to websites
- headers, footers and page numbers.

Your word-processing package can also perform the following formatting tasks for your images and illustrations.

- Wrapping – this refers to the way in which images are placed within the text, whether they are visible underneath the text (like a watermark) or whether the text flows around the image, as well as the space which is left between the edges of the image and text.
- Sizing – you can resize your images and charts to accommodate the space which you have available on the page.
- Positioning – you can move images from one spot to another in order to get the best presentation effect for your document.

Activity 8

In this activity you will be making your own newsletter template. Go to www.contentextra.com/businessadmin, view the materials that have been provided for this activity and download what you would like to use.

Portfolio task 312.9 → Links to **LO3**: assessment criterion 3.3

Write a short report which describes ways of integrating and laying out text and non-text. Include an example of a document from your own organisation – or else you may like to create a document of your own – which contains text and non-text elements, and say how the two elements were integrated to produce the finished document.

Functional skills

English: Speaking and listening

If your assessor asks you to take part in a discussion about this portfolio task as part of the assessment for this learning outcome, you may be able to count it as evidence towards Level 2 Functional English: Speaking and listening.

Checking finished documents for accuracy

Once you have finished compiling your document, you need to check it thoroughly to make sure it contains no errors before you distribute it to your colleagues. Errors can arise in documents due to:

● incorrect factual information given in articles – relating to dates, times, places and events

● the wrong spelling of people's names and job titles

● incorrect photos used in articles

● poor use of English

● spelling, grammar or punctuation errors.

There are many checks which must be made to the content of a document after it has been written. Each of these checks takes time and effort to complete, but must be carried out to ensure the accuracy of the content. Sending out documents which contain incorrect information or poor English will not reflect well on the person responsible for creating them.

Ways of checking your finished document for accuracy

Some of the checks that you must make to your finished document will involve checking information with the people the article was written about. They can confirm the accuracy of:

● the spelling of names

● job titles

● dates, times, places and events

● photos used in articles.

This process can usually be completed fairly easily by emailing them a draft of the document and asking for any corrections or comments. Always remember to give them a deadline by which they must reply to you, to prevent the completion of your document being delayed.

The other checks which relate to the quality of the writing (spelling, grammar and punctuation) need to be carried out either by yourself, if you are confident with the standard of your own English, or else by another member of staff. This can usually be carried out best by reading the document carefully to check for spelling mistakes, correct use of grammar and punctuation.

It is always better to check for this type of mistake on a printed copy of a document, rather than by reading from a computer screen, as it is well known that errors are more likely to be missed when reading on screen. It is also a very good idea to ask a second person to proofread the document for you, as they may well see errors that you have missed.

Your word-processing software will have an inbuilt spelling- and grammar-checking facility which you can use to help pick out mistakes in your document. However, take great care when using this facility and certainly never rely on it solely, as it will not pick up on certain errors such as the use of:

● 'there' instead of 'their'

● 'form' instead of 'from'

● 'manger' instead of 'manager'.

If you rely totally on the software's spelling- and grammar-checking facility to highlight all errors, mistakes will almost certainly remain in your document. For this reason, you must take the time to read through the document yourself.

✔ Checklist

Remember, when using your word-processing spell check facility:

• Always read the document yourself in addition to using the spell check facility.

• Do not rely on the spell checker to identify all errors.

The purpose of checking your finished document for accuracy

The reasons why it is important to carry out checks on your finished document for accuracy and correctness:

- to maintain the professional image of the organisation – a business document must be free from errors and produced to a high standard
- to avoid embarrassment to yourself and to others by having spelling mistakes and poor punctuation in documents
- to avoid potentially offending staff members or customers by printing incorrect information about them, or misspelling their name.

Portfolio task 312.10 → Links to **LO3**: assessment criterion 3.4

Produce a brief report which describes ways of checking finished documents for accuracy including:

- spelling
- grammar
- punctuation
- factual correctness.

You also need to include a section in your report which outlines the purpose of carrying out these checks on finished documents.

Storing documents safely and securely

Business documents, whether electronic or paper-based, are important items which are needed by the business. For this reason, they need to be stored in a safe and secure manner.

Purpose of storing documents safely and securely

Organisations need to have safeguards in place to guarantee the safety and security of their documents within the business. The reasons for this are as follows.

- Documents may well contain confidential or sensitive data relating to internal business issues which, if lost or stolen, could cause serious damage to the organisation.
- Lack of security and safety procedures means that it would be fairly easy for unauthorised staff to gain access to privileged information.
- Inadequate safety and security procedures for electronic documents would mean that they were at particular risk of attack from computer hackers.
- Loss of security concerning sensitive data constitutes a breach of the Data Protection Act 1998 and could cause the business to be brought before the **information commissioner**.

Key term

Information commissioner – the UK regulator concerned with data protection issues.

Checklist

You can find out more about the work of the UK information commissioner by visiting www.pearsonhotlinks.co.uk and clicking on this unit.

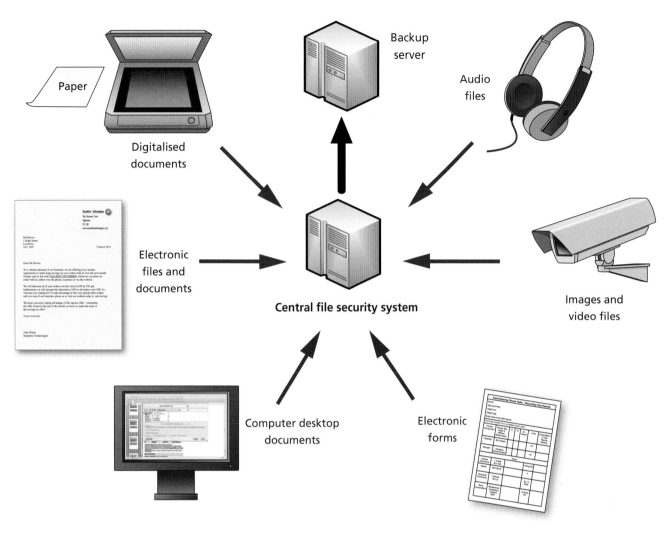

Backup server

Paper

Digitalised documents

Audio files

Electronic files and documents

Central file security system

Images and video files

Computer desktop documents

Electronic forms

Electronic control systems can ensure the safety and security of many different types of electronic resource

Ways of storing documents safely and securely

Safe and secure storage facilities for documents will include provision for both paper-based and electronic formats:

● Paper-based document storage will include lockable and fireproof filing cabinets with strictly controlled staff-access privileges.

● Electronic document storage will include password-protected access to computers, servers and archives where documents are stored. It will also include a back-up facility in order to guard against data loss.

Portfolio task 312.11 ➡ Links to **LO3**: assessment criterion 3.5

Produce a brief report which explains the purpose of storing documents safely and securely. Include a section in your report which describes ways of doing so. Remember to also include in your report any examples of safety and security measures which you are aware of from your own organisation and say why you think they are important.

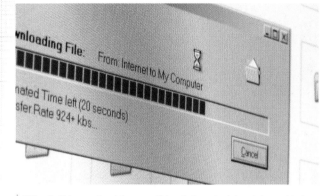

Why is it important for confidential material not to get into the wrong hands?

Confidentiality and data protection when preparing documents

Confidentiality and data protection are two key issues which need to be considered when documents are being prepared.

Confidentiality

You may need to keep documents private when they are being prepared if they contain confidential data relating to the organisation, its staff, customers or suppliers.

Confidential data can include staff salaries, new products in development, proposed mergers or takeovers by other businesses, customer contact lists, and grievance and disciplinary documentation. In fact, any information which, if it fell into the wrong hands, could cause damage to the organisation should be considered as confidential and should be handled very carefully so as not to be made public.

Confidential information should also be subject to special procedures to ensure its safe and secure storage. The organisation must have a policy on ways of dealing with such information and the specific steps which need to be taken by employees responsible for dealing with such types of information in order to ensure its safety and security.

Data protection

Organisations that deal with sensitive data relating to individuals (such as financial or medical information)

must take care to protect this data from being divulged to third parties, whether by accidental loss or by theft.

In fact, the Data Protection Act 1998 states that such organisations must have a security policy in place detailing the steps they will take to ensure the security of all sensitive data that they process as part of their business activities.

Activity 9

Carry out research on data protection. Speak to colleagues and your manager to find out whether the organisation which you work for processes sensitive data and is therefore affected by the Data Protection Act. Ask to be shown any relevant organisational policies which are in place to ensure that staff adhere to the regulations of the Data Protection Act.

Protection of data when preparing documents

Data protection applies to the preparation of business documents in the following ways.

- Any sensitive data relating to individuals which is to be included in documents must be kept secure and safe from unauthorised access.
- Sensitive data must be processed fairly and be kept up to date.
- Data must not be kept for longer than is needed by the organisation.

Portfolio task 312.12 → Links to **LO3**: assessment criterion 3.6

Write a short report which explains the purpose of confidentiality and data protection when preparing documents. Use two examples of documents from your own organisation in order to illustrate your answer and, for each one, say in what way confidentiality and data protection are important in document preparation.

Explain the purpose and benefits of meeting deadlines

Deadlines are the absolute latest times by which a project or task must be completed. The reason why managers in organisations issue deadlines to their staff is that most of the organisation's work is **interdependent**. In other words, for a person or department to be able to do their job effectively and on time, they rely on another person or department to do the same. Delays by one person in completing an element of their work can have huge consequences further down the chain.

What are the advantages of having a 'to do' tick list?

Key term

Interdependent – being dependent on one another.

Purpose of meeting deadlines

Meeting deadlines means completing work by the due date or time. This allows the smooth flow of work through the different departments of the organisation which, in turn, allows the organisation to achieve its wider goals.

The work of an organisation is a constant process and delays in one department can cause **bottlenecks** in another. This disruption in workflow can pass all the way through the organisation, resulting in lower organisational performance than expected, and reduced turnover and profit.

Key term

Bottlenecks – these hold up work flow and cause delays.

To illustrate the importance of this, imagine that a major software company is due to launch its latest software release. The launch will have taken months – or even years – of planning and the business will have invested a very large amount of money in the project. In addition, it will have involved the coordinated work efforts of hundreds of staff from many different departments:

- a team of highly skilled IT programmers to develop the software, test it and ensure it works properly

- marketing staff to generate a successful marketing campaign, making customers aware of the upcoming release and creating the demand for the new product
- sales teams to go out and secure orders for the new release
- production staff to make the CDs and packaging
- distribution staff to make sure the new product reaches its retailers in good time for the release date.

Any delays caused by any one of these departments at any stage of the production process will have consequences down the production flow for everybody else. Such delays may even mean that the scheduled release date must be put back by weeks or even months.

Delay may also mean an advantage to competitors who are able to release their own competing product first and threaten the company's market position.

Benefits of meeting deadlines

When all the staff in a department successfully meet their deadlines, the work of the department is completed on time, which means that output from the organisation meets the planned forecast. This, in turn, allows the wider goals of the organisation to be achieved in terms of production, costs and turnover. This illustrates how the contribution of each and every member of staff impacts upon the performance of the organisation as a whole.

The organisation benefits directly from staff and departments meeting their respective deadlines. It means that:

- workflow is controlled
- schedules run on time
- costs (for example, of extra time and staff needed to deal with delays) are adequately kept under control
- coordination of work with other departments (interdependence) is efficient
- business targets are successfully met.

Portfolio task 312.13 → Links to **LO3**: assessment criterion 3.7

Write a short report which explains the purpose and benefits of meeting deadlines. Use an example of a document which you have worked on in your own organisation in your answer. Say what the benefits were of meeting the deadline for completing the document.

Evidence collection

In order for you to complete the remaining assessment criteria to successfully pass this unit, you will need to carry out various tasks at work and then produce evidence to show that you have demonstrated the required skills and competence.

Evidence can be collected in a number of different ways. For example, it can be in the form of a signed witness testimony from a colleague or line manager, a copy of any related emails or letters you have produced, or a verbal discussion with your assessor.

Speak to your assessor to identify the best methods to use in order to complete each portfolio task and remember to keep copies of all the evidence that you produce.

Be able to design and produce documents to agreed specifications

Portfolio task 312.14 → Links to **LO4**: assessment criteria 4.1, 4.2, 4.3, 4.4, 4.5, 4.6, 4.7, 4.8, 4.9, 4.10 and 4.11

Gather evidence of your work to show your assessor that you have successfully carried out the tasks outlined in the table below. Check with your assessor on the best ways of gathering evidence for each of the tasks before you begin.

Task	Evidence
1 Agree the purpose, content, style and deadlines for documents.	
2 Identify and prepare resources needed to design and produce documents.	

A version of this table, ready for you to complete, is available to download from www.contentextra.com/businessadmin

Check your knowledge

1 Which of these styles would be most appropriate for a memo between two colleagues?

a) Formal and elaborate.

b) Formal and printed in colour with business logos and branding.

c) Informal and highly detailed.

d) Informal and brief.

2 Which of these is a format usually used in meeting agendas?

a) Red text on a black background.

b) A list ordered by presenter and topic.

c) A full-colour brochure.

d) A two-column newsletter template with illustrations.

3 Which of these is a resource typically needed to edit business documents?

a) A word-processing package.

b) An artwork-production package.

c) A game console.

d) A headset.

4 Why is it important to agree the deadline for the production of business documents?

a) To make sure that good grammar is used within the document.

b) To make sure the correct content is covered in the document.

c) To make sure the correct illustrations and photos are included.

d) To ensure that the document is produced by the required time.

5 Why would you need to research content for a business document?

a) To make sure that the document is factually correct.

b) To make sure that the correct style guide is used.

c) To make sure that the best layout is used.

d) To make sure that the most attractive headings are used.

6 Which of these are non-text elements which can be used in business documents?

a) Commas, apostrophes and full stops.

b) Paragraphs.

c) Columns.

d) Photos, illustrations and charts.

7 What is meant by grammar?

a) Remembering to use capitals and full stops.

b) Remembering to use the spell check facility.

c) The rules governing the correctness of words, phrases and sentence structure.

d) The rules about staying within the word count allowed for a document.

8 What is the main purpose of proofreading a document?

a) To make sure that it is produced by the deadline.

b) To make sure that it is the correct orientation.

c) To ensure that lots of illustrations are included in the document.

d) To ensure there are no spelling or grammatical errors in the document.

9 Why is it important to store documents safely and securely?

a) Because they may contain errors.

b) Because they may contain colourful illustrations.

c) Because they need to be kept safe from unauthorised access.

d) Because they may need to be corrected later on.

10 Why do you need to consider confidentiality and data protection when producing business documents?

a) Because the documents may contain formulae.

b) Because the documents may contain sensitive data relating to individuals.

c) Because the documents may contain sales promotion information.

d) Because the documents may contain links to external websites.

Answers to the Check your knowledge questions can be found at www.contentextra.com/businessadmin

Unit Q312

Design and produce documents in a business environment

What your assessor is looking for

In order to prepare for and succeed in completing this unit, your assessor will require you to be able to demonstrate competence in all of the performance criteria listed in the table below.

Your assessor will guide you through the assessment process, but it is likely that for this unit you will need to:

- complete short written narratives or personal statements explaining your answers
- take part in professional discussions with your assessor to explain your answers verbally
- complete observations with your assessor ensuring that they can observe you carrying out your work tasks

- produce any relevant work products to help demonstrate how you have completed the assessment criteria
- ask your manager, a colleague, or a customer for witness testimonies explaining how you have completed the assessment criteria.

Please note that the evidence which you generate for the assessment criteria in this unit may also count towards your evidence collection for some of the other units in this qualification. Your assessor will provide support and guidance on this.

The table below outlines the portfolio tasks which you need to complete for this unit, mapped to their associated assessment criteria.

Task and page reference	Mapping assessment criteria
Portfolio task 312.1 (page 166)	Assessment criterion: 1.1
Portfolio task 312.2 (page 168)	Assessment criterion: 1.2
Portfolio task 312.3 (page 169)	Assessment criterion: 1.3
Portfolio task 312.4 (page 170)	Assessment criterion: 2.1
Portfolio task 312.5 (page 171)	Assessment criterion: 2.2
Portfolio task 312.6 (page 172)	Assessment criterion: 2.3
Portfolio task 312.7 (page 175)	Assessment criterion: 3.1
Portfolio task 312.8 (page 176)	Assessment criterion: 3.2
Portfolio task 312.9 (page 178)	Assessment criterion: 3.3
Portfolio task 312.10 (page 180)	Assessment criterion: 3.4
Portfolio task 312.11 (page 181)	Assessment criterion: 3.5
Portfolio task 312.12 (page 182)	Assessment criterion: 3.6
Portfolio task 312.13 (page 184)	Assessment criterion: 3.7
Portfolio task 312.14 (page 184)	Assessment criteria: 4.1, 4.2, 4.3, 4.4, 4.5, 4.6, 4.7, 4.8, 4.9, 4.10 and 4.11

Unit Q322

Plan and organise meetings

What you will learn

- Understand the arrangements and actions required for planning and organising meetings
- Be able to prepare for a meeting
- Be able to support running a meeting
- How to follow a meeting

Introduction

This unit covers how to plan and organise meetings in the workplace. It also explains how to prepare for meetings, how to support and participate in meetings and how to undertake any follow-up activities.

Planning meetings can be daunting if you have never done it before, but by having a proper process in place you can become quite efficient at it. There are no special skills or knowledge required to plan and arrange meetings; you just need a methodical approach that you can follow every time.

Attending meetings can be quite nerve-racking, especially if it is something that you are doing for the first time. However, by being well prepared for the meeting you should be able to enjoy it and gain additional skills and knowledge along the way.

The arrangements and actions required for planning and organising meetings

After working through this section you will understand and be able to:

- explain the role of the person planning and organising a meeting
- describe the different types of meetings and their main features
- explain how to plan meetings that meet the agreed aims and objectives
- explain the purpose of agreeing a brief for the meeting
- explain how to identify suitable venues for different types of meetings
- outline the main points that should be covered by an agenda and meeting papers
- explain the purpose of meeting attendees' needs and special requirements and providing them with the information required for meetings

- describe the health, safety and security requirements that need to be considered when organising meetings
- explain the purpose and benefits of briefing the chair before a meeting
- explain the purpose of welcoming and providing suitable refreshments to attendees
- describe the types of information, advice and support that may need to be provided during a meeting
- describe the types of problems that may occur during a meeting and how to solve them
- explain what should be included in a record of a meeting and the purpose of ensuring the record is accurate and approved
- explain how to record actions and follow-up
- explain the purpose of collecting and evaluating participant feedback from the meeting
- describe how to agree learning points to improve the organisation of future meetings.

The role of the meeting planner and organiser

Consider your own organisation and think about what would happen if each employee planned their own meetings, but did not record the dates and times and did not inform other people where the meetings would take place. The situation would be chaotic and it is likely that:

- meetings would be impossible to plan and organise
- staff would not know where meetings were being held or when they started
- **resources** would not be used effectively.

> **Key term**
>
> **Resources** – Resources in a business environment can mean many things including: budgets or money available in the organisation; time available; people or staff availability; room or equipment availability.

Many organisations have a diary system in place. This may be a manual diary, usually held in the reception area, or it may be a central electronic diary system. When you are planning and organising meetings, it will be important to know how your organisation books meetings and rooms. An effective diary system can ensure that:

- activities, such as meetings and training events, can be planned and managed effectively
- resources are properly shared; for example, the booking of rooms, using equipment such as laptops or projectors, or utilising catering facilities.

Figure 322.1 below shows Microsoft Outlook, an example of an electronic diary system.

There are no specialist skills or knowledge required when organising meetings. It is important to undertake a logical approach and consider the implications of any actions that you take. By being organised you can plan meetings successfully. If you have a checklist, it is a useful way to make sure that you manage the process well. There is a detailed checklist provided for you on page 208 and also to download to adopt as your own checklist for when you organise meetings.

At the meeting venue

Arrive at the venue early so that you can check everything is in place as you agreed when you booked the room. Check that:

- the furniture layout is correct
- the correct resources and equipment are in place
- the room is clean and tidy and free from any hazards, e.g. trailing cables or steps that are hard to see
- that the lighting is adequate and the room is well ventilated and at an acceptable temperature
- there is adequate access to the room and other parts of the building if required, e.g. for the toilets or in case of evacuation
- there is adequate signage for the meeting attendees to find their way to the meeting room
- the catering arrangements are in place and the timings for refreshment and lunch breaks confirmed if relevant.

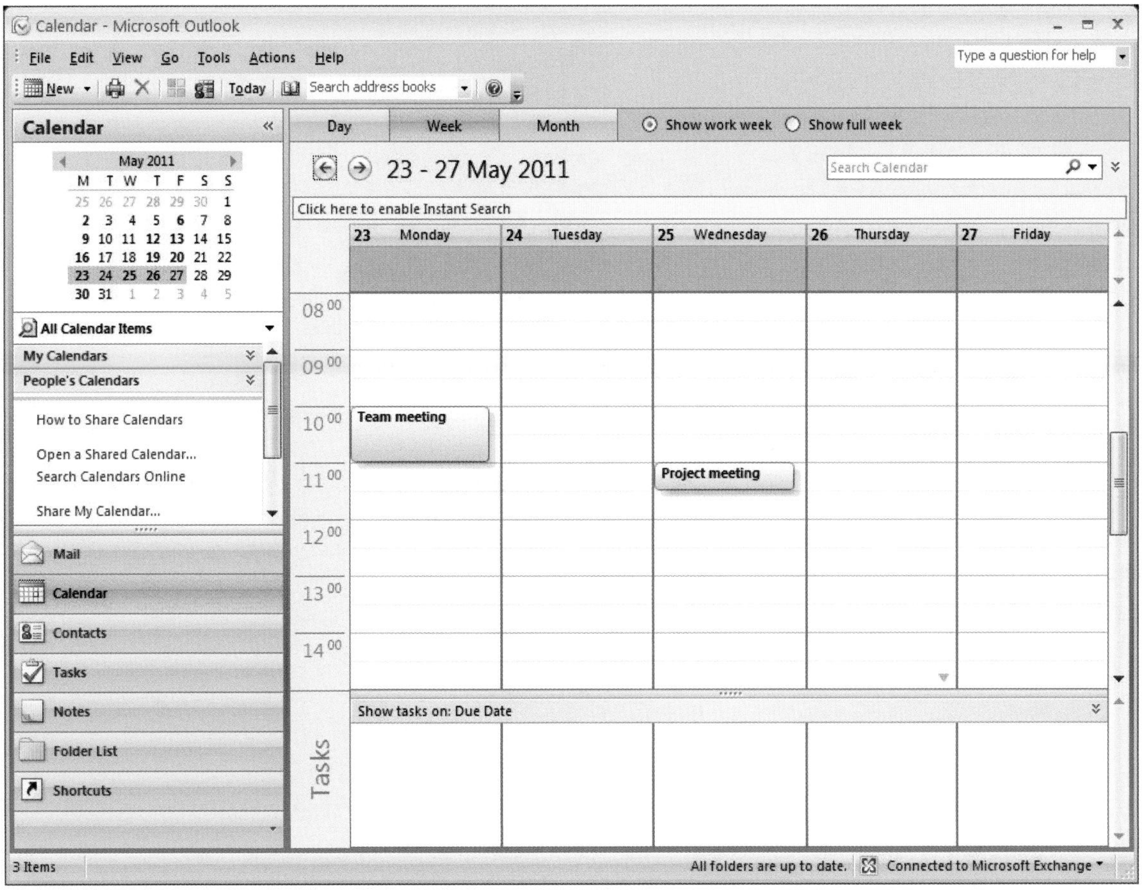

Figure 322.1: *Microsoft Outlook diary system*

Also, ask the person you are liaising with if there is anything else that you need to be aware of. For example, the venue may be planning a fire drill for that day and it is useful to know this type of information. Check whether visitors need to sign in and wear an identification pass.

Once you have checked that all the housekeeping issues are in place, you can then concentrate on making sure that you are well prepared and that all the equipment is working correctly. Decide where you are going to sit; this may be at the head of the table if you are providing a supportive role to the chairperson during the meeting. Put all your paperwork into a logical order as follows:

- Arrange in separate piles spare agendas and reports. This is in case someone arrives without their agenda, and you can quickly pass them a copy without having to look for them or search through some other paperwork.

- Put the files that you have brought with you next to where you are going to be seated. By doing this, if anyone wants some information during the meeting, perhaps relating to the minutes from a previous meeting, you will be able to quickly find the information.

- Place any items for the chairperson next to where they are going to be seated and remember to brief the chairperson before the meeting commences.

- Put any other paperwork or information in a logical order so that you can quickly refer to it if required.

As soon as you have completed sorting the paperwork, you need to check that all the equipment is working correctly. This could involve checking a computer or projector and uploading some files for a presentation. Generally speaking, you will know in advance of the meeting what is happening, but a colleague or perhaps a guest speaker may ask you to upload their presentation to the system. Make sure you know how to do this.

✔ Checklist

Presentations

Remember the following when setting up a presentation:

- Check before the meeting who is responsible for setting up the presentation so that you can refer to them if necessary.

- Make sure that the computer files are in the correct format.

- Check that the disc or memory stick has been virus-checked and that the files are not password-protected.

- Have with you the phone number to hand of an IT specialist back at the office who could help you if you have any difficulties.

Allow plenty of time for checking the presentation equipment as it is quite common to have a few minor problems when setting up presentations, particularly if you are away from your main office.

✔ Checklist

Organising a meeting

When organising a meeting, remember the golden rules:

- Apply a logical and systematic approach.

- Plan well ahead of the meeting date.

- Communicate the relevant information to all the people who are due to attend.

- If any problems arise, use your initiative to propose solutions.

- Book the room, refreshments and other resources, e.g. laptop or flipchart, well in advance of the meeting date.

Portfolio task 322.1 → Links to **LO1**: assessment criterion 1.1

List what resources would be required for a meeting to take place in your organisation.

Types of meetings and their main features

Meetings may be regular; for example, once a week, once a month or once a year. Meetings can also be irregular or organised for a one-off purpose. These are sometimes called ad hoc meetings which are arranged to deal with a specific issue. Examples of the various meetings are as follows:

● a team meeting held on a regular basis each week

● a health and safety committee meeting held each month

● an annual general meeting of a company or organisation which takes place once a year

● an ad hoc meeting arranged to discuss a specific issue; for example, a budget overspend or a new product

● training sessions held regularly or as one-off events.

Some large organisations, for example, local councils, will have a formal structured meeting process in place. The way that these committee meetings operate will be detailed in their written constitution. The constitution will set out how frequently they meet, what powers and responsibilities they have and how the decision-making process is undertaken. Some committees will only have specific powers and may have to refer decisions upwards to another committee; these are sometimes referred to as subcommittees. Other committees may have something called delegated powers, which enables them to make decisions within their remit. Limited companies will detail their committee structures within their 'Articles of Association' legal document.

Subcommittees will report to their main committee, which will then in turn report to the main overarching committee in the organisation; for example, the main board.

Figure 322.2 shows how a college might arrange its committee structure.

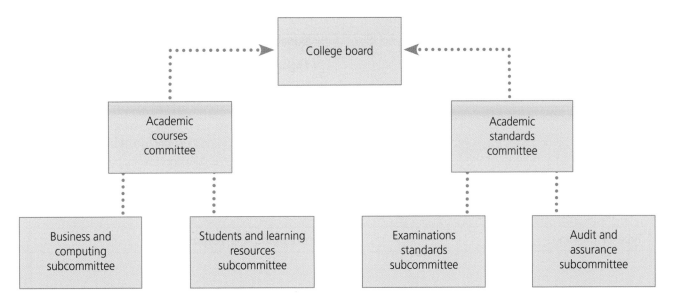

Figure 322.2: *A college committee structure*

Some meetings are formal and some are informal:

Formal meetings include:	Informal meetings include:
• Annual general meetings • Shareholder meetings • Board and committee meetings • Health and safety committee	• Team meetings • Working groups • Progress meetings

Don't worry about remembering whether a meeting is formal or not. The important things to remember are that a meeting will normally have the following features:

- at least two people in attendance
- someone running the meeting – this is the **chairperson**
- an agenda to discuss – this may be unwritten
- someone taking notes or minutes of the meeting
- an **outcome** from the meeting – e.g. a decision taken
- a record of what was said and any action points arising.

Key terms

Chairperson – the person leading a meeting.

Outcome – the decision taken.

It is also worth noting that a meeting can take place between just two people. An annual appraisal meeting would be a formal meeting held once a year between you and your manager.

Planning meetings to meet agreed aims and objectives

Some formal meetings can have written 'terms of reference'. These explain what the committee has been set up for and will also state the frequency of the meetings and details of the chairperson. For informal meetings a process and frequency of meetings will be agreed in advance and a schedule of forthcoming

Portfolio task 322.2

Links to **LO1**: assessment criterion 1.2

Make a list of the different meetings that take place in your organisation and describe their main features and purpose. You need to select three examples.

It may help you to use the table below to gather all the relevant information which you will need for your answer.

Functional skills

English: Reading

If you carry out research involving reading texts including work-related documents in order to complete your portfolio task, you may be able to count this as evidence towards Level 2 Functional English: Reading. Remember to keep records of all the documents, handbooks and guidelines which you study, as you will need to document any reading research you carry out.

Type of meeting	Main features and purpose

A version of this table, ready for you to complete, is available to download from www.contentextra.com/businessadmin

meetings is quite often drawn up. It is also quite common to rotate duties. For example, the minute-taker and chairperson might change from meeting to meeting. This is useful, as it provides additional skills and knowledge for the whole team.

The people who attend a meeting will normally be a chairperson, a minute-taker and the other attendees who will be participating in the meeting.

Meetings can use considerable resources and can be costly to the organisation. Before a new meeting is arranged, it is worth considering if you actually need the meeting at all. Consult with your colleagues and manager to check if there are any alternative ways to resolve the issue. Can the issue be resolved by email, for example?

Portfolio task 322.3 → Links to **LO1**: assessment criterion 1.3

If you were arranging a team meeting, describe what things you would need to consider before you arranged the meeting and sent the agenda out. You may want to record this as part of a professional discussion with your assessor.

Purpose of agreeing a brief for the meeting

A meeting brief sets out in a little more detail what the purpose is of the meeting and what issues need to be discussed during the meeting. By agreeing the brief, the meeting should focus on the specific issues that need to be discussed.

Planning the brief for the meeting forms part of the overall planning process for organising and supporting meetings. This planning stage before the meeting takes place is covered in the checklist later in the unit but, in principle, you need to ensure that you complete the following tasks:

- Check with the meeting **originator** what the purpose of the meeting is.
- Check who needs to be invited to attend.
- Check where the meeting will take place.
- Check what reports or agendas need to be prepared and who is writing them.

Portfolio task 322.4 → Links to **LO1**: assessment criterion 1.4

Explain the purpose of agreeing a brief for a meeting and describe the advantages that this can have. You may want to write this up as a personal statement.

Finding suitable venues for meetings

When you are booking a meeting venue, you will need to consider a number of elements to ensure that the meeting is accessible to all and that the specific needs of those people attending are met. This is sometimes easier when you are arranging a meeting at an external venue, because you are likely to check these elements as part of the booking process. However, try to be just as thorough when you are arranging a meeting at your own office, especially if people are attending who do not work for your organisation. When you arrange a meeting, make sure that you plan it well and inform everyone of the key information.

✓ Checklist

Essential requirements for all attendees to know are:

- the date, venue and time of the meeting
- the car-parking and other transport arrangements
- how long the meeting will last
- whether there will be refreshments or lunch provided
- who the secretary is for the meeting (this might be you).

Key term

Originator – the person who has decided the meeting is necessary (this may be the chairperson, but is not always).

Good housekeeping is critical to the success of a meeting. By planning the meeting and venue well and by making everyone comfortable in a pleasant, well-ventilated room with adequate lighting, you will stand the best chance of everyone enjoying the meeting and the meeting being a success. Always remember that the detail is important, and make sure that you know all the information required.

For example, someone is bound to ask you where the toilets are or where it is possible to smoke or at what time the lunch break will be.

Use the following checklist to help you with the practical elements of booking a meeting venue.

✓ Checklist

Booking meetings

For internal meetings remember to check:

- which meeting rooms you can use
- how to book the room correctly (there may be a central booking system)
- any additional costs in advance, e.g. the cost of the lunch, and agree them with the meeting originator
- that the room is the right size for the number of people attending the meeting.

For external venues remember to check:

- if there is a company policy to always meet at the same venue for external meetings
- that the budget for the event has been agreed with the meeting originator
- the correct procedure for booking the event; you may need to place an official order and get it signed
- the size of room you need – you may need more than one room
- that the room is well lit and adequately ventilated
- that you can have the room layout that you want
- the catering and refreshments arrangements, ensuring that the venue can cater for any special dietary needs
- what resources are available and what equipment needs to be taken to the meeting
- the car-parking arrangements and directions
- whether the venue is near to a railway station
- if overnight accommodation is required for any of the attendees.

Take a common-sense approach and check each element in detail. It may even be worth visiting the venue to check its suitability, especially if it is nearby. Always get confirmation from the venue of the booking.

What equipment is available in this meeting room? Could the layout of the room be improved?

Portfolio task 322.5

→ Links to **LO2**: assessment criterion 1.5

Undertake some research on the Internet and look at the different room layouts that can be used for different types of meetings. Name and draw three different meeting-room layouts and explain what type of meeting you would use each one for and describe the advantages of that particular layout for that type of meeting.

Functional skills

English: Reading

If you carry out research involving reading texts including work-related documents as well as internet research in order to complete your portfolio task, you may be able to count this as evidence towards Level 2 Functional English: Reading. Remember to keep records of all of the documents, handbooks and guidelines which you study, along with the websites which you visit, as you will need to document any reading research you carry out.

The resources needed for different meetings

At a meeting, there will be various resources required to ensure that the meeting takes place smoothly. When arranging a meeting, don't leave anything to chance and double-check things that you are not sure about in advance.

Think of all of the different elements required for your meeting and ask yourself the questions in Table 322.1 below:

Table 322.1: *Preparation for a meeting*

Paperwork	Practical elements	Equipment
Have the agenda and reports been sent out?	Does everyone know about the meeting?	Are the room and layout suitable?
Does any other paperwork need to be taken to the meeting such as spare copies of the previous minutes, the agenda or reports?	Does everyone know about the venue, including directions?	Is the right equipment in place e.g. laptop, flip chart, projector?
Take anything that you think you might need, e.g. list of people attending and their contact details, your phone, pens	Has the chairperson been properly briefed?	Are there adequate pens, paper, sticky notes and water?
	Does the venue meet the relevant health and safety requirements and are access facilities adequate?	

Table 322.2: *Key terms associated with meetings*

Phrases found on an agenda	
Apologies for absence	A note of those people who cannot attend the meeting.
Matters arising	Review of the previous meeting's minutes to check for accuracy and for the chairperson to give any relevant updates.
Reports	The main business of the meeting.
Regular items	Any items that always appear on the agenda; for example, training.
Any other business	The chance for anyone to raise an issue rather than wait for the next meeting.
Other phrases associated with meetings	
Ad hoc meeting	A meeting not within the normal schedule to cover a 'one-off' issue or project.
Quorum	The minimum number of people required for the meeting to take place. If the number falls below this amount, then the meeting is postponed.
Ultra vires	From the Latin 'beyond or outside the powers of'. This means that the decision that a meeting or committee is trying to make is beyond the powers or remit of the committee and they will need to refer the matter to another committee.

Portfolio task 322.6

➡ Links to **LO1**: assessment criteria 1.5 and 1.6

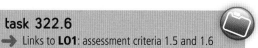

If you were arranging a team meeting, describe what things you would need to consider before you arranged the meeting and sent the agenda out. You may want to record this as part of a professional discussion with your assessor.

An agenda

The success of a meeting is often determined by the way in which it has been organised in advance. The document that is used to inform those people attending the meeting what is going to be discussed is called an agenda.

An agenda provides a framework to ensure that the meeting is undertaken in a methodical and structured way. Agendas follow a fairly standard format and an example is shown in Figure 322.3.

XYZ HEALTHCARE TRUST

HEALTH AND SAFETY COMMITTEE

16th May 2011 – 9.30 a.m., Committee Room 1

AGENDA

1. Apologies for absence
2. Minutes from the last meeting held on 18th April 2011
3. Matters arising from the minutes
4. Report from the health and safety officer
5. Verbal update from the health and safety representatives
6. Health and safety training plan
7. Any other business
8. Date of next meeting

Figure 322.3: *An agenda*

How to write an agenda

As already discussed, the agenda is a key document that will structure the meeting. If you are preparing an agenda for a meeting, make sure that you follow these steps:

● Use the standard 'house' format for the agenda.

● Check the minutes from the last meeting to see whether anything needs to be included on this agenda for the next meeting.

● Contact the chairperson and the other people who normally attend the meeting and ask them whether there are any items they want included on the agenda.

- Agree the final agenda with the chairperson and circulate the agenda and all the relevant paperwork well in advance of the meeting date.

✓ Checklist

The running order of an agenda

- Make sure that the items run in a logical sequence; for example, if there is an item that will affect another item, make sure that they are sequenced in the correct order as the earlier decision may have an impact on a following item.

- Deal with the simple items first before you get on to the main business.

- The main business can be dealt with in two sections, as follows: deal with the items that need input from all attendees first and then deal with any specific items that only need input from one person. By doing this, all those attending the meeting will be engaged in the discussion from the outset and are more likely to participate. When dealing with a specialist item first, there can be a tendency for some people to switch off as it is not relevant to them and then it is difficult to get them engaged and participating in the rest of the meeting.

- Deal with less urgent or less important items at the end of the agenda. Always remember that an item can be deferred to a future meeting if required. Imagine the scenario that you have had a long meeting, but there are still two or three items to deal with – what do you do? It is best practice to defer those items to the next meeting; otherwise you may not give them the time and discussion they deserve.

Your role will be to liaise with the chairperson and support them with the preparation of the agenda and arrange the meeting venue and **housekeeping** issues. Housekeeping can include such things as making sure that the room is tidy and ready before the meeting takes place and also ensuring that all the equipment is in place and that the refreshments have been ordered.

Key term

Housekeeping – Making sure the meeting room is tidy, all the equipment is working and that refreshments are ordered, etc., so that the meeting can run smoothly.

You will also need to ensure that you brief the chairperson before the meeting takes place. This should include any additional information or detail that you are aware of on any of the items on the agenda. An example could be an updated position on some expenditure or a report to reflect the latest proposal. By doing this, you will help the chairperson who can then inform the meeting of the most current information. Additionally, by having this up-to-date information, the chairperson will be better equipped to answer any questions that may arise.

Portfolio task 322.7 → Links to **LO1**: assessment criterion 1.7

Ask your manager if you can prepare the agenda for your next team meeting. This will provide useful evidence for your portfolio.

Meeting attendees' needs and special requirements

When you arrange a meeting, you always need to ensure that the needs of all attendees are met. If you are arranging a meeting in your own organisation, you may for example know about the parking facilities for disabled people. However, for external venues you will need to find out about the following:

- the access facilities for people with disabilities, including the parking arrangements

- whether there is an induction loop available in the meeting room for people with hearing difficulties

- whether the venue is able to provide food or refreshments to meet any special dietary requirements.

You will need to liaise with the venue to clarify these issues and you will also need to communicate this information to all the people who are attending the meeting. You can do this when you send the invitations out. When you send them out, also ask if anyone attending the meeting has any special dietary requests. An example could be:

'As you are aware, the next sales team meeting will be held at the Royal Oak hotel on Wednesday 15th November. Refreshments will be provided from 9.30 a.m. and the meeting will start at 10.00 a.m. prompt. Parking is available at the venue and a lunch of sandwiches and pastries will be provided after the close of the meeting at 1.00 p.m. If you have any special dietary requirements, would you please contact me on extension 4249. Thank you.'

What is the maximum gradient permitted for a wheelchair ramp?

How does an induction loop system work and who might use it?

✓ Checklist

Special requirements

It is important to find out well in advance of the meeting any special requirements attendees might have. Be aware of:

- any specific dietary requirements

- any specific access issues, e.g. are ramps and lifts provided?

- any specific requirements for hearing or sight, e.g. induction loops or large-print materials

- transport issues, e.g. some attendees may require a taxi home or to the train station — you may have to assist in arranging this for them.

Portfolio task 322.8

→ Links to **LO1**: assessment criterion 1.8

Research on the Internet to find out the different requirements needed to meet the needs of people with disabilities. For example, you might want to consider:

*   travel to and from the venue
*   arrangements at the venue itself.

Make a list of the main requirements that you should always meet when arranging a meeting.

Functional skills

English: Reading

If you carry out research involving reading texts including Internet research in order to complete your portfolio task, you may be able to count this as evidence towards Level 2 Functional English: Reading. Remember to keep records of all of the documents and websites which you visit, as you will need to document any reading research you carry out.

Health, safety and security requirements that need to be considered when organising a meeting

Having an effective health and safety system in place provides a framework to ensure that all activities and individuals are properly and adequately safeguarded against any potential hazards and associated risks. This includes customers and visitors who are visiting the organisation's premises.

Keeping your business premises safe, tidy and secure is something that your employer is required to do by law. Under Section 2 of the Health and Safety at Work Act 1974, your employer must 'ensure so far as reasonably practicable, the health, safety and welfare of employees at work'. This includes ensuring that employees are working in the correct temperatures, have enough lighting and ventilation, that they are working in a clean and tidy environment and that their health and safety is not compromised.

In respect of organising a meeting, you will need to ensure that the people who are attending the meeting do not have their health and safety compromised and that the organisation's security is adequate to protect the individual and the organisation. Use the following checklist to help you.

✓ Checklist

Health, safety and security issues when arranging a meeting

Ensure:

*   all people attending the meeting sign in at the front desk/reception
*   all people are made aware of the evacuation routes in the event of an emergency
*   all people are made aware of the welfare facilities available on site including where they can get a drink and where the toilets are
*   all people are made aware of any planned fire alarm tests or drills
*   all rooms that may contain confidential information or may pose a risk to a visitor are locked
*   all people are escorted around the building by a member of staff.

Portfolio task 322.9

→ Links to **LO1**: assessment criterion 1.9

Think about a meeting that you recently arranged and use the checklist above to see if you followed all the procedures. Also, can you think of anything else that you need to consider? You may want to record this as part of a professional discussion with your assessor.

Plan and organise meetings Unit Q322

Unit Q322 Plan and organise meetings

The purpose and benefits of briefing the chair before a meeting takes place

Before the meeting commences, it is important to undertake a briefing with the chairperson. This needs to be arranged in advance and often takes place one or two days before the meeting takes place.

At this briefing, you will be able to provide the chairperson with any relevant information. This might include:

- apologies for absence (people who are unable to attend)
- an update on any new information or issues that have recently arisen
- an update on any potential problems or awkward or contentious issues – you may even need to draft a response for the chairperson to consider
- a note of any new attendees
- any information relating to the next proposed meeting, e.g. agenda items or the date
- any specific things that you want the chairperson to mention.

The chairperson can then make any relevant notes on their copy of the agenda to assist them as they work through the meeting to make sure that the meeting runs smoothly. They will also include a provisional time allocation for each item.

The chairperson has an important role to undertake and, if the meeting is going to be structured and successful, it is essential that the chairperson:

- makes sure the meeting starts on time
- is well prepared and understands the purpose of the meeting and the anticipated outcomes
- introduces new members of staff to the rest of the group
- allows only one person to speak at once
- encourages input from all the people attending the meeting
- is able to summarise the discussion at the end of each item
- reaches a decision and agrees an action point or outcome.

Checklist

Attributes of a successful chairperson

A successful chairperson needs to be well-prepared, diplomatic, assertive and an effective communicator. They will be:

- well-prepared before the meeting and be able to clarify the exact purpose of the meeting
- comfortable that there is adequate business for the meeting to take place and that the key people will be in attendance
- able to manage the meeting effectively including encouraging discussion, challenging people, confirming actions and summarising information including the agreed decisions and responsibilities
- able to review the meeting, evaluate progress and check if the outcomes have been achieved.

Portfolio task 322.10 → Links to **LO1**: assessment criterion 1.10

Describe what information you would pass to the chairperson prior to a meeting taking place. Explain the importance of each piece of information and how it would ensure that the meeting was successful.

Welcoming attendees to a meeting

Once the room is set up correctly, be ready to welcome attendees arriving in the reception area. Introduce yourself and put them at ease by asking them about their journey, for example. Make sure you are well prepared to answer any questions, such as where the toilets are, or if there is a lift to the meeting room, or what time the meeting is expected to finish.

Don't leave things to chance. Finding out information at the last minute or out of the blue can be stressful; a successful meeting is more likely when everyone feels comfortable and relaxed.

Why is it important to provide refreshments at the right time and in the right place?

Portfolio task 322.11 → Links to **LO1**: assessment criterion 1.11

Ask your assessor to observe you welcoming attendees to a meeting. You may also chair or take the minutes during the meeting and this will also provide really useful evidence for your portfolio and your assessor will be able to cross-reference any other relevant assessment criteria.

The information, advice and support needed during a meeting

Once everyone has arrived, the meeting should be opened by you or the chairperson by announcing any general housekeeping issues. As a guide, the following announcements should be made.

- 'Please make sure that your mobile phones are switched off.'

- 'There are no fire drills planned for today, but if you do hear the fire alarm sounding, please follow me and I will escort you all out of the building. The muster point is in the car park at the front of the building.'

- 'The meeting today is likely to last until around 3.00 p.m., but we will have a short break at 10.30 a.m. and we will stop for lunch at 12 noon.'

- 'I will circulate an attendance list for you all to sign, please.'

As already discussed, the chairperson has an important role to undertake if the meeting is going to be structured and successful.

In terms of your role, you need to be clear with the chairperson what support they require and what your specific role will be. Your role might be to make a formal

Does it look like a successful meeting is taking place here?

record of the meeting (taking the minutes). You should also have a good general awareness of what is going on in the meeting; for example, be aware of people who are signalling to you that they want to speak. Make a note of their name and then gesture to the chairperson that this person wants to speak. During a busy meeting you may get several people wanting to speak on the same item and it will be important that you record their names in order and then cross each one off once they have spoken.

Portfolio task 322.12
→ Links to **LO1**: assessment criteria1.12 and 1.13

Ask your assessor to observe you providing advice or support during a meeting. This will provide useful evidence for your portfolio and your assessor will be able to cross-reference any other relevant assessment criteria.

The problems that might occur during a meeting

By applying a practical and well-organised approach, there is less chance of things going wrong in a meeting. If you plan well, then you have done as much as you can to ensure that the meeting is a success. At the start of the meeting, it needs to be agreed who is doing what; who is organising the refreshments, who is minute-taker, who is advising the chairperson, etc., as it may be difficult for you to do everything.

Sometimes, it is agreed that the minutes will be taken by different people on a rota basis, which works well as the responsibility does not always fall on one person and it also allows for more people to gain the relevant knowledge and skills in minute-taking. This approach works well for team meetings. The main disadvantage is that because different people are preparing the minutes, you can lose some consistency and the standard, detail and accuracy can vary. For formal meetings at a large organisation, it is normal for the same person to always take the minutes, such as the company secretary.

Most meetings run very smoothly, particularly if they are in your own offices and are with colleagues that you work with on a regular basis. However, you do need to be prepared to expect the unexpected. The following considers some scenarios and gives tips on how to resolve the difficulty.

- About five minutes before the meeting is due to start, three people have not turned up. You start to panic and begin making urgent phone calls. Then you remember that these same three people are always late for every meeting. In the future, make sure that you phone these people the day before and remind them of the meeting and reiterate the importance of everyone being there on time and starting the meeting promptly.

- Part way through the meeting, people start to wander into the room and look surprised that your meeting is taking place. The room has clearly been 'double-booked' and you will need to check if any other rooms are available for you. The worst case scenario is that you would need to adjourn the meeting for a short while or postpone until another day. The double-booking may not have been your fault, but it is always worth checking that the booking is in the diary either the day before or on the morning of the meeting.

● Someone in the meeting is insisting on repeating old arguments relating to a decision that was made months ago. They are also jumping to conclusions and interrupting everyone. Try to remain calm and keep the meeting flowing by working with the chairperson to give everyone a chance to participate. Ultimately, it is the chairperson's responsibility to keep control of the meeting. It is likely that the chairperson will speak to the person after the meeting and ask them to be more professional in their conduct at future meetings.

Portfolio task 322.13 → Links to **LO1**: assessment criterion 1.13

Ask your assessor to observe you helping to solve problems during a meeting.

Recording the meeting and making sure the record is accurate

Minutes are the definitive record of what happened at a meeting. The minutes must always be an accurate and **unbiased** record of the meeting. There are two main types of minutes:

● Verbatim minutes – this means a 'word-for-word' account of the meeting. These are used in some very specific situations; for example, a parliamentary debate or a public inquiry. These types of minutes are not used in a normal business environment.

● Narrative minutes – these are a detailed summary of the discussions that took place. It is also common to include an action column on the minutes to identify whose responsibility it is to action what was agreed.

Key term

Unbiased – something that is not influenced by anyone's opinions or desires.

✓ Checklist

Minutes

How to take accurate minutes of a meeting:

• Be prepared – have plenty of paper to hand, understand what is on the agenda and the types of things that will be discussed. Put subheadings on your notes of all the agenda items and leave plenty of space to record the discussion. If you are recording the minutes electronically, make sure the laptop is on and ready to use and has enough battery life if it is not plugged into the mains.

• Listen to what is being said – this sounds straightforward, but it is not always easy to follow carefully exactly the course of the discussion. You will need to concentrate and be objective in your summary of the discussion – state what was said and not your interpretation or own viewpoint. Work with the chairperson to get the group to agree a summary of the discussion and any decision or actions agreed.

• Summarise the main points and get used to writing abbreviations for names and main points. For example, if you are constantly referring to the chairperson, you could use the abbreviation 'Ch said…'.

• Don't worry if you miss something out. There are other people at the meeting who you can speak to afterwards. Either leave a gap in your minutes or maybe use a highlighter to remind you to clarify what was said at the end of the meeting. The chairperson will also be able to assist you with any issues.

• Always write minutes in the past tense as you are referring to something that has already happened. Use words like 'said', 'explained', 'gave', 'discussed', etc. An example would be 'David explained how the system worked.'

• Write up minutes as soon as possible after the meeting has taken place as all the information will be fresh in your mind.

• Use sentences rather than bullet points, if that is your house style, and use clear plain English that can be understood by all.

Minutes of a meeting should always include the date and time of the meeting, who attended, who sent their apologies, a record of items discussed and the date and time of the next meeting.

It is important to write up minutes for all meetings even if they are informal. The benefits of minutes enable:

● progress on particular issues to be tracked

● you and your team to demonstrate how they manage and improve performance

● the team to be informed even if colleagues miss meetings.

The layout and style of minutes will vary between organisations. Your team or organisation may well have its own house style. Figures 322.4 and 322.5 show two different styles, an informal and formal style respectively.

TEAM MEETING MINUTES

27th January 2011

Present:
Janet Staunton (chairperson)
John James, Sunil Patel, Nigel Dawson and Rachel Singleton

1. Apologies were received from Jolene Hart

2. New sales leads
The number of new sales leads were noted as follows:

- Jolene 9 + 2 new leads pending
- Janet 18
- Nigel 21
- Rachel 18

Janet explained an issue with a sales lead in Stoke whom she had difficulty contacting.

Agreed:
It was agreed that Nigel would attempt to contact the sales lead in Stoke in the next few days.

3. New brochure
Rachel gave an update on the new sales brochure and handed round a draft version. The team discussed the brochure and passed comments back to Rachel.

Agreed:
It was agreed that Rachel would take on board all the comments received and would incorporate them into the final brochure.

4. Sales targets for 2011/12
Each member of the team gave a verbal update on their progress to date.

Agreed:
It was agreed that Sunil would formalise the targets and agree them with each team member at the forthcoming appraisal meetings.

5. Interviews for new sales representatives
John explained that the proposed interviews had been delayed and they would now take place in mid-February.

Date of next meeting: 24th February 2011

Figure 322.4: *An informal set of minutes*

Minute No.	NORTHERNFLEET COLLEGE OF FURTHER EDUCATION	Action
	Minutes from the health and safety subcommittee held on Tuesday 8th March 2011, in room G45, 2 p.m. to 3.30 p.m. PRESENT: Jean Wilkinson (chairperson) Paul Edwards (secretary) Jason Poulter Joan Smith Janet Stevens Peter Tomlinson	
2011/10	1. Apologies were received from James Probert	
2011/11	2. Minutes of the last meeting The minutes of the meeting held on 3rd February 2011, previously circulated, were approved as a correct record.	PE
2011/12	3. Matters arising In respect of the boiler on the ground floor, Janet Stevens stated that this was still causing problems. Peter Tomlinson said that two of his engineers had been working on the boiler this morning and he understood that the boiler was now working correctly.	
2011/13	4. Accident statistics Jean Wilkinson stated that there had been no reportable accidents and only two minor accidents since the last meeting in February.	
2011/14	5. Review of the health and safety policy Jean Wilkinson presented a detailed report explaining the up-to-date position in relation to the annual review of the health and safety policy. She outlined that the review was now complete and recommended that the subcommittee accept the new policy with the minor amendments as agreed. **Agreed:** It was agreed that the new health and safety policy be accepted and presented for formal approval to the next academic standards committee meeting on 5th May 2011.	JW / PE
2011/15	6. Risk assessment updates Paul Edwards distributed to the group his up-to-date risk assessments. He explained that he would now implement these and provide the relevant training to staff. **Agreed:** It was agreed that Paul Edwards would implement the new risk assessments in his section and undertake the relevant training to his staff and ensure that safe systems of work were in place throughout the whole section by 31st May 2010.	PE
2011/16	7. Any other business Jean Wilkinson stated that the new health and safety adviser (Samira Mahmoud) would be commencing her employment with the College in early June. Jason Poulter formally wanted to thank James Probert (absent) for his recent assistance in relation to the final resolution of the parking issues at the front of the building.	
2011/17	Date of next meeting – 19th May 2011 The date was noted and agreed by all attendees. Joan Smith gave advance notice of her apologies for this meeting.	

Figure 322.5: *A formal set of minutes*

Portfolio task 322.14 → Links to **LO1**: assessment criterion 1.14

If you have never taken the minutes at a meeting, try it out. Ask your manager if you can sit in on a meeting and record the minutes, or maybe ask if you can take the minutes at your next team meeting. Also, explain what should be included in the record of a meeting and how you ensure that the record is accurate and is approved.

An accurate record of the meeting

Circulate the draft minutes to the chairperson to check for accuracy and for their comments. Also, dependent on the process that you have in place, you may need to circulate the minutes to other colleagues who attended the meeting for them to check accuracy. You may also need to speak to the chairperson to point out any specific, complicated or controversial parts of the minutes. They may then assist you in providing a diplomatic phrase or wording.

Once you have circulated the draft minutes and comments have been received back, you can make the relevant changes. It is also a good idea to then let the chairperson have a brief final check to confirm that they are happy that the minutes reflect a true and accurate record of the meeting. You can then circulate the minutes to all the people who attended the meeting (and also to anyone who sent their apologies to the meeting – they need a copy of the minutes as well). It might be easiest to do this by email and you can remind them of the date of the next meeting at the same time and also ask them to forward you any agenda items that they may have for the next meeting.

Recording actions and following up

An agenda helps to structure the sequence and proposed content of a meeting. The minutes agree what was discussed and list the action points arising from the meeting. What was agreed is often recorded as 'agreed by' and any relevant 'action' can also be recorded either on a separate action list or as another column in the minutes.

You will have noticed that the formal minutes shown in Figure 322.5 have an action column included in them. At the meeting it would have been agreed who would be undertaking the relevant actions and their initials would be put by the item. It is normal for the person who is nominated as the secretary for the meeting to manage this process – this could be part of your role. You could also try to ensure that these actions are completed within the timescales agreed. You could ask your colleagues to email you once they have completed their action. If it gets near to the next meeting and you haven't heard whether they have actioned the task, you will need to chase them up to find out what is happening.

Portfolio task 322.15 → Links to **LO1**: assessment criterion 1.15

Explain why it is important to record action points and to follow them up. Find a copy of some minutes from a meeting that took place in your organisation and identify some action points and find out if the action points have been followed up. This will provide useful evidence for your portfolio. This can be any type of meeting, but preferably a meeting which you attended.

Collecting and evaluating participant feedback from a meeting

In order to constantly improve, it is important to reflect on your experiences and think about what you can do better next time. By improving your performance, you should become more efficient in your role. Again, always remember that not everything is within your control. For example, if you booked a buffet lunch for a meeting and had written confirmation of the booking, but the lunch did not turn up, this is not your fault. It may be that the company had forgotten to put it on their schedule. In this situation it is impossible to make alternative arrangements and all you can do is apologise to the people at the meeting. However, you can reflect on whether you should use a different, more reliable catering service in the future.

You can review and reflect on the meeting in two different ways:

● Personal reflection — think back to a meeting that you have attended recently and ask yourself the following questions:

- What were the objectives of the meeting and were they achieved?
- How well did the chairperson manage the meeting?
- How did I do during the meeting?
- What were the best and worst aspects of the meeting?
- Overall, was the meeting successful?
- What can I do better next time?

By working through these questions, you will quickly establish your 'overall experience' and you will be able to identify any areas for improvement. If you have some areas for improvement, you might want to include them in your personal development plan, which is a key part of this qualification and is covered in more detail in Unit Q302.

● Formal feedback — For a large meeting, perhaps held at an external venue, it is sometimes useful to get the views of your colleagues. You could do this by sending everyone who attended the meeting an email or a brief questionnaire. Then, once you have received the feedback, you can summarise it and identify any improvements for next time. Your manager may be interested to see the feedback and suggestions too.

Some large conference centres and hotels have their own questionnaires and you may be able to utilise these and ask for a copy from the venue. If not, you can devise your own brief questionnaire with questions such as the following.

- Was the room tidy and comfortable in terms of heating, lighting and ventilation?
- Was the venue good for access and parking?
- Did the venue meet the needs of any special requirements that you had?
- Were the welcome arrangements, reception and signage adequate?

- Were the refreshments and lunch arrangements adequate?
- Was the meeting too long or too short?
- Would you want us to use this venue for future events?

Portfolio task 322.16 → Links to **LO1**: assessment criterion 1.16

Research using the Internet examples of feedback forms and design a feedback form for use in your organisation.

Functional skills

English: Reading

If you carry out research involving reading texts including work-related documents as well as Internet research in order to complete your portfolio task, you may be able to count this as evidence towards Level 2 Functional English: Reading. Remember to keep records of all of the documents, handbooks and guidelines which you study, along with the websites which you visit, as you will need to document any reading research you carry out.

Agreeing learning points to improve the organisation of future meetings

For any activity that you undertake in an office environment, it is a good idea to reflect on your experiences and try to improve for next time. Also, ask your colleagues for feedback. 'How did I do?' 'What could I do that would make it better for next time?'

You don't need any specific skills or knowledge to be able to plan and organise meetings, but you do need to be well-organised, have a methodical approach and plan all the elements well in advance. If you do this, things should run smoothly.

Figure 322.6 provides a brief summary to ensure that any problems can be resolved for all future meetings:

Before the meeting
Did I circulate all the paperwork, inform all attendees, book the room and brief the chairperson?
Was there anything that I did not do?

↓

At the meeting
Did the meeting run smoothly?
Were there any aspects that could be improved for next time?

↓

Follow-up activities
Were the minutes and the action list agreed by all attendees?
What needs to be done for the next meeting?

Figure 322.6: *A flow chart showing a summary of the tasks performed before, during and after a meeting*

Take time after the meeting to reflect on what went well and what needs improving for next time. Consider all elements including the venue, the paperwork and the refreshments.

Portfolio task 322.17 → Links to **LO1**: assessment criterion 1.17

Think about a meeting that you have recently organised. Consider what went well and what could be improved for next time. Prepare a personal statement or a reflective account to explain what action points you intend to complete to ensure that the next meeting that you organise is better.

✔ Checklist

How to plan, organise and support meetings – a summary

Before the meeting:

- Check the meeting brief – what is the purpose of the meeting?
- Identify a suitable venue, date and time for the meeting.
- Deal with any specific requirements for the meeting.
- Communicate the relevant details of the meeting to all the people who will be attending.
- Check who is formulating the agenda and check who is preparing the reports and coordinate this.
- Send out the agenda and reports.
- Book the room and all of the resources required including any equipment and refreshments needed.
- Confirm the booking just before the meeting is due to take place.
- Brief the chairperson prior to the meeting.

During the meeting:

- Make sure that the meeting starts on time.
- At the start of the meeting, communicate the housekeeping arrangements.
- Have all the information to hand including spare copies of the agenda and reports and copies of the old minutes for reference.
- Work closely with the chairperson and provide them with a high level of support as required.
- If you are taking the minutes, ensure that they are a true and accurate record of the meeting.

After the meeting:

- Prepare the draft minutes in your agreed house style.
- Circulate the minutes for comments.
- Evaluate the meeting and identify any improvements for next time.
- Follow up any action points with the relevant person.
- Prepare, plan and organise the next meeting in good time.

Evidence collection

In order for you to complete the remaining assessment criteria to successfully pass this unit, you will need to carry out various tasks at work and then produce evidence to show that you have demonstrated the required skills and competence.

Evidence can be collected in a number of different ways. For example, it can be in the form of a signed witness testimony from a colleague or line manager, a copy of any related emails or letters you have produced or a verbal discussion with your assessor.

Speak to your assessor to identify the best methods to use in order to complete each portfolio task and remember to keep copies of all the evidence that you produce.

Be able to prepare for a meeting

Portfolio task 322.18

→ Links to **LO2**: assessment criteria 2.1, 2.2, 2.3, 2.4, 2.5, 2.6, 2.7 and 2.8

Gather evidence of your work to show your assessor that you have successfully carried out the tasks outlined in the table below. Check with your assessor on the best ways of gathering evidence for each of the tasks before you begin.

Task	Evidence collected
1 Agree and prepare the meeting brief, checking with others if required.	
2 Agree a budget for the meeting if required.	

A version of this table, ready for you to complete, is available to download from www.contentextra.com/businessadmin

Be able to support running a meeting

Portfolio task 322.19

→ Links to **LO2**: assessment criteria 3.1, 3.2, 3.3 and 3.4

Gather evidence of your work to show your assessor that you have successfully carried out the tasks outlined in the table below. Check with your assessor on the best ways of gathering evidence for each of the tasks before you begin.

Task	Evidence collected
1 Welcome attendees and offer suitable refreshments (if required).	
2 Make sure attendees have a full set of papers.	

A version of this table, ready for you to complete, is available to download from www.contentextra.com/businessadmin

How to follow a meeting

Portfolio task 322.20

→ Links to **LO2**: assessment criteria 4.1, 4.2, 4.3, 4.4, 4.5, 4.6 and 4.7

Gather evidence of your work to show your assessor that you have successfully carried out the tasks outlined in the table below. Check with your assessor on the best ways of gathering evidence for each of the tasks before you begin.

Task	Evidence collected
1 Produce a record of the meeting.	
2 Seek approval for the meeting record and amend as required.	

A version of this table, ready for you to complete, is available to download from www.contentextra.com/businessadmin

Office life

Phil's story

My name is Phil Evans and I'm 23. I'm a human resource assistant in a housing trust in Sheffield where I arrange training events for staff. After the last 'away day' event for 150 people, I received some negative feedback about some problems with the conference venue.

I thought I should arrange a meeting with my manager, Sue, in order to discuss the issues raised. I prepared a detailed list of the problems my colleagues had raised and some of my own concerns. I also did some Internet research to see if there were any other suitable venues nearby.

Sue was pleased with all the information and impressed that I had researched some other suitable venues. We agreed that I would provide her with some more detailed information and costs on the new locations and have a further meeting to make a decision on whether to change venue.

I decided to write a checklist of things to do as follows.

- Visit possible new venues to check suitability.
- Create a comparison of costs for existing venue against proposed new venues.
- Phone the existing venue to discuss the problems raised, possible improvements or a discount for future events.
- Analyse the information, prepare a report and arrange a meeting with Sue.

Ask the expert

Q I have to find a meeting venue for 100 people to take place next month. What do I need to do?

A Gather as much information as you can from the meeting originator and make sure you are clear about the type of meeting that is going to take place.

You should check:

- the location, date and time of meeting
- the overall budget and projected costs
- availability of relevant resources and equipment
- the car-parking arrangements
- access facilities for people with disabilities
- size and layout of the room
- if overnight accommodation is available if required

Once you have gathered all the information, report back to the meeting originator.

Top tips

Phil received verbal feedback from his colleagues which implied there were no written processes in place. Phil could put a system in place, e.g. a short questionnaire, to get feedback after all training events and ensure any comments were dealt with appropriately.

Phil did well to make a checklist. This demonstrated he had thought about everything and started a structured process to try to find a solution.

When Phil goes out to the venues he could ask for contact details for other organisations that have used the venue. He could then contact them to ask for their feedback.

Can you think of anything else that Phil could have done better?

Unit Q322 Plan and organise meetings

Check your knowledge

1 What is the role of a chairperson?

a) To manage and lead the meeting.

b) To take the minutes.

c) To book the room and liaise with other staff.

d) To check if the budget is in place.

2 Who is the meeting originator?

a) The person who takes the minutes.

b) The person who has decided the meeting is necessary.

c) The person who actions all of the outcomes.

d) The person who checks all the minutes.

3 What does a meeting brief set out?

a) The time expected to complete the meeting.

b) Who is going to do what.

c) Plans for change.

d) The details and purpose of the meeting.

4 What does a meeting agenda set out?

a) The budget proposals.

b) How the issues are going to be agreed.

c) What is going to be discussed at the meeting.

d) The planned resources.

5 What is an annual general meeting?

a) A formal meeting held once a year.

b) An informal meeting held on an ad hoc basis.

c) A formal monthly meeting.

d) An informal meeting held once a month.

6 Which of the following resources may be required to run a meeting?

a) Staff/personnel.

b) Computer equipment.

c) A room.

d) All of the above.

7 What does 'ultra vires' mean?

a) Making sure the decision is right.

b) Beyond or outside the powers of.

c) Voting on a decision.

d) The way that the decision is made.

8 What does 'quorum' mean?

a) Helping out with tasks in your team.

b) Working with another team to gain additional skills.

c) The minimum number of people required for the meeting to take place.

d) Shadowing a team member to learn about their job.

9 At what stage of a meeting should you deal with 'apologies for absence'?

a) Anytime during the meeting as it arises.

b) After the meeting has taken place.

c) At the end of the meeting.

d) At the beginning of the meeting.

10 When organising a meeting, what health and safety issues should you consider?

a) Ensuring that the people who are attending the meeting do not have their health and safety compromised.

b) Meeting the attendees at the reception.

c) Planning all the resources effectively.

d) Ensuring that you issue an agenda for the meeting.

Answers to the Check your knowledge questions can be found at www.contentextra.com/businessadmin

What your assessor is looking for

In order to prepare for and succeed in completing this unit, your assessor will require you to be able to demonstrate competence in:

- planning, organising and preparing for meetings
- supporting and running meetings and also undertaking action points arising from meetings.

You will demonstrate your skills, knowledge and competence through the four learning outcomes in this unit. Evidence generated in this unit will also cross-reference to the other units in this qualification.

Please bear in mind that there are significant cross-referencing opportunities throughout this qualification and you may have already generated some relevant work to meet certain criteria in this unit. Your assessor will provide you with the exact requirements to meet the standards of this unit. However, as a guide it is likely that for this unit you will need to be assessed through the following methods:

- one observation of relevant workplace activities to cover the whole unit
- at least one witness testimony to be produced

- a written report or reflective account
- a professional discussion could be undertaken
- any relevant work products to be produced as evidence.

The work products for this unit could include:

- a diary entry or a meeting that you have booked
- research that you have undertaken for prices and availability of meeting venues
- emails that you have sent confirming or arranging a meeting
- a copy of an agenda that you have prepared or assisted with
- a copy of any minutes that you have produced.

Your assessor will guide you through the assessment process as detailed in the candidate logbook. The portfolio tasks cover the knowledge and understanding elements for this unit and the evidence will provide the remaining requirements to complete this unit. The detailed assessment criteria are shown in the candidate logbook.

Unit Q322 Plan and organise meetings

Task and page reference	Mapping assessment criteria
Portfolio task 322.1 (page 191)	Assessment criterion: 1.1
Portfolio task 322.2 (page 192)	Assessment criterion: 1.2
Portfolio task 322.3 (page 193)	Assessment criterion: 1.3
Portfolio task 322.4 (page 194)	Assessment criterion: 1.4
Portfolio task 322.5 (page 195)	Assessment criterion: 1.5
Portfolio task 322.6 (page 196)	Assessment criterion: 1.6
Portfolio task 322.7 (page 197)	Assessment criterion: 1.7
Portfolio task 322.8 (page 199)	Assessment criterion: 1.8
Portfolio task 322.9 (page 199)	Assessment criterion: 1.9
Portfolio task 322.10 (page 200)	Assessment criterion: 1.10
Portfolio task 322.11 (page 201)	Assessment criterion: 1.11
Portfolio task 322.12 (page 202)	Assessment criterion: 1.12
Portfolio task 322.13 (page 203)	Assessment criterion: 1.13
Portfolio task 322.14 (page 206)	Assessment criterion: 1.14
Portfolio task 322.15 (page 206)	Assessment criterion: 1.15
Portfolio task 322.16 (page 207)	Assessment criterion: 1.16
Portfolio task 322.17 (page 208)	Assessment criterion: 1.17
Portfolio task 322.18 (page 209)	Assessment criteria: 2.1, 2.2, 2.3, 2.4, 2.5, 2.6, 2.7 and 2.8
Portfolio task 322.19 (page 210)	Assessment criteria: 3.1, 3.2, 3.3 and 3.4
Portfolio task 322.12 (page 210)	Assessment criteria: 4.1, 4.2, 4.3, 4.5, 4.6 and 4.7

Deliver, monitor and evaluate customer service to internal customers

What you will learn

- Understand the meaning of internal customer
- Know the types of products and services relevant to internal customers
- Understand how to deliver customer service that meets or exceeds internal customer expectations
- Understand the purpose of quality standards and timescales for delivering customer service
- Understand how to deal with internal customer service problems
- Understand how to monitor and evaluate internal customer service and the benefits of this
- Be able to build positive working relationships with internal customers
- Be able to deliver customer services to agreed quality standards and timescales
- Be able to deal with internal customer service problems and complaints
- Be able to monitor and evaluate customer services to internal customers

Introduction

This unit is about providing good service to your internal customers. You will learn who your internal customers are, as well as investigating the sorts of products and services which these customers need.

Delivering a level of customer service that meets or exceeds the expectations of internal customers is a key requirement in many organisations and you will look at ways in which you can achieve this in your own role.

Working to quality standards is an integral part of providing good customer service and you will investigate the quality standards that relate to your own work as well as that of your organisation.

You will also look into the types of problems that may be experienced by internal customers as well as ways in which these problems can be effectively resolved.

Monitoring and evaluating internal customer service is an essential aspect of quality control in the organisation. You will look at different techniques which can be used to monitor and evaluate service standards, along with the benefits of this for the organisation.

Understanding internal customers

After working through this section you will understand and be able to:

● describe what is meant by internal customers
● identify internal customers within your own organisation.

Who are internal customers?

Customers are people or organisations which purchase goods and services from sellers such as shops and suppliers. As individuals we are all customers. Think about all the things you have purchased this week. If you were to write a list of all your purchases, you would probably be surprised at how much you have bought.

Organisations are also customers. For example, they purchase supplies from other organisations to keep their businesses running smoothly with everything they need.

These are all examples of **external customers** because the purchaser is external to the organisation which is selling the product or service.

Internal customers are different. Internal customers are people or departments within an organisation which depend on others within that organisation to supply them with products and services in order for them to be able to do their job.

The services they provide are often in the form of information such as reports, lists, prices, schedules and other types of data compiled into an easily usable format for the internal customer.

> ### Key terms
>
> **External customers** – customers from outside the organisation.
>
> **Internal customers** – people or departments within the organisation who depend on you in some way.

How does providing your internal customers with information when they need it help them to do their job?

Activity 1

The table shows some examples of internal customer relationships. For each one, identify:

- the internal customer
- the reason why they are the internal customer.

Internal customer relationship	Identify the internal customer	State the reason why they are the internal customer
The production manager needs the office administrator to generate weekly reports of new orders.		

A version of this table, ready for you to complete, is available to download from www.contentextra.com/businessadmin

If a salesperson relies on you to send them the weekly list of potential customers (also called sales leads), then they are your internal customer because they need this information from you. They need to be able to follow up the sales leads in order to generate new sales for the organisation.

Portfolio task 328.1 → Link to **LO1**: assessment criterion 1.1

Write a short summary which could be used in your organisation as part of a training pack to describe what is meant by internal customers. Write in a way which will be easily understood by your colleagues at work, especially new members of staff. To show your understanding, remember to include in your answer two examples of internal customers.

Functional skills

English: Speaking and listening

If your assessor asks you to take part in a discussion about this portfolio task as part of the assessment for this learning outcome, you may be able to count it as evidence towards Level 2 Functional English: Speaking and listening. You will need to prepare for this discussion by looking over your work and making sure you can explain the information which you chose to include. Also, be prepared to answer questions from your assessor.

If the office administration manager relied on you to send them the latest stock list of stationery, then they are also your internal customer. They need this information from you so that they can then order additional stationery to keep supplies maintained. Without adequate stationery supplies, the office staff would be unable to carry out basic tasks. For example:

- No paper would mean that no printing or photocopying would be possible.
- No pens or pencils would mean that staff would be unable to write notes.
- No staples would mean staff would be unable to collate work and keep it neat.

Products and services relevant to internal customers

After working through this section you will understand and be able to:

- describe the types of products and services which are offered to internal customers
- identify specific examples of products and services which are offered to internal customers within your own organisation.

Which products and services do internal customers need?

The types of products and services offered to internal customers can be anything which they may need in order to complete their work tasks and can include:

- price lists
- schedules
- project briefs
- marketing leads
- parts for products
- stationery
- IT support and advice
- typed-up reports
- filed documents
- training
- company vehicles
- assistance with booking travel and meetings.

The list shows that there are many different types of products and services an internal customer may need. Specific requirements will depend upon the exact nature of the internal customer's role, as well as the type of organisation in which they work.

It may surprise you to know that your manager is probably one of your main internal customers! Think about all the things that they ask you to do for them each day and all the products and services that they need in order to be able to do their job.

Delivering customer service that meets or exceeds expectations

After working through this section you will understand and be able to:

- explain the purpose and value of identifying internal customer needs and expectations
- explain why customer service must meet or exceed internal customer expectations
- explain the value of meeting or exceeding internal customer expectations
- explain the purpose and value of building positive working relationships.

Portfolio task 328.2

→ Link to **LO2**: assessment criterion 2.1

In order to complete this portfolio task, you need to describe the products and services that are offered by your own organisation to four of its internal customers.

Remember that internal customers are people or departments within your organisation who rely on

others to provide them with products and services to be able to do their job.

It may help you to complete the table below in order to gather all the information you need to complete your answer.

Internal customer	What products or services do they need?	Who within the organisation supplies these products or services to them?

A version of this table, ready for you to complete, is available to download from www.contentextra.com/businessadmin

Identifying internal customer needs and expectations

Your internal customers at work are those people who need you to provide products and services to them so that they can carry out their job **effectively**. Together, you are both ultimately serving the wider goals of the organisation itself.

Colleagues from different teams and departments need to be able to work well together when obtaining and providing products and services to each other as a part of their work routine.

Key term

Effectively – working well to produce good results.

Reasons why you should identify internal customer needs

In order to work effectively with your own internal customers, it is important to begin by examining both their needs and their expectations from you. In fact, you should do this in the same way as you would if they were an external customer.

The main reason why you should do this is that only once you are fully aware of these customer requirements can you begin to work supportively and effectively together to support the wider goals of the organisation.

In order to establish good working relationships with your internal customers, you should work out with them in very clear terms what you are to provide to them, when and how. This sets out the ground rules for your working relationship.

Remember, you cannot satisfy the needs and expectations of your internal customers if you do not know what they are!

Examining internal customer needs and expectations

One way of looking at internal customer needs and expectations is as follows:

- The needs of the internal customer are the specific things that they need you to provide to them. For

example, they may need you to provide them with the latest list of product prices, or details of this month's special discounts and promotions.

- The expectations of the internal customer include issues such as how quickly and in what way you will provide these things to them. For example, they may expect an emailed list from you daily or a hard-copy printout each week.

✓ Checklist

Remember:

- Internal customers' needs consist of the products and services which they require from you.

- Internal customers' expectations relate to the way in which these things need to be delivered (i.e. when and how).

Portfolio task 328.3 → Link to **LO3**: assessment criterion 3.1

In order to complete this portfolio task, you need to write a short report which explains the purpose and value of identifying internal customer needs and expectations. Include two examples of internal customer needs and expectations and, for each one, say why it is important to be able to identify these needs.

Functional skills

English: Writing

If you take care to produce a professional and well-presented report for your answer to this portfolio task, you may be able to count it as evidence towards Level 2 Functional English: Writing. Remember to use headings and subheadings and check that you have used correct spelling and grammar. You will need to keep copies of all the drafts of the report which you produce and then print out the final corrected version, once you have made all your corrections.

Why meeting or exceeding internal customer expectations is essential

Establishing with your internal customers what you will provide them, when you will provide it and how (see page 219), is the process of setting out the minimum level of customer service which you will provide to them.

Meeting minimum expectations

Meeting this minimum level of customer service is essential and something you must achieve. This is the minimum requirement from your internal customers – without these things, they will be unable to carry out their job.

Problems where minimum customer service levels are not met

Figure 328.1 shows what might happen if, for example, it was your job to email the telesales team leader the weekly list of potential customers for the team to call, and you failed to do this.

> Telesales staff would be unable to make their follow-up calls to generate business for the organisation.

> Sales orders would consequently be lower.

> Less **revenue** would be generated for the business.

> Sales results for the telesales team would be lower than usual.

> Performance-related bonuses for the telesales team members would consequently be lower – or even not awarded at all.

Figure 328.1: *Example of a problem created when internal customer expectations are not met*

As illustrated, other employees depend on you to provide products and services to them in order for them to be able to carry out their jobs. This is called **interdependency**.

✓ Checklist

Remember, if you do not meet minimum internal customer service requirements, your internal customers will be unable to carry out their jobs.

Failing to meet the minimum internal customer service levels may cause problems such as:

- strained working relationships between you and your internal customers

- lower job satisfaction for both you and your customers

- reductions in business efficiency due to delays in the internal customer receiving necessary products or services

- possible secondary effects which extend to reduction in service levels to external customers.

The potential consequences of failing to meet minimum customer service levels are far-reaching and can ultimately end in external customer dissatisfaction. This can then escalate into serious problems, with **detrimental** effects on the overall performance of the organisation.

Key terms

Revenue – the money which comes into an organisation via sales.

Interdependency – where people or departments are dependent on one another.

Detrimental – causing harm or damage.

Activity 2

Think about the effects on your organisation of its internal customers being dissatisfied. Write down three effects and, for each one, say why this would be bad for the organisation.

Effect on your organisation of internal customers being dissatisfied	Reason why this would be bad for the organisation

A version of this table, ready for you to complete, is available to download from www.contentextra.com/businessadmin

✓ Checklist

Remember:

- There should be the same level of customer service for internal customers as for external customers (see Unit Q329).

- The customer service which you provide to your internal customers is a key part of the process which contributes towards external customer service.

The value of meeting or exceeding internal customer expectations

Excellence in customer service is widely associated with improved business performance, increased revenue and profits for the organisation. This is because satisfied customers are more likely to remain with the organisation in the future. It is also a very successful way of attracting new customers if your organisation already has a reputation for outstanding levels of customer service. Achieving excellent customer service levels is of great value to the organisation.

Role of internal customers

Figure 328.2 shows that there is a very close and dependent relationship between external and internal customers. Good external customer service (the front line of the business) depends upon the provision of equally good internal customer service (from the people working behind the scenes to make sure the front line staff are well supported).

Figure 328.2: *Internal and external customer service are both essential elements of the total customer service process*

Portfolio task 328.4

➜ Link to **LO3**: assessment criterion 3.2

In order to complete this portfolio task, you need to write a short summary which explains why customer service must meet or exceed internal customer expectations.

Try to include examples of internal customer expectations from your own work experience and say why it is important for these expectations to be met.

Example of internal customer expectations	Why it is important for these expectations to be met

A version of this table, ready for you to complete, is available to download from www.contentextra.com/businessadmin

By providing positive experiences for your internal customers, you are directly helping them to:

- be more **productive**
- enjoy their role more
- be more motivated
- perform to a higher standard.

Key term

Productive – producing positive results.

They, in turn, will be better placed to pass on this positive experience to their external customers. This helps the business to achieve its goals, creates satisfied customers and also enhances the reputation of the organisation.

Figure 328.3: *Total customer service*

Total customer service within an organisation can only be achieved by having both internal and external customer service working alongside each other.

Why you should aim to delight your customers

Key points to be aware of in understanding the value of exceeding – rather than just meeting – the minimum internal customer expectations are that:

Portfolio task 328.5

→ Link to **LO3**: assessment criterion 3.3

In order to complete this portfolio task, you need to write a short summary which explains the value of meeting or exceeding internal customer expectations.

You also need to give two examples of meeting internal customers' expectations from your own work experience. Your answer needs to include all the benefits involved in meeting or exceeding these expectations. These benefits apply to you, your internal customers and the organisation. You may also wish to carry out some additional research for this portfolio task, which can include organisational documents as well as Internet research.

You can complete the table below to gather the information which you need to write your answer.

Functional skills

English: Reading

If you carry out research involving reading texts, including work-related documents as well as Internet research, in order to complete your portfolio task, you may be able to count it as evidence towards Level 2 Functional English: Reading. Remember to keep records of all of the documents, handbooks and guidelines which you study, along with a record of the websites which you visit, as you will need to provide evidence of any reading research you carry out.

Internal customer expectations	Value of meeting or exceeding internal customer expectations

A version of this table, ready for you to complete, is available to download from www.contentextra.com/businessadmin

- by only meeting the minimum customer service levels, you are merely preventing your customers from complaining

- by exceeding the minimum, and going above and beyond what is expected of you, you will delight your customers!

> ### ✓ Checklist
>
> Great customer service is a key part of the whole package of the purchase-making process. Remember:
>
> - Customers do not simply want the cheapest product.
>
> - Customers want to be treated well.
>
> - Customers want to feel looked after by the organisation with which they are dealing.

The purpose and value of building positive working relationships

You cannot underestimate the enormous benefits that can be achieved through building and maintaining positive working relationships with your internal customers.

How does building positive working relationships with your internal customers help create a dynamic environment?

Key benefits include:

- good two-way communications between you and your customers

- effective **interpersonal relationships**

- a climate of trust and openness

- a well-coordinated approach to getting tasks completed

- a team culture

- support for each other when problems need to be solved and – importantly – collaboration to achieve successful outcomes.

By building positive working relationships with your internal customers, the **ethos** of good customer service will quickly spread across the work of the whole organisation.

> ### Key terms
>
> **Interpersonal relationships** – relationships between two or more individuals.
>
> **Ethos** – character or spirit.

Useful techniques for building positive working relationships

There are certain techniques that you can employ at work in order to build positive working relationships with your internal customers. These include:

- keeping in regular communication with your internal customers; face-to-face communication is the best method, wherever possible

- asking for feedback including comments, criticism and praise from your internal customers; this will demonstrate to them how important it is to you to provide a good level of service to them

- acting on feedback relating to areas in which you could improve

- reporting any problems or issues to your internal customers immediately so that they can prepare themselves for any work delays in advance; they may even be able to help resolve the issue

- responding quickly and politely to any enquiries from your internal customers – returning phone calls promptly, responding to emails quickly and dealing with staff in person when they call by to see you with a query.

Portfolio task 328.6 → Link to **LO3**: assessment criterion 3.4

In order to complete this portfolio task, you need to write a short summary which explains the purpose and value of building positive working relationships.

It may help you to mention in your answer examples of positive working relationships which you have experienced within your own organisation.

You could split your answer into two main sections as follows:

* The first section could give an outline of the reasons why it is important to build positive working relationships.

* The second section could list the benefits of positive working relationships.

The purpose of quality standards for customer service

After working through this section you will understand and be able to:

● identify quality standards for your organisation and your own work

● explain the value of agreeing quality standards and timescales

● explain how to set and meet quality standards and timescales with internal customers.

Identifying quality standards

In this section you will investigate the quality standards which apply to organisations, as well as looking at the specific quality standards and requirements which you have to meet in your own role within the organisation.

Organisational quality standards

Organisations can have many quality standards, kite marks, accreditations and charters, which encompass the high standards to which they work. Some quality standards are international and can apply to all organisations, whereas others are national, regional or industry-sector-specific. Some are also **regulatory** — and it is therefore a legal requirement for the organisation to meet them — whereas others are voluntary.

Key term

Regulatory – subject to government regulations, which must be obeyed.

What do organisational quality standards cover?

The quality standards of an organisation are concerned with aspects of the organisation such as:

● the products and services that the organisation provides

● the suppliers and distributors which they use

● the way in which they recruit, manage, train and develop their staff

● their commitment to customer service

● their approach to management and leadership.

Some examples of organisational quality standards include the following:

● ISO9001 — this is an international quality standard which is achieved by organisations for their quality management systems, where they can demonstrate their conformity not only to customer service but also to regulatory requirements which apply to their products and services.

● Investors in People — this is a standard which is awarded to those organisations which demonstrate their commitment to developing their staff and providing good training and career opportunities. It can be awarded to organisations across any sector.

● The disability symbol is awarded by Jobcentre Plus to employers in England, Scotland and Wales who have made specific commitments regarding the employment of disabled people. In order to be awarded this symbol, organisations must make five commitments to disabled employees including agreeing to interview all disabled candidates who satisfy the minimum criteria for a job vacancy, as well as raising awareness among all of their staff about disability issues.

- Customer First® – this is a standard awarded to organisations for the achievement of excellent customer service and involves a three-point framework against which organisations wishing to become accredited must be assessed: building customer relationships, maximising market awareness and staff development.

Quality standards for your own work

Quality standards for your job may involve things such as:

- how quickly you must reply to email queries
- checks which you must make on the accuracy of your work
- the format and wording of the letters that you send out to customers
- the way in which you must speak to customers on the phone
- the speed with which customer complaints must be dealt with
- the number of calls that you must handle per hour or per day
- the number of complaints that you must resolve

Examples of various types of organisational quality standards

- the settings that you must use on your work telephone answering machine, for example, so that callers are attended to by a colleague when you are unavailable.

Activity 3

For this activity, you are going to find out about the specific quality standards that apply to your job. First, use the table below to list all the quality standards that apply to your role at work.

Next, take a copy of this list along to your manager or mentor and ask them to add any other quality standards that are relevant to your position. The results from this activity will be very useful for you in completing the portfolio task for this section.

Quality standards that apply to my job	Why this quality standard is important to my job

A version of this table, ready for you to complete, is available to download from www.contentextra.com/businessadmin

Portfolio task 328.7 → Link to **LO4**: assessment criteria 4.1

In order to complete this portfolio task, you need to write a short summary which identifies all of the relevant quality standards which apply to:

- your organisation
- your own work.

For each of the quality standards that you mention relating to your organisation, carry out Internet research in order to understand what the quality standard is for, how the organisation has achieved it and when it will expire. You can also research organisational documents relating to these quality standards to help you in this respect.

You can use the work you did for the previous activity to outline the quality standards which apply to your own work. For each one, explain why you think these are important in helping you to perform to a high standard in your role.

Functional skills

English: Reading

If you carry out research involving reading texts, including work-related documents as well as Internet research, in order to complete your portfolio task, you may be able to count it as evidence towards Level 2 Functional English: Reading. Remember to keep records of all of the documents, handbooks and guidelines which you study, along with a record of the websites which you visit, as you will need to provide evidence of any reading research you carry out.

Agreeing quality standards and timescales

Value of agreeing quality standards

Agreeing quality standards with internal customers throughout the organisation is the best way to get their involvement in quality improvement initiatives. This is central to the success of the initiatives because simply imposing new standards upon staff may alienate them and the take-up rate is certain to be low.

Working in collaboration with your internal customers from different departments engenders a sense of commitment and ownership from both sides which is vital in the implementation of quality standards. You will each need full commitment from the other in order for quality standards to be successful, as you are each dependent upon the other for an effective working relationship.

A plan must be agreed and drawn up between you and your internal customers which sets out what specific quality standards are to be achieved and by whom. A very good technique for securing agreement is to have meetings with the internal customers involved and ask their opinions as to what standards they need you to work to.

They will be well placed to offer their suggestions in this respect because they are already doing the job at the front line. Harnessing agreement and cooperation from both sides — from you as the supplier and from them as the customer — will set the foundation for a solid and effective working relationship.

Value of agreeing timescales

Once you have established with your internal customers the nature of the quality standards to be introduced, you also need to get agreement on timescales which you will work to, as part of your service commitment to your customers.

Activity 4

Can you think of any additional quality standards which in your opinion would improve your job performance? List them in the table below.

Additional quality standards for my job	How this would improve performance

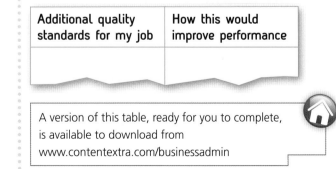

A version of this table, ready for you to complete, is available to download from www.contentextra.com/businessadmin

How can planning in collaboration with your internal customers ensure the most effective outcomes?

Timescales can typically relate to issues such as how quickly:

- customers can expect to be dealt with
- phone calls will be returned
- emails will be replied to
- letters will be sent out
- information will be supplied.

In addition to the above, it is important to have a clear working procedure for communicating with your internal customers in the event of a problem. If, for example, there is going to be a delay in providing required information to your internal customers, you should alert them as early on as possible. This is both courteous and good business practice. Ensure you make them aware that you are doing everything possible to rectify the situation as soon as you are able.

In summary, you could argue that the true value of agreeing quality standards and timescales lies in the fact that you, as the supplier, will know exactly what is expected of you and by when, in your working relationship with your internal customers.

Portfolio task 328.8 → Link to **LO4**: assessment criterion 4.2

In order to complete this portfolio task, you need to write a short summary which explains the value of agreeing quality standards and timescales for delivering internal customer service.

It may help you to include examples of quality standards and timescales from your own work experience and say how you think that having these in place benefits both you and your internal customers.

Setting and meeting quality standards and timescales with internal customers

Setting quality standards with internal customers

In order to do this, take the following steps:

- Make sure that the quality standards are **aligned** to the needs of the internal customers. There is no point spending your time working to a high level of detail on areas which are not relevant to their needs.

- **Proactively** work together with your internal customers at each stage of the process when you are establishing quality standards, so that they are aware of exactly what you are trying to do. This way, the resulting standards will be a **collaborative** effort, which will be much more effective for both you and your internal customers.

- Ask for input from your internal customers so that you have the benefit of this information from the outset. This will prevent irrelevant standards from being developed. It will also ensure standards are in place for all the areas in which they are needed.

Key terms

Aligned – relevant to and in accordance with the needs of the business.

Proactively – in a way that controls a situation before it happens, by using your initiative.

Collaborative – working together with other people or departments to achieve goals.

Setting timescales with internal customers

The two main considerations when setting timescales for delivery of service are to:

- identify how quickly they need the various services from you
- establish how quickly you are able to deliver these services.

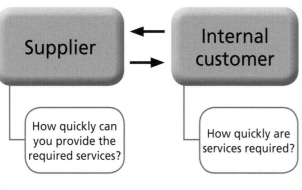

Figure 328.4: *Setting timescales with internal customers*

Meeting quality standards and timescales with internal customers

Once you have successfully set out the quality standards and timescales with your internal customers, you now need to make sure that they are met, both to the required standard and on time.

In order to achieve this, you could produce a weekly schedule of the routine tasks that you need to carry out in order to ensure all internal customer requirements are supplied on time. You can use either a desk diary or else an electronic calendar or 'to do' list on your computer. If using the computer calendar or 'to do' list facility, you can also set reminders which can recur daily, weekly, monthly or even annually to remind you to complete tasks by the required deadline. Your weekly task list might look something like the one in Table 328.1.

> **Portfolio task 328.9** → Link to **LO4**: assessment criterion 4.3
>
> In order to complete this portfolio task, you need to write a short summary which explains how to set and meet quality standards and timescales with internal customers.
>
> Give three examples of quality standards and corresponding timescales which you have set with your internal customers. For each one, say how you made sure that you were able to meet the required timescales.

Dealing with internal customer service problems

After working through this section you will understand and be able to:

- describe the types of problems that internal customers may have
- explain ways of dealing with problems
- explain the purpose and value of a complaints procedure.

Table 328.1: *An example of a weekly task list for satisfying internal customer requirements*

	Monday	Tuesday	Wednesday	Thursday	Friday
a.m.	Generate report from website of sales leads received over the weekend and email to the sales manager.			Complete filing and notify office manager of any missing files.	
p.m.			Update current stationery stock list and email to the office manager.		Compile a list of the week's customer feedback and email to the customer service manager.

Problems that internal customers may have

The types of problems that internal customers may experience from time to time include:

- delays in receipt of products and services from other staff or departments
- incorrect products or services delivered
- poor quality products and services delivered.

Delays in receipt of products and services

Delays in receiving products and services from within the organisation can arise for a number of reasons including staff absence, new or inexperienced staff taking longer to supply items or items having been delayed in transit in the case of the movement of physical items from one location to another.

Incorrect products and services

Internal customers may also find themselves in receipt of the wrong products and services. This can happen where, for example, there has been a misunderstanding about what was needed. It can also happen as a result of simple **clerical error**. In either of these situations, the problem is quite easily remedied.

Poor-quality products and services

If internal customers receive poor-quality products and services on a regular basis, this will probably have a significant negative impact on their own performance and ability to do their job. This will impact on **productivity** as well as **morale**.

Key terms

Clerical error – an error in processing a task by an employee in the office.

Productivity – the rate at which work is completed.

Morale – enthusiasm and willingness of employees, or a measure of how happy they are at work.

Examples of poor-quality products and services might include badly compiled information reports with missing or incomplete data, schedules with unfeasible dates or customer contact lists containing errors which make it impossible to make contact with them.

Activity 5

Try to think of three more examples of poor products or services that could be delivered to the internal customers within your own organisation. Write your examples in the table below.

Poor products or services that could be delivered to internal customers	Effect that this would have on internal customers

A version of this table, ready for you to complete, is available to download from www.contentextra.com/businessadmin

Portfolio task 328.10 → Link to **LO5**: assessment criterion 5.1

In order to complete this portfolio task, you need to write a short summary which describes three types of problems that internal customers may have. You may like to include in your answer examples of customer service problems which you have experienced at work. You will be reusing these three examples of problems again in Portfolio task 328.11.

Ways of dealing with problems

There are some key principles which hold good across many situations where you find yourself faced with a problem:

- Good communications – this is a vital ingredient in problem-solving with colleagues.

● Promptness – act promptly to prevent a problem from becoming **protracted**.

● **Integrity** – if you say you are going to do something, do it! Showing integrity to your colleagues is an essential element of building trust.

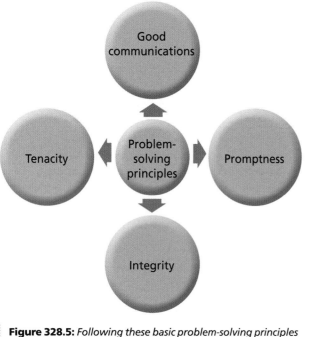

Figure 328.5: *Following these basic problem-solving principles will help you deal effectively with many types of problems*

● **Tenacity** – keep going until the problem is actually resolved. Don't leave problems to continue as they will undoubtedly hamper your working relationships with internal customers.

Key terms

Protracted – long and drawn out, often tedious.

Integrity – honesty or keeping to your word.

Tenacity – the ability to remain focused on the completion of a task or project.

If you are an internal customer who has experienced problems with the products or services that you have received, you need to do the following.

● Inform the supplier about the problem as soon as you can. A phone call or a face-to-face meeting is better in these situations than an email or a letter because it is both quicker and more personal.

● Explain the effect of the problem on your work.

● Ask when the corrected supplies will be able to be sent to you.

● Keep the exchange polite but to the point.

● Thank the other person for their efforts to correct the problem.

Portfolio task 328.11

→ Link to **LO5**: assessment criterion 5.2

In order to complete this portfolio task, you need to write a short summary which explains ways of dealing with three problems.

Using the three examples of internal customer service problems which you wrote about in the previous portfolio task, for each one, say how you went about dealing with that problem. Mention, too, whether you

had any difficulties in dealing with each problem or whether they were straightforward to resolve. Did you have to get assistance from another colleague to deal with any of the problems you identified?

Use the table below to gather all the information which you need to write your answer.

Example of an internal customer problem (from Portfolio task 328.10)	Explanation of how you dealt with this problem	Were there any difficulties and did anybody else help to resolve the problem?

A version of this table, ready for you to complete, is available to download from www.contentextra.com/businessadmin

The purpose and value of a complaints procedure

In this section you will investigate the reasons why having a complaints procedure is a good thing, along with some of the benefits which this brings to the organisation.

Purpose of a complaints procedure

The purpose in any organisation of having a complaints procedure is to provide a standard and controlled way for employees to voice their concerns about things that are not working well and find a resolution. In the case of internal customers, it is a procedure for ensuring that, in the future, products and services that are needed will arrive in a timely fashion and to the required standard.

Value of a complaints procedure

There are several benefits of having a complaints procedure:

- Employees know that there is a procedure in place which they can employ if and when they are unhappy with some aspect of service provision. In other words, there is something that they can do about it.

- Everyone is treated fairly and equally, in accordance with the standard sequence of actions laid out in the procedure.

- The main point of the procedure is to iron out **inefficiencies** where they exist and to enhance productivity – all of which ultimately improve the performance of the organisation.

- A complaints procedure allows a problem to be documented and brought to the attention of the manager who is responsible for resolving it.

- Problems can be tackled quickly and **objectively**.

Key terms

Inefficiencies – things that are wasteful and do not help achieve results.

Objectively – based on facts, unbiased.

Monitor – to keep track of.

Portfolio task 328.12 → Link to **LO5**: assessment criterion 5.3

In order to complete this portfolio task, you need to write a short summary which explains the purpose and value of a complaints procedure.

If there is an internal customer service complaints procedure in your organisation, you can discuss this in your answer and mention the benefits that it offers. If your organisation does not have a complaints procedure, you may wish to carry out Internet research to find an example of one which you can use as the basis for your answer.

Monitoring and evaluating internal customer service

After working through this section you will understand and be able to:

- explain the purpose and benefits of monitoring internal customer satisfaction and how to do so

- describe techniques for collecting and evaluating customer feedback

- explain the benefits of continuous improvement.

The purpose and benefits of monitoring internal customer satisfaction

In this section you will investigate the reasons why it is important to **monitor** internal customer satisfaction. You will also look at some of the ways in which you can do this.

Why you need to monitor internal customer satisfaction

You need to monitor internal customer satisfaction levels in order to establish the quality of the service that is being given to the internal customers in the organisation.

If you do not monitor satisfaction levels, it is possible for problems to go unreported. Internal customers may be unhappy and demotivated and this could result in serious problems for the business.

Monitoring satisfaction ensures that any such issues are highlighted early on, so that they can be dealt with as quickly as possible. This is important because the longer a problem goes on, the more damage is done to the business. The performance of the organisation may suffer and employees may feel unhappy.

Regular monitoring of satisfaction levels is very important:

- Firstly, it allows you to highlight areas of concern.
- Secondly, it allows you to take action to remedy situations causing dissatisfaction among internal customers.

Methods of monitoring internal customer satisfaction

Some of the main methods that can be employed to monitor satisfaction levels among internal customers include the use of:

- questionnaires
- focus groups
- one-to-one meetings.

Questionnaires

Questionnaires are a good method for collecting feedback from a large volume of respondents in a relatively short time. They can also be sent out via email and the results collected electronically, which makes the subsequent collation of results extremely easy.

Careful preparation is required, however, in planning the exact questions to be used on the questionnaire, along with the way in which they should be worded. It is very important for all questions to be clear, **unambiguous** and not in any way leading. **Leading questions** direct the respondent towards a certain answer and so the answers to these types of questions are not meaningful as they are skewed one way or another.

A good example of a leading question could be, 'Why do you prefer product x — because of its superior performance, value for money or staying power?' This question assumes that the respondent does in fact prefer

product x — which may not be the case. The question should be reworded to remove the leading element which pushes the respondent into a certain answer.

It would be preferable to ask, 'Which of the products do you prefer: product x or product y?' Then a second question could be used to establish the reason for the preference.

Questionnaires should ideally be quick and straightforward for the respondent to complete. The questions themselves should be mainly closed or structured in nature. This means that they are worded in such a way as to offer the respondent only a limited choice of replies. The responses to these types of questions are very easy to collate afterwards.

Some typical examples of **closed questions** ask for responses in the form of:

- yes/no
- true/false
- tick-box answers from listed choices
- scaled responses, where 1 = poor and 5 = excellent
- multiple-choice questions.

Open questions should be very carefully used, if at all, on questionnaires. The reason for this is that open questions allow respondents to answer freely in their own words and, as a result, are very difficult to collate.

Key terms

Unambiguous – having only one meaning.

Leading questions – questions which plant a pre-supposed answer into the mind of the respondent.

Closed questions – questions where there are only certain possible answers, such as yes/no.

Open questions – questions which allow the respondent freedom to write any answer.

A good example of an open question is, 'What do you think of our customer service?' Respondents could answer in many different ways, either going into a great amount of detail or else by giving a one-word reply. Imagine if you had to collate the responses to 500 of these questions. It would be almost impossible!

Probably the most useful information you will get from reviewing answers to questions such as these is that any extreme examples of good or bad feedback will be spotted.

Look at Table 328.2. Some examples of open questions are listed in the left-hand column. The questions have then been reworked as closed questions in the right-hand column, offering the respondent only a limited choice of answer.

Table 328.2: *Open and closed questions*

Open question	Closed question
What do you think of this new brand of washing powder?	Tick one of the boxes below to say what is the most important factor for you in choosing a brand of washing powder: ☐ Price ☐ Brand loyalty ☐ Special offers ☐ Cleaning power at low temperatures
What do you think of our new range of menswear?	Indicate by circling the numbers below how you rate our new menswear range. 1 = poor and 5 = excellent Price 1 2 3 4 5 Choice 1 2 3 4 5 Quality 1 2 3 4 5
What do you think of our new range of cakes?	Say how often you would purchase one of our new range of cakes: a) once or more per week b) once or more per month c) occasionally d) never

Activity 6

Read the open questions in the table below and reword them in such a way as to make them into closed questions which will be more suitable for use in a questionnaire. (Please note that the table below shows one sample question and the rest are in the document on the website.)

Remember that you can use response choices such as:

* yes/no
* true/false
* tick boxes
* multiple-choice questions
* scaled responses.

Open question	Closed question
What do you think of our customer service?	Rate the quality of our customer service on a scale of 1 to 5, where 1 = poor and 5 = excellent. Put a circle around your answer. 1 2 3 4 5

A version of this table, ready for you to complete, is available to download from www.contentextra.com/businessadmin

Focus groups

Focus groups are special groups of customers who are brought together to discuss and give their opinions about certain issues. They usually consist of up to ten members and the group discussions can last quite a long time. The group is usually led by a **facilitator** who will guide the members through the process and keep them on track if they become sidelined by a certain issue. The facilitator will also **arbitrate** in situations where group members become deadlocked into arguments. The focus group discussions are also normally recorded so that the points made and issues voiced can be analysed later on and the results reported back.

Focus groups are a good method to use for monitoring internal customer satisfaction because the group members are able to contribute freely to the group's discussion and they are also free to go into as much detail as is necessary to explain their opinions or

Key terms

Facilitator – someone who helps a group with their discussions without taking sides.

Arbitrate – to help resolve a dispute.

Eliciting – evoking or drawing out.

concerns. This level of detail is also very useful for getting to the bottom of problems that may exist with customer satisfaction.

Another good use of focus groups is to test out new approaches for making improvements to current systems at work. Group members can give their honest opinions and can provide extremely useful information for the organisation to inform them about what would and would not work in practice – and the reasons why.

One-to-one meetings

One-to-one meetings can be either formal or informal, depending on the circumstances. Whichever way they are run, they are a very good method of **eliciting** feedback from internal customers. One-to-one forums are beneficial when internal customers may need to feed back negative comments in relative privacy, and they allow for an open and honest exchange which may be more difficult in a focus-group situation. They also allow for a more detailed account of a particular situation than you would be able to glean from a questionnaire.

Table 328.3 shows a summary of the relative advantages and disadvantages of the different methods of monitoring internal customer satisfaction levels which we have discussed in this section.

Table 328.3: *Monitoring internal customer satisfaction*

Method	Advantages	Disadvantages
Questionnaires	Quick to administer. Can reach a large number of people in a short time. Easy to collate the results.	Can only get limited amount of detail. Questions need careful preparation so as not to confuse or lead respondents.
Focus groups	Can obtain very detailed accounts from group members. Can obtain very useful information for new ideas for improvements.	Time consuming to administer. Results can be difficult to collate into a report due to the in-depth nature of the discussions.
One-to-one meetings	Very good method for getting open and honest individual feedback. A good level of detail can be obtained.	Time-consuming to administer. People may be overly focused on one particular issue.

Portfolio task 328.13 → Link to **LO6**: assessment criterion 6.1

In order to complete this portfolio task, you need to write a short summary which explains the purpose and benefits of monitoring internal customer satisfaction and how to do so.

It may help to divide up your answer into two main sections as follows:

1 The purpose and benefits of monitoring internal customer satisfaction.

2 Three methods of monitoring internal customer satisfaction. Remember to include in this section examples of techniques which are employed for this purpose in your own organisation.

Collecting and evaluating customer feedback

The techniques for collecting and evaluating customer feedback will depend on the method which was used to monitor satisfaction levels. In the previous section we discussed three ways of monitoring internal customer satisfaction:

- questionnaires
- focus groups
- one-to-one meetings.

For each of these, you will now look at the techniques which you can employ to collect and evaluate the feedback received.

Questionnaires

The results of questionnaires have the advantage of being fairly easy to collate, as each respondent has answered the same set of mainly structured and closed questions. This means that a lot of feedback can be quickly analysed and summarised in report format.

Focus groups

Feedback received via focus groups is more time-consuming to collate and summarise. This is because focus groups are open discussions between groups of

people. They can also contain significantly more detail than that which is typically involved in a questionnaire. Therefore the issues raised and the opinions expressed during focus-group discussions are largely unpredictable and no two focus groups are ever likely to be the same. The analysis of the discussions will involve in-depth study of the notes or recordings taken during each of the focus-group sessions and a report will subsequently be generated. This will usually be along the lines of a summary of each of the main topics raised and the feelings of the majority of the group on each issue.

One-to-one meetings

Collecting and evaluating customer feedback received via one-to-one meetings can be particularly time-consuming, especially when many internal customers have had one-to-one meetings with a particular manager.

Careful notes need to be taken during each of the meetings in order that all of the feedback is accurately recorded. A template feedback sheet containing various category headings would be a very useful way of recording the conversations of such meetings. This will make it easier to collate all the meeting outcomes in a summary form later on. Possible category headings might include:

- positives
- areas for improvement
- any specific issues or special concerns needing to be addressed
- overall satisfaction.

Portfolio task 328.14 → Link to **LO6**: assessment criterion 6.2

In order to complete this portfolio task, write a short summary which describes three techniques for collecting and evaluating customer feedback.

Include examples of some of the techniques that are employed for this purpose in your own organisation. For each technique that you identify, make sure you give an outline of how they operate and say what information is obtained from them.

✔ Checklist

Collecting and evaluating customer feedback

Remember:

- Separate the positive from the negative feedback – it is the negative feedback which indicates where action needs to be taken.

- Be careful of individual feedback which is extreme – it may reflect the personality of the respondent rather than the existence of a particular problem.

- Monitor any trends which become apparent in feedback and investigate these types of issues further. The identification of trends is central in evaluating all feedback, as these may indicate potential problems in certain areas. The fact that the same issue is highlighted numerous times validates, to some extent at least, the existence of the problem.

Small, incremental changes can make a significant improvement to business performance over time

The benefits of continuous improvement

'Continuous improvement' is a business strategy sometimes referred to as '*kaizen*', the Japanese word for improvement. It is based on the idea of making continuous, small, incremental changes to all business processes. The underlying principle is that by making small changes on a continuous basis, over time large improvements in business efficiency will ensue.

Some of the key benefits of continuous improvement include:

- employee involvement at all levels – from the boardroom to the shop floor – which is a very good way of raising morale
- an increase in team-working initiatives
- improvements in business efficiency
- reductions in activities that do not add value to the business
- the production of better products in a shorter time

- better customer service leading to increased levels of customer satisfaction and therefore more customers remaining with the business for the long term.

One of the founding principles of continuous improvement is that everybody's ideas for improvements are equal, no matter what their position within the organisation. The team ethos which is involved with continuous improvement adds again to this culture of **inclusivity**.

Key term

Inclusivity – including everybody from all levels of the organisation.

It is widely acknowledged that organisations which implement strategies of continuous improvement benefit greatly from improvements in business efficiency in many areas. The results of this speak for themselves in the performance figures for the organisations: improved profits, reduced waste and improvements in the business' reputation.

Portfolio task 328.15

→ Link to **LO6**: assessment criterion 6.3

In order to complete this portfolio task, you need to write a short summary which explains the benefits of continuous improvement. Include examples of any continuous improvement initiatives from your own organisation in your answer. If your own organisation does not use the strategy of continuous improvement, carry out some Internet research to find examples of organisations that do and use your research findings from these on which to base your answer.

Evidence collection

In order for you to complete the remaining assessment criteria to successfully pass this unit, you will need to carry out various tasks at work and then produce evidence to show that you have demonstrated the required skills and competence.

Evidence can be collected in a number of different ways. For example, it can be in the form of a signed witness testimony from a colleague or line manager, a copy of any related emails or letters you have produced, or a verbal discussion with your assessor.

Speak to your assessor to identify the best methods to use in order to complete each portfolio task and remember to keep copies of all the evidence that you produce.

Be able to build positive working relationships with internal customers

Portfolio task 328.16

→ Links to **LO7**: assessment criteria 7.1, 7.2, 7.3 and 7.4

Gather evidence of your work to show your assessor that you have successfully carried out the tasks outlined in the table below. Check with your assessor on the best ways of gathering evidence for each of the tasks before you begin.

Task	Evidence collected
1 Identify internal customers.	
2 Confirm internal customer needs in terms of products and services.	

A version of this form, ready for you to complete, is available to download from www.contentextra.com/businessadmin

Be able to deliver customer services to agreed quality standards and timescales

Portfolio task 328.17

→ Links to **LO8**: assessment criteria 8.1, 8.2 and 8.3

Gather evidence of your work to show your assessor that you have successfully carried out the tasks outlined in the table below. Check with your assessor on the best ways of gathering evidence for each of the tasks before you begin.

Task	Evidence collected
1 Provide customer service to agreed quality standards.	

A version of this form, ready for you to complete, is available to download from www.contentextra.com/businessadmin

Be able to deal with internal customer service problems and complaints

Portfolio task 328.18

→ Links to **LO9**: assessment criterion 9.1

Gather evidence of your work to show your assessor that you have successfully carried out the tasks outlined in the table below. Check with your assessor on the best ways of gathering evidence for each of the tasks before you begin.

Task	Evidence collected
1 Follow procedures, within agreed timescales, to: a) process problems and complaints b) resolve problems and complaints c) refer problems and complaints, where necessary.	

A version of this form, ready for you to complete, is available to download from www.contentextra.com/businessadmin

Be able to monitor and evaluate customer services to internal customers

Portfolio task 328.19

→ Links to **LO10**: assessment criteria 10.1, 10.2 and 10.3

Gather evidence of your work to show your assessor that you have successfully carried out the tasks outlined in the table below. Check with your assessor on the best ways of gathering evidence for each of the tasks before you begin.

Task	Evidence collected
1 Obtain and record internal customer feedback.	

A version of this form, ready for you to complete, is available to download from www.contentextra.com/businessadmin

Office life

Jahanzeb's story

My name is Jahanzeb Kahn and I am 19 years old. I have been working for a telecoms and Internet service provider as a telesales assistant for four months. I enjoy my job but I am beginning to notice that there are some problems when we work with the administration department.

For example, sometimes when we are on the phone with customers, they request us to post them out details of our special terms or promotions, so that they can review them at their leisure at home before deciding whether to purchase them or not. We have to send this mailout request to the administration department and they fulfil the request. This is meant to happen the same day.

However, I have had several calls from upset customers who have not received the promotion information that was promised to them. This is not just an isolated case – it is quite a regular complaint. This is causing some concern in our team and people are beginning to complain among themselves. I am worried that this is making our team look unprofessional.

Ask the expert

Q I work in a telesales department and we are having problems getting the staff in the administration department to do the things which we need them to do for our external customers. This is causing many customers to become upset and I am concerned that we are going to have issues with losing business in the future if this is not addressed.

A Departments with internal customer relationships need to establish service levels between one another, including the key tasks that are necessary for the organisation as a whole to provide good service to the external customers. Without this basic level of cooperation, the business will not perform efficiently in servicing the needs of its external customer base.

Top tips

In order for the administration and telesales departments to work more effectively together, their work tasks and priorities need to be better synchronised so that they better serve the needs of the external customers of the organisation. The two departments have an internal customer relationship in as much as they each depend on the other for certain tasks in order to serve the wider goals of the organisation. A good next step in this situation would be for Jahanzeb to relay his concerns to his line manager so that a meeting for the two departments can be set up to identify the core interdepartmental tasks which need to be achieved, along with the required quality standards and timelines.

Check your knowledge

1 What is an internal customer?
a) Someone who shops in indoor retail outlets only.
b) Someone who only shops via the Internet.
c) A person or department within an organisation who relies on another person or department for something.
d) A mystery shopper.

2 Which of these products or services would not normally be offered to internal customers?
a) Weekly sales reports.
b) Daily customer-complaint reports.
c) Free tickets for the local nightclub.
d) Weekly roundup of website enquiries.

3 Why is it essential to meet at least the minimum level of customer service to internal customers?
a) Because without this, they will resign.
b) Because without this, they will keep phoning you.
c) Because without this, they will be very unhappy.
d) Because without this, they will be unable to do their job.

4 What does it mean to have a positive working relationship with someone?
a) You have a fiery relationship with one another.
b) You are only allowed to say positive things at work.
c) You work very effectively and supportively with one another.
d) You really cannot work with that person.

5 Which of these might be a suitable quality standard for producing a letter to one of your customers?
a) It must be done urgently.
b) It must be printed on A4 letterhead paper, typed in 12-point font with full contact details including your direct telephone line.
c) It must be pretty.
d) It must be laminated and sent by courier.

6 Which of these statements about timescales is true?
a) It is always up to you when you do things for other departments.
b) Timescales need to be agreed for the completion of services between internal customers and their suppliers.
c) Timescales can always be changed at the last minute.
d) Timescales will always depend on what the managing director says.

7 What is the best approach to take when dealing with internal customer problems?
a) Ignore their phone calls and emails.
b) Establish good communications, be proactive in dealing with the situation and follow through on everything that you have promised to do.
c) Just hope that it will sort itself out.
d) Refer all problems to your manager.

8 What is the main purpose of having a complaints procedure?
a) You can divert all of the annoying customers to it.
b) Good companies have no need for a complaints procedure.
c) It allows you to ignore the angry customers.
d) It allows for a fair and consistent way for issues to be investigated and resolved quickly.

9 What is the main reason for monitoring internal customer satisfaction?
a) Unhappy staff need to be brought back into line.
b) You should always monitor your staff.
c) If levels of satisfaction are found to be low, this can then be addressed.
d) You need to know which of your staff are shopping on the Internet at work.

10 What is meant by continuous improvement?
a) It means cutbacks will increase.
b) It means that by making small changes each week or each month, significant improvements in business efficiency can be achieved over time.
c) It means that you must always work harder tomorrow than you did today.
d) It means that you must never miss work.

Answers to the Check your knowledge questions can be found at www.contentextra.com/businessadmin

What your assessor is looking for

In order to prepare for and succeed in completing this unit, your assessor will require you to be able to demonstrate competence in all of the performance criteria listed in the table below.

Your assessor will guide you through the assessment process, but it is likely that for this unit you will need to:

● complete short written narratives or personal statements explaining your answers

● take part in professional discussions with your assessor to explain your answers verbally

● complete observations with your assessor ensuring that they can observe you carrying out your work tasks

● produce any relevant work products to help demonstrate how you have completed the assessment criteria

● ask your manager, a colleague, or a customer for witness testimonies explaining how you have completed the assessment criteria.

Please note that the evidence which you generate for the assessment criteria in this unit may also count towards your evidence collection for some of the other units in this qualification. Your assessor will provide support and guidance on this.

The table below outlines the portfolio tasks which you need to complete for this unit, mapped to their associated assessment criteria.

Task and page reference	Mapping assessment criteria
Portfolio task 328.1 (page 217)	Assessment criterion: 1.1
Portfolio task 328.2 (page 218)	Assessment criterion: 2.1
Portfolio task 328.3 (page 219)	Assessment criterion: 3.1
Portfolio task 328.4 (page 221)	Assessment criterion: 3.2
Portfolio task 328.5 (page 222)	Assessment criterion: 3.3
Portfolio task 328.6 (page 224)	Assessment criterion: 3.4
Portfolio task 328.7 (page 226)	Assessment criterion: 4.1
Portfolio task 328.8 (page 227)	Assessment criterion: 4.2
Portfolio task 328.9 (page 228)	Assessment criterion: 4.3
Portfolio task 328.10 (page 229)	Assessment criterion: 5.1
Portfolio task 328.11 (page 230)	Assessment criterion: 5.2
Portfolio task 328.12 (page 231)	Assessment criterion: 5.3
Portfolio task 328.13 (page 235)	Assessment criterion: 6.1
Portfolio task 328.14 (page 235)	Assessment criterion: 6.2
Portfolio task 328.15 (page 237)	Assessment criterion: 6.3
Portfolio task 328.16 (page 237)	Assessment criteria: 7.1, 7.2, 7.3 and 7.4
Portfolio task 328.17 (page 238)	Assessment criteria: 8.1, 8.2 and 8.3
Portfolio task 328.18 (page 238)	Assessment criterion: 9.1
Portfolio task 328.19 (page 239)	Assessment criteria: 10.1, 10.2 and 10.3

Unit Q329

Deliver, monitor and evaluate service to external customers

What you will learn

- Understand the meaning of external customers
- Know the types of products and services relevant to external customers
- Understand how to deliver customer service that meets or exceeds external customer expectations
- Understand the purpose of quality standards and timescales for customer service to external customers
- Understand how to deal with customer service problems for external customers
- Understand how to monitor and evaluate external customer service and the benefits of this
- Be able to build positive working relationships with external customers
- Be able to deliver external customer services to agreed quality standards and timescales
- Be able to deal with customer service problems and complaints for external customers
- Be able to monitor and evaluate services to external customers

Introduction

Providing excellent customer service to external customers is central to the ongoing success of organisations. Organisations which consistently provide excellent customer service will achieve significant business benefits and will stand apart from their competitors in the market.

In this unit you will explore what is meant by external customers and you will look at the products and services which are relevant to these customers.

Meeting customers' needs is the foundation of providing good customer service to external customers and you will investigate what this means for you, in practice, as well as looking at ways in which you can make sure that you successfully meet – and even exceed – the needs of your customers.

Quality standards for customer service are designed to clearly establish the minimum requirements that must be met in service provision. These standards are issued by the organisation to staff to make sure that everyone knows what is expected of them when providing customer service.

You will investigate the quality standards that are relevant to your organisation and your own work and look at ways in which you can implement these in your role. You will also investigate the importance of being able to set and meet timescales with your external customers.

Skills for effectively dealing with problems are a key requirement for all employees who work in a customer-facing role. You will look into some of the typical problems which you may be presented with from external customers and at possible ways of handling these.

In the final section of this unit you will examine the reasons why it is important for organisations to monitor and evaluate external customer service as well as look at different ways in which this can be done.

Understanding external customers

After working through this section you will understand and be able to describe what is meant by external customers.

Defining who external customers are

External customers are any customers who make a transaction to purchase products and services from an organisation which they do not work for. Remember, too, that external customers can be individuals (members of the public) or other businesses. The diagram below shows the relationship between supplier and purchaser in the external customer relationship.

Most businesses are external customers of other businesses. This is because they need to purchase raw materials, and parts and services from other businesses in order for their own business to function effectively.

Organisations as external customers

If an organisation **outsources** its payroll function, for example, to a third-party service provider, then this organisation purchases this service from the provider and is an external customer to them.

> ### Key term
>
> **Outsources** – subcontracts work to a third party.

If a parts supplier is contracted to the same organisation to supply all the parts needed for the machinery in the factory, then the organisation is also a customer of this parts supplier.

Customer A pays Organisation B an agreed amount of money

Customer A

Organisation B

In return, Organisation B provides products and/or services to Customer A

Figure 329.1: *The external customer relationship*

Parts supplier has a contract to supply all machine parts to the organisation

The organisation as a customer

Third-party payroll service provider carries out payroll function for the organisation

Distribution company carries out all the distribution of the organisation's products to national retailers

Figure 329.2: *The organisation is an external customer of the payroll service provider, the parts supplier and the distribution company*

If the organisation outsources the distribution of its products from the factory to its retailers, then the organisation is also a customer of the distribution company. This organisation is a customer of three other businesses: the payroll company, the parts supplier and the distributor. This relationship is illustrated in Figure 329.2.

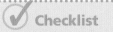

Checklist

Remember:

- External customers are individuals and organisations which purchase products and services from other organisations.

Portfolio task 329.1 → Links to **LO1**: assessment criterion 1.1

Write a short report which describes what is meant by external customers. Use three examples of external customers from your own experience to show your understanding of the term. These can be taken either from your work experience or from your own personal experience.

Activity 1

Look at the information in the table below and decide which of these relationships show examples of external customers.

Scenario	Example of an external customer relationship (Y/N)?	Reason
A student goes into her local phone shop to buy herself a new phone.		
An account manager requests a detailed breakdown of the sales report from the sales manager.		

A version of this table, ready for you to complete, is available to download from www.contentextra.com/businessadmin

Products and services relevant to external customers

After working through this section you will understand and be able to describe the products and services offered by the organisation to external customers.

Products and services offered by the organisation to external customers

In this section, you are going to carry out some research of your own to identify the products and services which your organisation provides to its external customers.

Portfolio task 329.2 ➡ Links to **LO2**: assessment criterion 2.1

Write a short report which describes the products and services offered by an organisation to external customers. You need to describe at least four products or services in your answer. You can describe your own organisation's products or services, or you can use another organisation whose products and services you are familiar with, on which to base your answer.

Functional skills

English: Speaking and listening

If your assessor asks you to take part in a discussion about this portfolio task as part of the assessment for this learning outcome, you may be able to count it as evidence towards Level 2 Functional English: Speaking and listening.

Activity 2

Carry out research within your organisation to compile a list of all the products and services which your company provides to its external customers. Ask your manager or mentor to help you to make sure you do not miss any products or services from your list.

If there is a company list of all available products and services, for example, from the company website or sales brochure, it would be a good idea to take a copy of this as it will be useful for you in completing your next portfolio task.

You may wish to complete the table below.

The products and services which my organisation provides to its external customers are:	

A version of this table, ready for you to complete, is available to download from www.contentextra.com/businessadmin

Delivering customer service that meets or exceeds expectations

After working through this section you will understand and be able to:

- explain the purpose and value of identifying customer needs and expectations
- explain why customer service must meet or exceed customer expectations
- explain the value of meeting or exceeding customer expectations
- explain the purpose and value of building positive working relationships.

The purpose and value of identifying customer needs and expectations

Identifying customer needs and expectations is the starting point for any organisation wishing to provide excellent customer service. If you don't know what your customers value from your organisation and what they expect you to provide for them, you cannot possibly develop a level of customer service provision that will satisfy their wants and needs.

Figure 329.3: *The provision of customer service is a continuous process*

Therefore, carrying out a thorough needs identification is a fundamental activity for all professionals involved in providing customer service for an organisation. The provision of excellent customer service can be illustrated as a cycle of activities as shown in Figure 329.3.

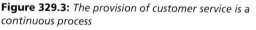

Checklist

Remember:

- Customers' needs are the top priority and must be satisfied.

- Customers' expectations are second in priority to their needs, although they are still important.

Activity 3

Carry out some research in your organisation to establish the methods used to identify customer service needs and expectations. Compile a list of your findings in the table below.

The methods which are used in my organisation to identify customer needs and expectations are:	

A version of this table, ready for you to complete, is available to download from www.contentextra.com/businessadmin

Portfolio task 329.3 → Links to **LO3**: assessment criteria 3.1

Write a short report which explains the purpose and value of identifying customer needs and expectations. You can use examples from your own organisation, or another of your choice, on which to base your answer. You need to include at least two examples.

Why customer service must meet or exceed customer needs and expectations

In this section, you are going to investigate how to meet and then exceed customers' needs and expectations, the reasons for doing this and the consequences for the organisation if it fails to do this.

Meeting customer needs

Once you have successfully identified your customers' needs, you can then begin to plan how you are going to develop your customer service provision in order to satisfy these needs.

You can do this by setting out a plan of actions and policies which addresses each need that has been identified (see Table 329.1).

By first identifying and then taking action to address each of the identified customer needs, the organisation will be sure of meeting these needs.

Activity 4

Now it's your turn to practice your management skills! Take a look at the table which is reproduced below from Table 329.1 and, for each identified customer need, say what you could do to take it one step further to exceeding, rather than simply just meeting, customers' needs.

Customer need	How the organisation will address this need	How the organisation could exceed, rather than just meet customer needs
1 Customers need quicker home delivery of products.	Arrange for next-day delivery to be offered as an option to customers.	

A version of this table, ready for you to complete, is available to download from www.contentextra.com/businessadmin

Table 329.1: *An example of how an organisation may decide to plan to satisfy its customers' needs*

Customer need	How the organisation will address this need
Customers need quicker home delivery of products.	Arrange for next-day delivery to be offered as an option to customers.
Customers need to be able to speak to a customer service advisor more easily via the automated telephone system.	Arrange a review of the current system to eliminate delays and aim to achieve a maximum wait time of less than two minutes for 95% of callers.
Customers need product support after they have made a purchase.	Add a specialist product support advice team to the customer service department with their own dedicated routing through the telephone system.

Exceeding customer needs

You have seen how an organisation can go about meeting customers' needs. But how can you take this one step further and really impress your customers by exceeding their needs?

Meeting minimum standards of customer expectations

Meeting customer expectations is the minimum standard which customer service teams must achieve to avoid causing customer dissatisfaction. Failing to meet these minimum standards will cause problems for the customer service team and also for the organisation in terms of customer complaints, returned products and cancellation of future orders. The ultimate action of dissatisfied customers is to take their custom elsewhere – usually to a competitor.

Customer service charters

Most large organisations have a publicly available customer service charter which states their commitment to excellent customer care. According to the Institute of Customer Service:

'The main purpose of a Customer Charter/Code of Practice is to improve access to an organisation's services and promote quality. It does this by telling customers the standards of service to expect, what to do if something goes wrong, and how to make contact. A Customer Charter/Code of Practice helps employees too, by setting out clearly the services their organisation provides.'

Source: www.instituteofcustomerservice.com.

As described above, the key reasons why organisations have customer service charters is to set out the minimum standards which customers can expect. When organisations fail to live up to the promises given in their charters, customers have the right to complain using the official complaints procedure.

Below is some of the information given in the Vale of White Horse District Council Customer Service Standards Charter. Read it and notice how it sets out exactly what the public can expect from the council:

'Whatever the service, whichever way they contact us, we promise our customers to:

● deal with enquiries in a friendly, helpful and courteous manner

● ensure we act without discrimination to meet customer needs

● provide accurate and timely information and advice

● treat any information given to us or held by us sensitively and discreetly, respecting any confidentiality

● meet the targets set out in our service standards

● treat any comments and complaints about our service seriously and handle them in a positive way.'

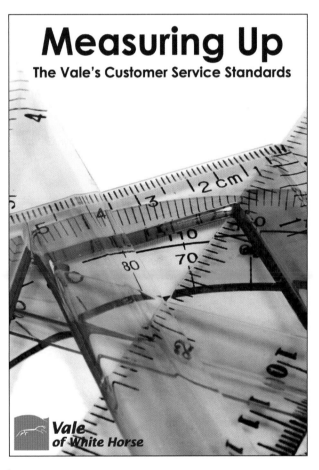

The Customer Service Charter for Vale of White Horse District Council

Portfolio task 329.4 → Links to **LO3**: assessment criterion 3.2

Write a brief report which explains three reasons why customer service must meet or exceed customer expectations. Use examples from your own organisation, or another of your choice, to illustrate your answer.

Functional skills

English: Reading

If you carry out research involving reading texts including work-related documents as well as Internet research in order to complete your portfolio task, you may be able to count this as evidence towards Level 2 Functional English: Reading. Remember to keep records of all of the documents, handbooks and guidelines which you study, along with the websites which you visit, as you will need to document any reading research you carry out.

The value of meeting or exceeding customer expectations

As you have seen on page 249, it is important to meet customers' needs, first and foremost, in order to prevent them from becoming dissatisfied with your organisation.

Organisations which strive to meet and exceed customer expectations benefit in many ways. The most obvious benefit is that they create a base of satisfied customers, who are therefore more likely to stay with that

✓ Checklist

Remember:

- Meeting customers' needs satisfies customers.

- Exceeding their needs delights them.

organisation in the future. This gives the organisation a long-term **revenue stream**, which is hugely valuable to any organisation because it has a solid **customer retention** profile.

Competitors

Your organisation most likely operates in a very competitive industry or sector and, if your competitors are offering better levels of customer service provision, you are risking losing your valuable customers to these companies.

Customer expectations

Remember, customers do not simply want good products and services from organisations nowadays. They also expect certain levels of service to go hand-in-hand with making a purchase – especially when the purchase is a large one such as a car or a house.

If your organisation provides a perfectly satisfactory level of customer service, but your competitor provides one which is excellent in every respect, your organisation is at a disadvantage. It needs to provide customer service which is at least as good as that of its competitors to be sure of retaining its customers – and of maintaining its **competitive position** in the market.

Key terms

Revenue stream – a method by which income is made by the company.

Customer retention – keeping hold of your customers so that they do future business with your company.

Competitive position – the position of an organisation in the market relative to that of its competitors.

Creating long-term relationships with your customers

Organisations which constantly strive to achieve or exceed customer expectations will create longer-term relationships with their customers than organisations which do not have this customer service focus.

Traditionally the customer relationship was viewed by organisations as a simple purchasing transaction where the focus of the organisation was simply to sell its products to make as much profit as possible.

This is sometimes referred to as a **product orientation**. The organisation would have no interest in any further contact with the customer, would maintain no contact details for them and no data on that customer's purchase history or future requirements.

Nowadays, however, businesses have realised that there is enormous value to be gained from developing ongoing relationships with customers and finding new ways of adding value to the customer experience. This is known as **customer orientation**. Keeping customers happy by providing excellent customer service is a very good way of doing this.

What kind of customer service might a car dealer offer?

Key terms

Product orientation – where a supplier purely concentrates on making sales.

Customer orientation – where a supplier focuses on developing a long-term relationship with its customers.

Customer First UK

Customer First UK is the awarding body responsible for overseeing implementation of the National Standard for Customer Service by organisations wishing to deliver the very highest standards of customer service. They identify five key benefits to organisations which adopt their high standards of customer service excellence:

- increased financial turnover
- improved services
- winning new customers
- competitive differentiation
- customer loyalty.

For more information on the National Standard for Customer Service, visit www.pearsonhotlinks.co.uk, search for this book title and click on the relevant unit.

Reputation

Being known as a business which has at its core the achievement of excellence in customer care will enhance the reputation of the organisation. This, in turn, will generate further benefits such as:

- attracting new customers – as people hear good things about a company, they are very quick to transfer their custom to that company
- retaining old customers – if customers are happy, they are very unlikely to go elsewhere
- generating good PR for the organisation, which is often picked up by the media, in effect giving the company free publicity.

Activity 5

Spend five minutes thinking of as many companies as you can which are well known for having an excellent customer service focus. Make a list of them and show it to your assessor.

Unit Q329 Deliver, monitor and evaluate customer service to external customers

Portfolio task 329.5 → Links to **LO3**: assessment criterion 3.3

Write a short summary which explains the value of meeting or exceeding customer expectations. Use two examples from your own organisation, or another of your choice, to illustrate your answer. It may help you to strengthen your answer if you carry out your own additional research for this task and include your findings from this in your answer.

Building positive working relationships

A positive working relationship is one in which two or more employees get along well, listen and respect each other's views, help each other out during challenging times and generally support one another in the achievement of work goals and tasks. This is especially important in dealing with external customer service issues as the quality of the work of the team or department is immediately obvious and visible to external customers. If they experience some negativity in working relationships, they may well begin to wonder what other problems are lurking.

Operating in a positive working relationship is very different to working in a negative working relationship.

To illustrate this, consider the example of one particularly busy day in the office. You are overloaded and cannot get through your workload. Meanwhile your colleague seems to have very little to do. He does not offer to help you, however, and considers it 'your problem' that you are drowning in work. Instead he decides to while away an hour on the phone, chatting to his friend – much to your astonishment and dismay. This is typical of the behaviour of colleagues in a culture of individualistic working where team-working is not valued.

In contrast, if there were a positive team ethos, your colleague would notice that you were overloaded and would offer to help you. You, in turn, would thank them and pass over some of your work so that between you

the work would be completed before the end of the day. Which of these two arrangements would you prefer?

Positive working relationships with external customers

Positive working relationships are not only important between internal colleagues, but they are also vital between customer service staff and their external customers. Whether a customer decides to stay with your organisation or go elsewhere often depends on the quality of the relationship which exists with the customer service staff.

Benefits of building positive working relationships

Building positive working relationships with colleagues and customers has several benefits:

● The organisation produces better results.

● Teamworking can be effective in achieving results, especially in challenging situations.

● The organisation is a more attractive place in which to work.

● Staff remain for longer with the company and enjoy a much more pleasant working life.

Activity 6

Think of three things which you could do in your present job role to ensure that you help to maintain positive working relationships with your colleagues and manager.

✓ Checklist

Remember, positive working relationships require the ability to:

• respect other people's views and opinions

• listen to alternative viewpoints

• behave in ways which do not cause harm or upset to others.

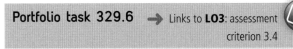

Portfolio task 329.6 → Links to **LO3**: assessment criterion 3.4

Write a short report which explains the purpose and value of building positive working relationships. Use two examples from your own organisation, or another of your choice, to illustrate your answer.

Quality standards and timescales for customer service

After working through this section you will understand and be able to:

● identify quality standards for your own organisation and work

● explain the value of agreeing quality standards and timescales

● explain how to set and meet quality standards and timescales with external customers.

Quality standards for your organisation and your work

In this section you will examine some of the quality standards that apply to your organisation and your job.

Organisational quality standards

Organisations can have many quality standards, kite marks, accreditations and charters, which encompass the high standards to which they work. Some quality standards are international and can apply to all organisations, whereas others are national, regional or industry-sector specific. Some are also **regulatory** – and are therefore a legal requirement for the organisation to meet, whereas others are voluntary.

Key term

Regulatory – subject to government regulations, which must be obeyed.

What do organisational quality standards cover?

The quality standards of an organisation are concerned with aspects of the organisation such as:

● the products and services that the organisation provides

● the suppliers and distributors that they use

● the way in which they recruit, manage, train and develop their staff

● their commitment to customer service

● their approach to management and leadership.

Some examples of organisational quality standards include the following:

● ISO9001 – this is an international quality standard which is achieved by organisations for their quality management systems, where they can demonstrate their conformity not only to customer service but also to regulatory requirements which apply to their products and services.

● Investors in People – this is a standard which is awarded to those organisations which demonstrate their commitment to developing their staff, providing good training and career opportunities. It can be awarded to organisations across any sector.

● Positive about disabled people – this symbol is awarded by Jobcentre Plus to employers in England, Scotland and Wales who have made specific commitments regarding the employment of

Look for this sign on job adverts – it shows the company is positive about employing disabled people

disabled people. In order to be awarded this symbol, organisations must make five commitments to disabled employees including agreeing to interview all disabled candidates who satisfy the minimum criteria for a job vacancy, as well as raising awareness among all of their staff about disability issues.

● Customer First® – this is a standard awarded to organisations for the achievement of excellent customer service and involves a three-point framework against which organisations wishing to become accredited must be assessed: building customer relationships, maximising market awareness and staff development.

putting the
Customer First®

If an organisation displays this logo, it has achieved the Customer First® Standard

✓ Checklist

Remember:

- Organisational quality standards are in recognition of excellence in a particular area.

- Organisations must provide evidence to the awarding standard body to demonstrate that they practise excellence in that particular area.

- Quality standards do not last forever; each will usually have a time limit after which the organisation must reapply to keep its quality standard.

Quality standards for your own work

Depending on your role in the organisation, there may be many different quality standards which have been set to define the way in which you must perform your work tasks. Using an example of a customer service assistant, typical quality standards which may apply could include:

● being polite and courteous to external customers at all times

● answering the phone within three rings

● resolving customer complaints within two business days.

Activity 7

Carry out some research within your organisation to identify all the quality standards that your organisation possesses. Make sure you know what each quality standard is for and what your organisation needs to do in order to keep the quality standard. You can use the table below to record your findings. The information from this activity will be very useful for you in completing portfolio task 329.7.

Organisational quality standard	What is it for?	How often must the quality standard be renewed?

A version of this table, ready for you to complete, is available to download from www.contentextra.com/businessadmin

Work quality standards can be further broken down into specific elements including:

- to what level of accuracy (so, 95 per cent of all calls, 100 per cent of all complaints)
- by when (and whether 'within seven days' includes weekends or bank holidays or whether it refers to business working days only).

Breaking down standards into very detailed elements in this way is really beneficial to all involved with their use. This is because the detail removes any ambiguity that may exist in the initial standard. For example, if the phone is to be answered within three rings, does this mean by an automated answering service or an employee? Precise detail makes it clear to employees the exact requirements of them. That way, they are more likely to succeed in achieving them.

Activity 8

Identify all the relevant quality standards that relate to your job. Ask your manager to help you to identify these if you are unsure of them. Make a list of the relevant standards in the table below. This information will be very useful for you in completing the next portfolio task.

Quality standard relating to my job	Reason for having this quality standard

A version of this table, ready for you to complete, is available to download from www.contentextra.com/businessadmin

Portfolio task 329.7

Links to **LO4**: assessment criterion 4.1

Write a short summary which identifies the relevant quality standards for your own organisation and work. You can use the information which you presented in the activities on pages 254 and above to complete this portfolio task.

Make sure you select two organisational standards and two work-related standards to use in your answer. You may like to complete the tables below in order to compile all the information needed for your portfolio task.

Quality standard for my organisation	How this affects my organisation

A version of this table, ready for you to complete, is available to download from www.contentextra.com/businessadmin

Quality standard for my own work	How this affects my work

A version of this table, ready for you to complete, is available to download from www.contentextra.com/businessadmin

Agreeing quality standards and timescales

Value of agreeing quality standards

The benefit of agreeing quality standards for your work is that they set out very clearly exactly what is expected of you and by when. These types of detail are often included in customer service charters.

Having standards laid down is also a very good way for you to keep track of your achievements at work, which will be valuable to present to your manager at your performance review meeting.

If you keep a diary, write up each job you are given to do and the time it took you. If you receive positive feedback and thanks from satisfied customers by letter or email, keep copies of these, as they are evidence of your successful performance against your work standards.

Activity 9

Carry out some Internet research to locate customer service charters for two different organisations, one of which can be your own organisation if it has a customer service charter.

Look over the content of each charter and highlight two similarities and two differences between them.

Value of agreeing timescales

Agreeing timescales with external customers for the completion of work is a very valuable activity as it demonstrates your service commitment to them. It is helpful to both you and the customer as it sets out, unambiguously, by when the particular task will be completed. This also gives you as the employee the opportunity to demonstrate **integrity** to your customer, which will show them that the organisation and its staff value their customers and their needs.

Key term

Integrity – honesty or keeping to your word.

Activity 10

Give two examples of ways in which you can agree timescales with external customers in your organisation. For each, say what you would do in that situation if there were difficulties with keeping to these timescales.

✓ Checklist

Establishing and agreeing timescales with external customers

Remember:

- Do not get pushed into agreeing to a time which you cannot possibly achieve, as this will only cause further frustration to the customer later on.

- If things change and a timescale later becomes a problem, let the customer know straightaway and negotiate a new timescale with them.

Portfolio task 329.8 → Links to **LO4**: assessment criterion 4.2

Write a brief report which explains the value of agreeing quality standards and timescales. In order to complete this portfolio task, you need to give two benefits of securing agreement on quality standards and two benefits of securing agreement on timescales to show your understanding. Use your own organisation, or another of your choice, on which to base your answer.

Functional skills

English: Writing

If you take care to produce a professional and well-presented report for your answer to this portfolio task, you may be able to count it as evidence towards Level 2 Functional English: Writing. Remember to use headings and subheadings, check you have used correct spelling and grammar and then print out the final version of your report, once you have made all your corrections.

Setting and meeting quality standards and timescales with external customers

A good technique for you to adopt in order to successfully negotiate quality standards and timescales with external customers is to make sure the agreement is in enough detail (see page 255). You will now investigate how this works in practice.

Setting and meeting quality standards with external customers

Quality standards relevant to your external customers could include:

● dealing with a delayed product delivery

● replacing a faulty product

● arranging for a special discount.

The setting of quality standards in any of these instances will involve stating what you are going to do for the customer and how you are going to do it. For example, to deal with a delay in a product being delivered to a customer, you may say that you will:

● track the despatch of the order by the end of the current working day and confirm back to the customer the status of the order

● investigate the tracking of the order and, depending on what you discover, offer to place a new order for the customer with next-day delivery, free of charge.

Setting and meeting timescales with external customers

In order to meet timescales which you agree with customers, you must be very careful not to over-promise. This means avoiding promising to deliver things in an unrealistic time for them. This will require a degree of **assertiveness** on your part, as the customer may be skilled in persuading others to agree to their wishes.

Setting timescales

Before you embark on a discussion with a customer about timescales, you need to do some preparation by identifying minimum lead times which you will need to work to. This will effectively be your fallback position with the customer, but you should always try to build in a margin for error, just in case things cannot proceed quite as quickly as you would like.

Meeting timescales

Once you have set and agreed timescales with a customer, you must then work hard to track the progress of the work to make sure it is processed as per your timescale. This may involve significant coordination of others on your part. Achieving a timescale which you have agreed with a customer is a very valuable accomplishment. Your customer will no doubt be very pleased with your efforts and will know that you put their needs and expectations as your top priority.

> **Key term**
>
> **Assertiveness** – standing up for yourself in a non-aggressive manner.

> **Portfolio task 329.9** → Links to **LO4**: assessment criterion 4.3
>
> Write a short report which can be used to train new members of staff in your organisation and which explains how to set and meet quality standards and timescales with external customers. Give two examples each of how to meet (a) these standards and (b) these timescales in your answer.

Dealing with customer service problems for external customers

After working through this section you will understand and be able to:

● describe the types of problems that external customers may have

● explain the consequences of not meeting external customer needs and expectations

● explain ways of dealing with external customer services problems

● explain the purpose and value of a complaints procedure.

Types of problems that external customers may have

Typical problems which external customers may experience from time to time may include the following.

- The product they ordered is not delivered on time – or at all.
- The wrong product is delivered to them.
- The product is faulty.
- They need advice on how to use a product from the company (such as the correct installation of new software, for example).
- The product is not as it was described by the company.
- The customer is not happy with the service which they received from a company.
- The customer cannot get through on the phone to the company to complain.
- The customer does not like the automated telephone answering system which they have to go through to get to speak to an advisor.

Portfolio task 329.10 → Links to **LO5**: assessment criterion 5.1

Write a brief report which describes three types of problems that external customers may have. You may use examples of customer problems from your own organisation, or another of your choice, in your answer. Remember to say in each case why these problems occur and whether they are simple or difficult things to resolve for the customer.

Functional skills

English: Speaking and listening

If your assessor asks you to take part in a discussion about this portfolio task as part of the assessment for this learning outcome, you may be able to count it as evidence towards Level 2 Functional English: Speaking and listening.

Activity 11

The problems above are just a small sample of the types of problems which external customers may experience – you can probably think of more to add to this list. Think of three key issues which can be the cause of customer problems, using examples either from your work experience or from your own personal experience as an external customer.

Complete the table:

Three key issues which can be the cause of customer problems are:	

A version of this table, ready for you to complete, is available to download from www.contentextra.com/businessadmin

Consequences of not meeting external customer needs

The customers of any organisation will have certain needs and expectations of minimum service levels which they expect from that organisation. When these are not met, the customer – understandably – will become upset and frustrated.

This can cause a number of problems such as:

- an increase in the number of customer complaints received by the organisation
- customers deciding to take their business to a competitor
- customers telling others about the bad service which the company has given them (if this is expressed online via social network sites, the remarks will spread rapidly and cause huge damage to the company's reputation).

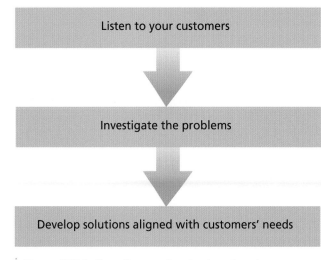

Figure 329.4: *Flow diagram showing how to act on customer feedback*

In order for a business to survive, it needs to make sales. In order to make sales, it has to sell products and services which meet customers' needs. If a business fails to address the issue of customers' needs not being met, or does not adapt its product and services to cater for changing customer needs, ultimately the business will fail.

This is why it is so vitally important for organisations to regularly listen to the feedback that it receives from its customers and, importantly, act on it where areas of concern are highlighted (see Figure 329.4).

Activity 12

Carry out research within your own organisation to find out whether there is a policy or guidance document in place for dealing with customer needs. Find out what compensation, if any, is offered by the company to unhappy customers. If there is no documentation available to you which mentions dealing with customer needs, draft a one-paragraph document which outlines the ways in which you believe customers' needs should be dealt with by the customer service staff in your organisation.

Portfolio task 329.11 ➡ Links to **LO5**: assessment criterion 5.2

Write a brief report which explains three consequences of not meeting external customer needs and expectations. You may include examples from your own organisation, or another of your choice, in your answer.

Office life

Sue's story

My name is Sue Wright and I have been working as an administrative executive in the customer services department of a large telecoms company for six months. During this time, I have noticed that certain customer issues are beginning to take longer to resolve than they used to. As a result, we are starting to see an increased volume of upset and angry callers coming through to us on the telephone.

This problem seems to have arisen since we recruited a new team of customer service representatives, all of whom are quite inexperienced. There is a distinct lack of team spirit among these new recruits and they are all fiercely competitive with each other. I am sure that if something is not done soon, the problems will only escalate.

I want to raise this with my line manager but I am hesitant to be seen to be airing negative views about the company. After all, I do enjoy my position and I hope to make a long-term career out of my position with this organisation.

Ask the expert

Q The performance of the external customer service team in our company is suffering due to a lack of positive working relationships among the new recruits. These new customer service representatives are more concerned with competing with each other than providing good customer care. I am concerned that this situation is going to result in disaster for the team if something does not change. What do you recommend?

A The new recruits to the team need to be given some extensive training, which would definitely include some team-building initiatives, as well as customer-care training and team-working skills training. It seems that their lack of team spirit is a result of their inexperience, and their very individualistic personalities. This is compounded by their short time with the company, so they have not yet had time to assimilate the customer service culture.

Top tips

Positive working relationships among customer service representatives are a vital component of a good customer service ethos. When new team members are recruited in such customer-facing positions, it should be a priority for the department that they undergo certain training initiatives to ensure they can quickly learn the critical skills and abilities required of them to work in harmony with the existing team members and adopt the prevailing team spirit. As the problems Sue has identified are of vital importance to the organisation, she should have no hesitation in reporting the situation to her line manager, who should in turn organise training for the relevant customer service representatives.

Dealing with external customer services problems

Every organisation will experience customers who have problems from time to time. This is why all organisations should have a set of guidelines for staff who deal with these situations, so that when customer service staff come across such a situation, they are well prepared to handle it in the most professional way.

The key to successfully managing customer service problems is to remember that the customer is most likely quite upset and needs to vent their feelings. Once they have expressed their initial complaint, they will usually become calmer and be ready to listen to you. This is where you have the golden opportunity to turn the situation around and find the most appropriate form of compensation for their inconvenience. If they are satisfied with both the manner and the outcome of your dealings with them, it is more likely that they will remain a customer of the organisation in the future.

Why is it important to remain calm and friendly when talking to customers?

Guidelines for dealing with external customer service problems

Below is a step-by-step guide for dealing with customer service problems.

> ### ✓ Checklist
>
> **Remember**
>
> 1 Listen – really listen – to the customer.
> 2 Do not interrupt them.
> 3 Make notes on what they say so that you can refer to these later. Also, this will help you to establish the facts even if the conversation becomes heated. Try to find out exactly what has gone wrong.
> 4 Pause for one or two seconds before you begin to reply to them.
> 5 Be polite and calm in all that you say.
> 6 Carry out a damage limitation exercise with your customer – after all, you want to keep this customer if at all possible.
> 7 Gauge what outcome from this situation will make the customer happy.
> 8 Offer replacement products, alternatives or a refund.
> 9 Make sure that these compensatory offers are given to the customer immediately.

Activity 13

Carry out research within your organisation to identify the ways in which external customer service problems and issues are generally dealt with. Find out:

- whether there is a policy document or charter which details the company's approach to dealing with customer problems (and ask to be given a copy of it); and

- whose responsibility it is for dealing with customer service issues in your organisation.

Unit Q329

Deliver, monitor and evaluate customer service to external customers

✓ Checklist

Remember:

- If you can successfully manage customer service problems, the organisation is more likely to keep these customers.

- If you can establish what compensation the customer wants and arrange for this to be given to them, you can turn the situation around and provide a positive outcome.

Portfolio task 329.12 → Links to **LO5**: assessment criterion 5.3

Write a short report which is to be used to train new members of staff in your organisation and which explains three ways of dealing with external customer services problems. You may include examples from your own organisation, or another of your choice, in your answer.

The purpose and value of a complaints procedure

A complaints procedure is a very important business document which all organisations should have. It is important because it outlines to all concerned that the organisation:

- takes complaints seriously – and will act on them
- has an official procedure in place to look into complaints consistently
- wants to resolve complaints as quickly and efficiently as possible
- is keen to address any issues within the organisation which may need improvement.

Purpose of complaints procedures

The key purpose of a complaints procedure is to resolve all complaints that come into the organisation as quickly as possible. This will ensure that there are no negative issues left unresolved – with all the associated problems that are brought along with them.

Beyond complaints resolution, other purposes of complaints procedures include:

- ensuring consistency and control in the treatment of all complaints
- giving customers a **transparent** process by which they can seek a solution to their issues
- providing vital information to the organisation on areas where improvements need to be made.

Key term

Transparent – clear and open for all to see.

Value of complaints procedures

The key benefits of having a complaints procedure are that:

- customers can see that the organisation cares about the level of quality which it provides to its customers
- it encourages speedy and informal resolution of issues
- it shows the organisation to be fair in its treatment of complaints.

A complaints procedure also details the exact steps that are being taken by both the customer and the organisation throughout the procedure, along with the time by which each step is to be completed. It should ensure both confidentiality and privacy for the person making the complaint.

Portfolio task 329.13 → Links to **LO5**: assessment criterion 5.4

Write a short report which is to be used to train new members of staff in your organisation and which explains the purpose and value of a complaints procedure.

You should include two examples showing the benefits of complaints procedures which are relevant to your own organisation, or another of your choice, in your answer.

Monitoring and evaluating external customer service

After working through this section you will understand and be able to:

- explain the purpose and benefits of monitoring external customer satisfaction and how to do so
- describe techniques for collecting and evaluating external customer feedback
- explain the benefits of continuous improvement.

The purpose and benefits of monitoring external customer satisfaction

Why monitoring external customer satisfaction is important

Organisations must monitor external customer satisfaction levels to make sure that customers are happy and that there are no issues which need to be addressed. Monitoring customer satisfaction levels gives very valuable information to the organisation and allows it to make any necessary changes or improvements to products and services when problems come to light.

Failing to keep track of customer satisfaction levels may mean organisations miss opportunities to make improvements because, by the time they realise that there is an issue to be dealt with, its customers have already gone elsewhere. Losing customers in this way is very bad for the organisation. This is because it is very expensive to attract new customers to replace those which it has lost. It would be smarter for the organisation to focus time and effort instead on keeping its existing customers.

Ways in which monitoring of external customer satisfaction can be carried out

The main methods which organisations can use to monitor external customer satisfaction include:

- questionnaires
- focus groups
- suggestion boxes
- the website.

Questionnaires

Questionnaires are a good method for collecting feedback from a large volume of respondents in a relatively short time. They can also be sent out via email and the results collected electronically, which makes the subsequent collation of results extremely easy.

Focus groups

Focus groups are special groups of customers who are brought together to discuss and give their opinions about certain issues. They usually consist of up to ten members and the group discussions can last quite a long time. The group is usually led by a **facilitator** who will guide the members through the process and keep their discussions on track. The focus group discussions are also normally recorded so that the points made and issues voiced can be analysed later on and the results reported back.

> **Key terms**
>
> **Facilitator** – someone who helps a group with their discussions without taking sides.

Focus groups are a good method to use for monitoring customer satisfaction because the group members are able to contribute freely to the group's discussion and they are also free to go into as much detail as is necessary to explain their opinions or concerns. This level of detail is also very useful for getting to the bottom of problems that may exist with customer satisfaction.

Suggestion boxes

Suggestion boxes are often used in organisations such as supermarkets in order to allow customers a convenient and quick method for giving their opinions and feedback on their customer experiences. Customers are invited to give both positive and negative information, depending on the nature of their experience.

Information gathered from suggestion boxes can be difficult to collate and analyse, however, as there is no particular structure to the information which is provided. Usually it is a blank piece of paper which the customer completes in whatever way they wish.

Have you ever written a suggestion for a suggestion box?

Websites

Organisations often use their websites to invite feedback from their customers. The main advantage of this method of collecting feedback is that it is very quick and easy to complete. In addition, because it is electronic in format, it is easy to collate and analyse.

Activity 14

Carry out some research within your organisation to identify the methods that are used to monitor external customer satisfaction levels. Make a list of the methods that you find as these will be useful for you in completing the next portfolio task.

Portfolio task 329.14 → Links to **LO6**: assessment criterion 6.1

Write a short report which explains:

- the purpose and benefits of monitoring external customer satisfaction

- three ways in which monitoring external customer satisfaction can be carried out.

You should include examples from your own organisation, or another of your choice, in your answer to show your understanding.

Techniques for collecting and evaluating external customer feedback

Questionnaires

Information received in the form of questionnaires has the advantage of being fairly easy to collate, as each respondent has answered the same set of mainly structured and **closed questions**. This means that a lot of feedback can be quickly analysed and summarised in report format. The headings in the report can be tailored to the key results found, and the report can be further enhanced by the inclusion of graphs and charts to add a visual impact (see Figure 329.5 below).

Key term

Closed questions – questions where there are only certain possible answers, such as yes/no.

Focus groups

Feedback received via focus groups is more time-consuming to collate and summarise. This is because focus groups are open verbal discussions between groups of people. They can also contain significantly more detail than that which is typically involved in a questionnaire. The issues raised and the opinions expressed during focus group discussions are largely unpredictable and no two focus groups are ever likely to be the same. The analysis of the discussions will involve an in-depth study of the

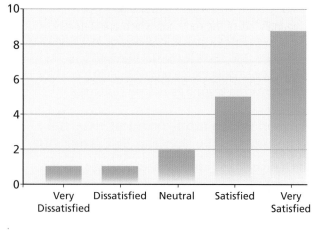

Figure 329.5: *Bar graph showing the response to a survey*

notes or recordings taken during each of the focus-group sessions and a report will subsequently be generated. This will usually be along the lines of a summary of each of the main topics raised and the feelings of the majority of the group on each issue.

Suggestion boxes

Feedback received via suggestion boxes is potentially complicated to analyse. This is because of the huge variety of information which can come in via this method. The most obvious way to begin an analysis of suggestion-box feedback would be to separate the positive from the negative feedback. The positive comments can be relayed back to staff via email, team meetings and internal company newsletters. The negative feedback will require more detailed processing to examine any common complaints and to split these up by giving each a rating of urgency or severity. If, for example, twenty complaints are received about lengthy delays at the supermarket checkouts, then this issue must be flagged up for further investigation and action by management. Once the results have been reviewed, a summary report can be produced which gives the main topics of complaint along with the severity of the issue for the customers.

Websites

Feedback received via the website is quick and easy to analyse and evaluate if imported into a spreadsheet for detailed analysis. A report can then be generated to highlight the main issues received.

Activity 15

Carry out research within your organisation to identify all of the methods which are currently used to collect external customer feedback. Keep a note of your findings as they will be useful for you in completing the next portfolio task.

✓ Checklist

Remember:

• Different methods of collecting customer feedback will require different approaches to analysing and reporting.

Portfolio task 329.15 → Links to **LO6**: assessment criterion 6.2

Write a short report which describes three techniques for collecting and evaluating external customer feedback. Use examples of techniques which are used in your own organisation, or another of your choice, in your answer.

The benefits of continuous improvement

Continuous improvement is a term used in business to mean the implementation of ongoing initiatives to make improvements to all aspects of the work which a business undertakes. Continuous improvement techniques include:

● *kaizen* – a Japanese approach which aims to foster continuous improvement, which involves contributions from all members of staff regardless of seniority

● lean production – this is a technique used to eliminate waste and unnecessary costs in production and manufacturing processes

● quality circles – where groups of staff meet on a regular basis to discuss how they can make improvements to efficiency in their roles.

Activity 16

Carry out some research within your own organisation to find out whether your company uses any continuous improvement techniques. If so, keep notes of any initiatives which they undertake as these will be very useful for you in completing the next portfolio task.

If your organisation does not use any continuous improvement techniques, carry out some Internet research to identify an example of an organisation which does. Make notes on your chosen company and the techniques which it uses, as you will need these to complete the next portfolio task.

Benefits of adopting continuous improvement techniques

The key benefits which are associated with using continuous improvement techniques within an organisation are:

- reduction in waste and therefore costs
- improvements to efficiency of processes which bring about savings of both time and money
- improved satisfaction, commitment and morale among staff, as they feel involved with and can directly contribute to the improvements which are achieved by the business.

Activity 17

1 Carry out some Internet research to identify three organisations which adopt continuous improvement techniques.

2 Research and describe two different continuous improvement techniques which can be used by organisations. Write one paragraph on each technique that you identify.

Portfolio task 329.16 → Links to **LO6**: assessment criterion 6.3

Write a short report which explains three benefits of continuous improvement. You may use examples from your own organisation, or another of your choice, in your answer to show your understanding.

Evidence collection

In order for you to complete the remaining assessment criteria to successfully pass this unit, you will need to carry out various tasks at work and then produce evidence to show that you have demonstrated the required skills and competence.

Evidence can be collected in a number of different ways. For example, it can be in the form of a signed witness testimony from a colleague or line manager, a copy of any related emails or letters you have produced, or a verbal discussion with your assessor.

Speak to your assessor to identify the best methods to use in order to complete each portfolio task and remember to keep copies of all the evidence that you produce.

Be able to build positive working relationships with external customers

Portfolio task 329.17

→ Links to **LO7**: assessment criteria 7.1, 7.2, 7.3 and 7.4

Gather evidence of your work to show your assessor that you have successfully carried out the tasks outlined in the table below. Check with your assessor on the best ways of gathering evidence for each of the tasks before you begin.

Task	Evidence collected
1 Identify external customers.	
2 Confirm external customer needs in terms of products and services.	

A version of this form, ready for you to complete, is available to download from www.contentextra.com/businessadmin

Be able to deliver external customer services to agreed quality standards and timescales

Portfolio task 329.18

→ Links to **LO8**: assessment criteria 8.1, 8.2 and 8.3

Gather evidence of your work to show your assessor that you have successfully carried out the tasks outlined in the table below. Check with your assessor on the best ways of gathering evidence for each of the tasks before you begin.

Task	Evidence collected
1 Provide external customer service(s) to agreed quality standards.	
2 Provide external customer service(s) to agreed timescales.	

A version of this form, ready for you to complete, is available to download from www.contentextra.com/businessadmin

Unit Q329

Deliver, monitor and evaluate customer service to external customers

Be able to deal with customer service problems and complaints for external customers

Portfolio Task 329.19

→ Links to **LO9**: assessment criteria 9.1

Gather evidence of your work to show your assessor that you have successfully carried out the tasks outlined in the table below. Check with your assessor on the best ways of gathering evidence for each of the tasks before you begin.

Task	Evidence collected
1 Follow procedures, within agreed timescale, to: a) process problems and complaints	

A version of this form, ready for you to complete, is available to download from www.contentextra.com/businessadmin

Be able to monitor and evaluate services to external customers

Portfolio task 329.20

→ Links to **LO10**: assessment criteria 10.1, 10.2 and 10.3

Gather evidence of your work to show your assessor that you have successfully carried out the tasks outlined in the table below. Check with your assessor on the best ways of gathering evidence for each of the tasks before you begin.

Task	Evidence collected
1 Obtain and record external customer feedback.	

A version of this form, ready for you to complete, is available to download from www.contentextra.com/businessadmin

Check your knowledge answers

1 Which of the following is an example of an external customer?

a) A colleague requesting some sales figures.

b) A manager from head office asking for a coffee.

c) A car driver filling his tank with petrol at the local garage.

d) An account manager asking for customer contact records.

2 Which of these are typical products or services available to external customers?

a) Sensitive personal employee data.

b) Televisions, DVD players and other consumer electronics.

c) Monthly sales reports.

d) Annual performance appraisals.

3 Which of these is a typical external customer need?

a) To be able to access product advice and support after making a purchase.

b) To be able to chat to employees by text message.

c) To be given access to stock-control information.

d) To be able to read confidential company information.

4 Why does customer service have to meet customer expectations?

a) Customer service does not necessarily have to meet customer expectations.

b) Because expectations are legally binding.

c) Because failure to meet customer expectations will result in dissatisfaction among customers.

d) Because failure to meet customer expectations will result in instant dismissal.

5 Which of these would not be a typical quality standard for your work?

a) To make ten cups of coffee per day for your team.

b) To answer the telephone within three rings.

c) To respond to ten customer queries per day.

d) To be polite and attentive to all customers who approach you with queries.

6 What is the main benefit of agreeing timescales for the completion of work?

a) You can extend the deadline afterwards.

b) You establish clearly with colleagues the time when the work will be completed so that there is no misunderstanding.

c) You can argue for longer to complete the work.

d) You will be forced into working long hours to get the work done on time.

7 Which of these is not a typical problem which a customer may have?

a) The product is the wrong colour when it arrives.

b) The product is late arriving.

c) The customer service team are very helpful.

d) The product does not work.

8 What is the main consequence of not meeting external customer needs?

a) The organisation will achieve its customer service standards.

b) The organisation will have dissatisfied customers.

c) The organisation will have delighted customers.

d) The organisation will double its customer numbers.

9 What is the key purpose of monitoring customer satisfaction?

a) To spy on customers.

b) To spot any issues which may arise with customer satisfaction and to address these as quickly as possible.

c) To generate some interesting facts and figures.

d) To reduce satisfaction.

10 Which of these is not a typical method of collecting feedback from customers?

a) Surveys.

b) Questionnaires.

c) TV interviews.

d) Suggestion boxes.

Answers to the Check your knowledge questions can be found at www.contentextra.com/businessadmin

What your assessor is looking for

In order to prepare for and succeed in completing this unit, your assessor will require you to be able to demonstrate competence in all of the performance criteria listed in the table below.

Your assessor will guide you through the assessment process, but it is likely that for this unit you will need to:

● complete short written narratives or personal statements explaining your answers

● take part in professional discussions with your assessor to explain your answers verbally

● complete observations with your assessor ensuring that they can observe you carrying out your work tasks

● produce any relevant work products to help demonstrate how you have completed the assessment criteria

● ask your manager, a colleague, or a customer for witness testimonies explaining how you have completed the assessment criteria.

Please note that the evidence which you generate for the assessment criteria in this unit may also count towards your evidence collection for some of the other units in this qualification. Your assessor will provide support and guidance on this.

The table on the next page outlines the portfolio tasks which you need to complete for this unit, mapped to their associated assessment criteria.

Task and page reference	Mapping assessment criteria
Portfolio task 329.1 (page 245)	Assessment criterion: 1.1
Portfolio task 329.2 (page 246)	Assessment criterion: 2.1
Portfolio task 329.3 (page 248)	Assessment criterion: 3.1
Portfolio task 329.4 (page 250)	Assessment criterion: 3.2
Portfolio task 329.5 (page 252)	Assessment criterion: 3.3
Portfolio task 329.6 (page 253)	Assessment criterion: 3.4
Portfolio task 329.7 (page 255)	Assessment criterion: 4.1
Portfolio task 329.8 (page 256)	Assessment criterion: 4.2
Portfolio task 329.9 (page 257)	Assessment criterion: 4.3
Portfolio task 329.10 (page 258)	Assessment criterion: 5.1
Portfolio task 329.11 (page 259)	Assessment criterion: 5.2
Portfolio task 329.12 (page 262)	Assessment criterion: 5.3
Portfolio task 329.13 (page 262)	Assessment criterion: 5.4
Portfolio task 329.14 (page 264)	Assessment criterion: 6.1
Portfolio task 329.15 (page 265)	Assessment criterion: 6.2
Portfolio task 329.16 (page 266)	Assessment criterion: 6.3
Portfolio task 329.17 (page 267)	Assessment criteria: 7.1, 7.2, 7.3 and 7.4
Portfolio task 329.18 (page 267)	Assessment criteria: 8.1, 8.2 and 8.3
Portfolio task 329.19 (page 268)	Assessment criterion: 9.1
Portfolio task 329.20 (page 268)	Assessment criteria: 10.1, 10.2 and 10.3

Glossary

Aligned – relevant to and in accordance with the needs of the business.

Arbitrate – to help resolve a dispute.

Assertiveness – standing up for yourself in a non-aggressive manner.

Best practice – a method seen as the most effective at achieving an outcome.

Body language – the gestures, postures or facial expressions of a person.

Bottlenecks – these hold up work flow and cause a delay.

Brand – a brand is an identifiable trade name, product or logo.

Chairperson – the person leading a meeting.

Clerical error – an error in processing a task by an employee in the office.

Closed questions – questions where there are only certain possible answers, such as yes/no.

Collaborative – working together with other people or departments to achieve goals.

Competitive advantage – when an organisation is able to secure profits above the average gained by its competitors.

Competitive position – the position of an organisation in the market relative to that of its competitors.

Consistently – always the same.

Constructive feedback – feedback which is designed to focus on the positives, helping the employee to find ways of improving, while avoiding personal criticism.

Contingency plan – an alternative plan of action set up to minimise disruption to a business where an original plan did not go as scheduled.

Culture – many unspoken rules which develop in an organisation over time and which simply become the way things are done.

Customer orientation – where a supplier focuses on developing a long-term relationship with its customers.

Customer retention – keeping hold of your customers so that they do future business with your company.

Delegating – giving authority or responsibility to another person to carry out a task.

Detrimental – causing harm or damage.

Differentiate – to find a way of making a company or product different from its competitors.

Diligence – a high degree of care and attention.

Disciplined – reprimanded for some aspect of your behaviour or performance; in a work situation this is usually part of a disciplinary procedure.

Discrimination – when someone is treated unfairly at work on the basis of their ethnic origin, age, sexual orientation, gender or ability.

Dismissed – told you no longer have a job.

Effectively – working well to produce good results.

Efficient – able to complete a task quickly and to a high standard.

Eliciting – evoking or drawing out.

Empathy – being understanding and sensitive.

Empowerment – the process of enabling or authorising an individual to think, behave, take action, control their work and take part in decision-making processes.

Ethos – character or spirit.

External customers – customers from outside the organisation.

Facilitator – someone who helps a group with their discussions without taking sides.

Finite – something which only has a limited supply.

Goals and targets – short-term plans for the achievement of specific aims.

Housekeeping – Making sure the meeting room is tidy, all the equipment is working and that refreshments are ordered, etc., so that the meeting can run smoothly.

Inclusivity – including everybody from all levels of the organisation.

Inefficiencies – things that are wasteful and do not help achieve results.

Information Commissioner – the UK regulator concerned with data protection issues.

Integrity – honesty or keeping to your word.

Interdependency – where people or departments are dependent on one another.

Interdependent – being dependent on one another.

Intellectual property – intangible items such as ideas, art or brands which have a value to organisations.

Interdependent – being dependent on one another.

Internal communication – communication (face to face, emails, memos) between staff in an organisation.

Internal customers – people or departments within the organisation who depend on you in some way.

Interpersonal relationships – relationships between two or more individuals.

Job satisfaction – being happy in your job.

Key competencies – tasks performed to meet the basic requirements of a job.

KISS – Keep It Short and Simple – a useful acronym to remember in verbal and written communication.

Leading questions – questions which plant a pre-supposed answer into the mind of the respondent.

Learning organisations – organisations which encourage learning, thereby creating a knowledgeable workforce, or are willing to accept and adapt to new ideas and change.

Learning plan – a plan containing specific measurable targets, drawn up for each member of staff to help plan their learning and development needs.

Milestones – scheduled events signifying the completion of a task.

Mission and objectives – a statement outlining an organisation's overall objective and reason for being in business.

Mission statement – a short statement setting out the reason why an organisation exists.

Monitor – to keep track of.

Morale – enthusiasm and willingness of employees, or a measure of how happy they are at work.

Motivated – has the desire to do something, such as to work hard.

Non-verbal – unspoken.

Objectively – based on facts, unbiased.

On-the-job training – training which is provided to staff while they are at work doing their job.

Open questions – questions which allow the respondent freedom to write any answer.

Operational – regular, short-term tasks and activities which must be carried out by staff in an organisation.

Orientation – the way round a document is presented; either portrait or landscape.

Originator – the person who has decided the meeting is necessary (this may be the chairperson, but is not always).

Outcome – the decision taken.

Outcomes – the end results of activities which can also be measured or quantified.

Outsources – subcontracts work to a third party.

Paid advertising – advertising which has to be paid for such as TV adverts, and adverts in magazines and newspapers.

Patronising – talking down to someone.

Performance standards – the requirement that must be met for a particular level of performance.

Person specification – a list of the skills and abilities that the post-holder must possess.

Plain English – language that the intended audience can read and act upon the first time they read it.

Primary research – research that you carry out yourself, which can include questionnaires, surveys, interviews and focus groups.

Prioritisation – setting out the order in which you must do your various work tasks.

Private sector – the sector of the economy that consists of profit-making organisations.

Proactive — acting in anticipation and dealing with any potential problems.

Proactively — in a way that controls the situation before it happens, by using your initiative.

Product orientation — where a supplier purely concentrates on making sales.

Productive — producing positive results.

Productivity — the rate at which work is completed.

Protracted — long and drawn out, often tedious.

Public sector — the sector of the economy run by the government. This includes schools, hospitals, the NHS, as well as local councils.

Reflecting — looking back over a situation and considering what you might do differently next time.

Regulatory — subject to government regulations, which must be obeyed.

Reporting line — the line showing which position reports in to which manager.

Resources — Resources in a business environment can mean many things including: budgets or money available in the organisation; time available; people or staff availability; room or equipment availability.

Revenue — the money which comes into an organisation via sales.

Revenue stream — a method by which income is made by the company.

Secondary research — research which already exists in some form.

Self-assessment questionnaire — a questionnaire used in many organisations to identify an individual's current skills or knowledge gaps.

Self-evaluation — looking at both the positives and negatives of some aspect of yourself.

Self motivated — be able to work independently and with enthusiasm without pressure from others.

Stereotypes — characteristics of groups of people that are simplistic and often exaggerated.

Stereotypes — characteristics of groups of people that are simplistic and often exaggerated.

Sustainability — the ability to continue with an activity without depleting the world's natural resources.

Synergy — the total is greater than the sum of the parts.

Systematic — organised and consistent.

Tenacity — the ability to remain focused on the completion of a task or project.

Time management — working out how to make the best use of your time.

Transparent — clear and open for all to see.

Unambiguous — having only one meaning.

Unbiased — something that is not influenced by anyone's opinions or desires.

Unified — working together towards a common purpose.

Verbal — spoken.

Virgin resources — new resources which have not yet been processed or recycled.

Working culture — the way that an organisation works, based on its history, traditions, values and vision.

Index

Key terms are indicated by **bold** page numbers